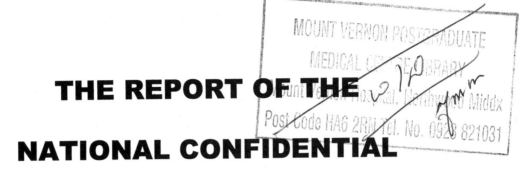

THE REPORT OF THE

NATIONAL CONFIDENTIAL

ENQUIRY

INTO

PERIOPERATIVE DEATHS

1994/1995

(1 April 1994 to 31 March 1995)

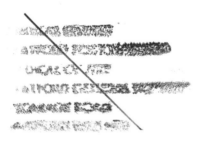

S C Gallimore	**BA**
R W Hoile	**MS FRCS**
G S Ingram	**MBBS FRCA**
K M Sherry	**MBBS FRCA**

Published 30 September 1997

by the National Confidential Enquiry into Perioperative Deaths

35-43 Lincoln's Inn Fields
London
WC2A 3PN

Tel: 0171 831 6430

Requests for further information should be addressed to the Chief Executive

ISBN 0 9522069 3 5

The National Confidential Enquiry into Perioperative Deaths is a company limited by guarantee. Company number 3019382

ROYAL COLLEGE OF ANAESTHETISTS

✦

ROYAL COLLEGE OF OBSTETRICIANS AND GYNAECOLOGISTS

✦

ROYAL COLLEGE OF OPHTHALMOLOGISTS

✦

ROYAL COLLEGE OF PATHOLOGISTS

✦

ROYAL COLLEGE OF PHYSICIANS OF LONDON

✦

ROYAL COLLEGE OF RADIOLOGISTS

✦

ROYAL COLLEGE OF SURGEONS OF ENGLAND

✦

FACULTY OF DENTAL SURGERY OF THE ROYAL COLLEGE OF SURGEONS
OF ENGLAND

✦

FACULTY OF PUBLIC HEALTH MEDICINE OF THE ROYAL COLLEGES OF
PHYSICIANS OF THE UK

✦

ASSOCIATION OF ANAESTHETISTS OF GREAT BRITAIN & IRELAND

✦

ASSOCIATION OF SURGEONS OF GREAT BRITAIN & IRELAND

4

Contents

Surgery

Pathology

References

Appendices

Foreword

It is ten years since the report of the Confidential Enquiry into Perioperative Deaths,[1] and the annual National CEPOD reports continue to highlight improvements and areas where improvement is still needed. In the 12 months, 1 April 1994 to 31 March 1995, nearly 19,000 deaths were reported within the first 30 days of operation. We chose to focus on a more detailed sample, the first death for each consultant surgeon or gynaecologist within three days of operation. There were 1818 such cases.

It is a pleasure to thank all those local reporters, surgeons and anaesthetists who have voluntarily supplied details of patients and it is gratifying to note that more than 75% of all the questionnaires were returned, a proportion which rose to 86% in gynaecology and 90% in head and neck surgery and which reflects the support we receive from our colleagues.

In surgery and anaesthesia in the UK the overall standards remain very high, and the decade has seen a further increase in the level of consultant involvement in decision-making. Audit has now become almost universal. In anaesthesia pulse oximetry in the recovery room is now the norm. Anaesthetists of all grades freely seek advice. So much is commendable.

On the negative side during the period of this review there was evidence of a dearth of ICU/HDU beds, especially in paediatric and cardiovascular surgery, which has since been addressed by the development of the National Intensive Bed Register and a very large investment of new money. Difficulty in obtaining medical notes was often the reason why consultants could not return their questionnaires. Emergency vascular surgery was still having to be undertaken by surgeons without regular vascular surgical practice. All too often the very old patients seemed to receive substandard care. Some trainee surgeons in the grade of senior house officer were still working without supervision, especially out of hours.

NCEPOD is a peer-review system which depends on the voluntary cooperation of thousands of surgeons, gynaecologists and anaesthetists who take the trouble to complete our forms. In return, NCEPOD assures complete confidentiality. NCEPOD does not have the denominator figures from which it could, even if it wished, compare the death rate for any given procedure of Mr X with that of Mr Y; or Hospital A with Hospital B. It cannot and does not produce league tables.

NCEPOD does examine the circumstances surrounding deaths after operation in the hope of identifying ways in which care might have been better. It does ask the question "If preventable, why not prevented?" in the hope that asking the question will prompt action, and in our recommendations we indicate possible remedial measures. The present report suggests that NCEPOD has been successful at least in part. For this we not only must thank all our colleagues who have cooperated in answering our questionnaires, but also those who have worked in the hospitals and professional organisations to implement our previous recommendations and bring about changes. Much remains to be done.

J P Blandy CBE FRCS
Chairman
National Confidential Enquiry into Perioperative Deaths
July 1997

Acknowledgements

This is the sixth report of National CEPOD and we continue to be indebted to the local reporters and administrative and clinical audit staff who provide the initial data on perioperative deaths.

Many consultant and trainee anaesthetists and surgeons have, once again, voluntarily contributed to the Enquiry by completing detailed questionnaires.

Thank you to all of these people without whom this report would not have been possible.

The management and day-to-day running of National CEPOD depends on the efforts, good humour and enthusiasm of the administrative staff. The Steering Group members wish to record here their appreciation of the efforts of Peter Allison, Anne Campling, Fatima Chowdhury, Paul Coote, Jennifer Drummond, Sean Gallimore and Dolores Jarman. All data analysis was carried out by Sean Gallimore.

General recommendations 1994/95

- Essential services (high dependency and intensive care beds) are still inadequate and resources need to be increased to correct deficiencies.

- Communication between specialists and between grades needs to be more frequent and more effective.

- There are special circumstances of patients (those over 90 years of age, those with aortic stenosis, those who need radical pelvic surgery, those who need transfer to neurosurgical units and those for emergency vascular operations) which require special individual attention by consultant anaesthetists and consultant surgeons.

- Organisation for effective clinical audit needs still to be improved in all disciplines but particularly in gynaecology and ophthalmology.

- Clinical records and data collection still need to be improved.

- The abilities of locums should be ascertained before appointments are made.

Management of the Enquiry

Corporate structure

The National Confidential Enquiry into Perioperative Deaths (NCEPOD) is an independent body to which a corporate commitment has been made by the Associations, Colleges and Faculties related to its areas of activity. Each of these bodies nominates members of the Steering Group.

Steering Group (as at July 1997)

Chairman
Emeritus Professor J P Blandy CBE

Vice-Chairman
Emeritus Professor V R Tindall CBE   (Royal College of Obstetricians and Gynaecologists)

Secretary
Mr H B Devlin CBE   (Royal College of Surgeons of England)

Treasurer
Dr J N Lunn   (Royal College of Anaesthetists)

Other members
Mrs M Beck   (Royal College of Ophthalmologists)

Mr K G Callum   (Association of Surgeons of Great Britain and Ireland)

Dr J F Dyet   (Royal College of Radiologists)

Dr M J Goldacre   (Faculty of Public Health Medicine)

Dr H H Gray   (Royal College of Physicians of London)

Dr J Lumley   (Royal College of Anaesthetists)

Professor V J Lund   (Royal College of Surgeons of England)

Dr D A Saunders   (Association of Anaesthetists of Great Britain and Ireland)

Dr P J Simpson   (Royal College of Anaesthetists)

Mr M F Sullivan   (Royal College of Surgeons of England)

Professor P G Toner   (Royal College of Pathologists)

Mr J Ll Williams   (Faculty of Dental Surgery, Royal College of Surgeons of England)

Co-opted members

Mr R W Hoile   (NCEPOD Clinical Coordinator)

Dr G S Ingram   (NCEPOD Clinical Coordinator)

Dr P A Knapman   (Coroners' Society of England and Wales)

Mr T J Matthews   (Institute of Health Services Management)

Dr M McGovern   (Department of Health - England)

Coordinators

Anaesthesia	Dr G S Ingram
	Dr J N Lunn (until June 1997)
Surgery	Mr H B Devlin (until June 1997)
	Mr R W Hoile
Chief Executive	Ms E A Campling

Assistant Coordinators

Anaesthesia	Dr K M Sherry (from October 1996)
	Dr A J G Gray (from April 1997)
Surgery	Mr M A C Leonard (until September 1996)
	Mr F E Loeffler (until October 1996)

Funding

The total annual cost of NCEPOD is approximately £424,000 (1996/97). We are pleased to acknowledge the continued support of;

Department of Health (England)
Welsh Office
Health and Social Services Executive (Northern Ireland)
States of Guernsey Board of Health
Jersey Group of Hospitals
Department of Health and Social Security, Isle of Man Government
BUPA Hospitals Limited
Benenden Hospital
Nuffield Hospitals
St Martins Hospitals Limited

This funding covers the *total* cost of the Enquiry, including administrative salaries and payments for clinical coordinators, assistant clinical coordinators, office accommodation charges, computer and other equipment as well as travelling and other expenses for the coordinators, Steering Group and advisory groups.

Data collection and review

NCEPOD reviews clinical practice and identifies potentially remediable factors in the practice of anaesthesia, all types of surgery and, from 1 April 1998, other invasive procedures. We consider the *quality* of the delivery of care and not specifically causation of death. Data are supplied on a voluntary basis; consultant clinicians in the relevant specialties are invited to participate. NCEPOD also reviews requests for and reporting of postmortem examinations. The commentary in the reports is based on peer review of the data, questionnaires and notes submitted to NCEPOD: it is not a research study based on differences against a control population, and does not attempt to produce any kind of comparison between clinicians or hospitals.

Scope

All National Health Service and Defence Medical Services hospitals in England, Wales and Northern Ireland, and public hospitals in Guernsey, Jersey and the Isle of Man are included in the Enquiry, as well as hospitals managed by BUPA Hospitals Limited, General Healthcare Group PLC, Nuffield Hospitals, St Martins Hospitals Limited and Benenden Hospital.

Reporting of deaths

NCEPOD collects basic details on all deaths in hospital within 30 days of a surgical procedure, through a system of local reporting (see Appendix H). When the Equiry started, the local reporters in each hospital were usually consultant clinicians, but this role is increasingly being taken on by information and clinical audit departments who are often able to provide the data from hospital information systems. In the independent sector, hospital or nursing managers provide the data. When incomplete information is received, the NCEPOD staff contact the appropriate medical records or information officer, secretarial or clinical audit staff.

Deaths of patients *in hospital* within 30 days of a surgical procedure (excluding maternal deaths) are included. If local reporters are aware of postoperative deaths at home, they report them to us. A surgical procedure is defined by NCEPOD as;

> *"any procedure carried out by a surgeon or gynaecologist, with or without an anaesthetist, involving local, regional or general anaesthesia or sedation".*

Reporters provide the following information:

```
Name of authority/trust
Name/sex/hospital number of patient
Name of hospital in which the death occurred (and hospital where surgery took place, if different)
Dates of birth, final operation and death
Surgical procedure performed
Name of consultant surgeon
Name of anaesthetist
```

From 1 April 1998, NCEPOD will also review data relating to interventional cardiological and radiological procedures.

Sample for more detailed review

The data collection year runs from 1 April to 31 March. Each year, a sample of the reported deaths is reviewed in more detail. The sample selection varies for each data collection year, and is determined by the NCEPOD Steering Group.

For each sample case, questionnaires (see Appendices C and D) are sent to the consultant surgeon or gynaecologist and consultant anaesthetist. These questionnaires are identified only by a number, allocated in the NCEPOD office. Copies of operation notes, anaesthetic records and fluid balance charts and postmortem reports are also requested. Surgical questionnaires are sent directly to the consultant surgeon or gynaecologist under whose care the patient was at the time of the final operation before death. When the local reporter has been able to identify the relevant consultant anaesthetist, the anaesthetic questionnaire is sent directly to him or her. However, in many cases this is not possible, and the local tutor of the Royal College of Anaesthetists is asked to name a consultant to whom the questionnaire should be sent.

NCEPOD may collect data about patients who have survived more than 30 days after a procedure. These data are used for comparison with the data about deaths, or to review a specific aspect of clinical practice. Data from other sources may also be used.

Consultants

We hold a database, regularly updated, of all consultant anaesthetists, gynaecologists and surgeons in England, Wales and Northern Ireland.

Analysis and review of data

The collection, recording and analysis of data are managed by the Project Manager and Chief Executive of NCEPOD. All questionnaires are examined by the NCEPOD administrative staff to identify any inconsistency in the information provided and to prepare the data for entry to the computer database. The data are aggregated to produce the tables and information in the reports. Overall data are aggregated to regional or national level only so that individual trusts and hospitals cannot be identified.

Advisory groups

The completed questionnaires and the aggregated data are reviewed by the advisory groups for anaesthesia and surgery, together with the NCEPOD clinical coordinators. These groups are drawn from hospitals in England, Wales and Northern Ireland. The advisory group in pathology reviews postmortem data from the surgical questionnaires as well as copies of postmortem reports.

Clinical Coordinators

The Trustees, on the recommendation of the Steering Group, appoint for a defined tenure clinical coordinators who lead the review of the data relating to the annual sample and advise the Steering Group and the Trustees.

They may also from time to time appoint assistant clinical coordinators, who must be engaged in active academic/clinical practice (in the NHS) during the full term of office.

Production of the report

The advisory groups comment on the overall quality of care within their specialty and on any individual cases which merit particular attention. These comments form the basis for the sections in the published reports on anaesthesia and surgery, and all advisory groups contribute to the draft for their specialty, prepared by the coordinators. The draft report for pathology is prepared by the chairman of the group and is based on a proforma used by the group (see Appendix E). All the anaesthetic, surgical and pathology drafts are then reviewed and amended by the coordinators and by the NCEPOD Steering Group.

Confidentiality

NCEPOD is registered with the Data Protection Registrar and abides by the Data Protection Principles. We do not provide individual data to any person or organization outside the NCEPOD staff, coordinators or Steering Group other than in the published Report.

All reporting forms, questionnaires and other paper records relating to the sample are shredded once an individual report has been published. Similarly, all patient-related data are removed from the computer database.

Data in the reports are aggregated to regional or national level so that individual Trusts, hospitals, authorities and patients and clinicians (who treat them) cannot be identified.

Before review of questionnaires by the clinical coordinators or any of the advisors, all identification is removed from the questionnaires and accompanying papers. The source of the information is not revealed to any of the coordinators or advisors.

General data 1 April 1994 to 31 March 1995

Points

> - Lost medical notes continue to be a major problem.
> - The return rate of anaesthetic and surgical questionnaires was 76%; regional rates of return ranged from 53% to 100%.

Reporting of deaths

Local reporters (see Appendix H) provided data to NCEPOD about patients who died in hospital between 1 April 1994 and 31 March 1995 within 30 days of a surgical procedure. We were also informed of a few deaths which occurred at home within the 30-day period.

Tables G1 to G4 refer to the total number of 18728 reported deaths. This total does not include seven reports where, despite all efforts, the data were incomplete, 517 reports received too late for inclusion in the analysis, and 416 inappropriate reports (see table G5). The regional breakdown of total deaths reported to NCEPOD, together with the totals of reports for previous years, are shown in table G1. The year-on-year fluctuations are in part caused by local (hospital) problems with data collection, complicated for the 1994/95 year by changes in the regional structure of the NHS. This means that the figures for previous years are not necessarily directly comparable.

Table G1
Deaths reported to NCEPOD

	1994/95	Previous years				
		1993/94	1992/93	1991/92	1990	1989
Anglia & Oxford	**1361**	1577	1862	1556	1367	1371
North Thames	**1944**	2703	2515	2127	2554	2609
North West	**2618**	2636	2378	2509	2736	2864
Northern & Yorkshire	**2549**	2637	2671	2267	2464	2685
South & West	**2469**	2561	2493	1847	1997	2306
South Thames	**2246**	2531	2445	2465	2457	2840
Trent	**2386**	2342	2036	2014	1722	1849
West Midlands	**1531**	1578	1565	1578	1826	1902
Wales	**933**	1078	1072	1079	1102	1162
Northern Ireland	**497**	529	474	375	316	380
Guernsey	**12**	33	26	18	39	32
Jersey	**17**	27	32	25	22	26
Isle of Man	**-**	25	41	25	25	7
Defence Medical Services	**17**	36	40	75	60	94
Independent sector	**148**	149	166	172	130	120
Total	**18728**	20442	19816	18132	18817	20247

Table G2
Calendar days from operation to death
(i.e. not 24 hour periods)

		%	%
0 (i.e. day of operation)	1998	*10.7*	
1	2267	*12.1*	
2	1548	*8.3*	
3	1192	*6.4*	*37.5*
4	1091	*5.8*	
5	923	*4.9*	
6	865	*4.6*	
7	792	*4.2*	
8	718	*3.8*	*19.2*
9	621	*3.3*	
10	598	*3.2*	
11	539	*2.9*	
12	503	*2.7*	
13	475	*2.5*	*12.5*
14	424	*2.2*	
15	414	*2.2*	
16 to 20	1677	*9.0*	
21 to 25	1202	*6.4*	*20.0*
26 to 30	881	*4.7*	
Total	**18728**		

Figure G1 (see table G2)
Calendar days from operation to death
(i.e. not 24 hour periods)

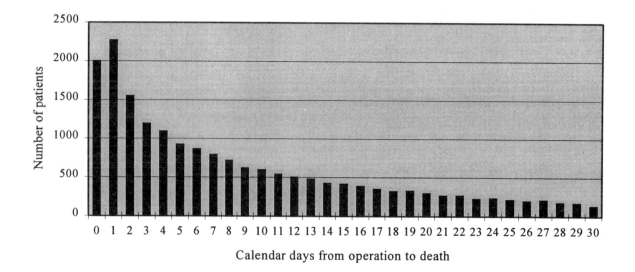

Calendar days from operation to death

Table G3
Age/sex distribution of reported deaths

Age in years			Male	Female	Total
0	to	*4	140	94	234
5	to	9	16	12	28
10	to	14	22	14	36
15	to	19	43	15	58
20	to	24	48	20	68
25	to	29	62	25	87
30	to	34	68	39	107
35	to	39	71	67	138
40	to	44	113	109	222
45	to	49	204	157	361
50	to	54	305	203	508
55	to	59	450	350	800
60	to	64	861	480	1341
65	to	69	1265	859	2124
70	to	74	1890	1336	3226
75	to	79	1611	1383	2994
80	to	84	1393	1617	3010
85	to	89	799	1347	2146
90	to	94	267	672	939
95	to	99	55	194	249
100	+		11	41	52
Total			**9694**	**9034**	**18728**

* *i.e. day of birth to the day preceding the fifth birthday*

Table G4
Calendar days between death and receipt of report by NCEPOD
(i.e. not 24 hour periods)

1	to	29	5547
30	to	59	3915
60	to	89	2733
90	to	119	1800
120	to	149	1146
150	to	179	830
180	or	more	2757
Total			**18728**

It is disappointing that only 30% of the deaths were reported to us within 30 days of the patient's death, compared with 33% in 1993/94 and 40% in 1992/93. As more hospitals provide data from computer systems, rather than reports of deaths being sent to NCEPOD as they occur, computer-generated reports of all perioperative deaths occurring during a set period (monthly, quarterly or even yearly) are increasingly being provided. This method of reporting, whilst being more convenient for the local reporters, and also possibly more accurate than manual methods, does regrettably bring with it an inevitable time-lag in reporting.

Table G5
Inappropriate reports received and not included

264	More than 30 days *(day of operation to day of death)*
52	No surgical procedure performed or inappropiate procedure *(according to NCEPOD criteria)*
50	Procedure not performed by a surgeon
41	Duplicate report
5	Maternal death
4	Patient still alive (death wrongly reported)
1	Procedure performed in non-participating hospital (overseas)
416	**Total**

These figures do not include inappropriate reports included in computer printout format. Some hospital systems cannot easily filter out inappropiate reports such as deaths following procedures by physicans, or deaths following procedures excluded by NCEPOD.

Sample for detailed review

The detailed sample for 1994/95 was based around the **first** perioperative death reported for each consultant surgeon or gynaecologist, **occurring on the day of surgery itself or within the next three calendar days.** The day <u>following</u> the operation was counted as the first postoperative day. Using this method, each consultant surgeon or gynaecologist received a maximum of one questionnaire. Certain procedures (as they were described on the local report forms) were excluded, e.g. purely diagnostic endoscopic procedures, in which case the next perioperative death (if any) for that surgeon or gynaecologist was chosen. From a total of 18728 deaths reported to NCEPOD, the sample for this year comprised 1818 (9.7%) cases.

Surgical questionnaires

Questionnaires were sent to consultant surgeons for further information on all 1818 cases, and 1384 completed questionnaires were returned to NCEPOD. The overall return rate (see table G6) was therefore 76.1% (1384/1818).

After excluding 16 questionnaires which were returned incomplete, or related to the wrong operation or patient, and two questionnaires which were returned too late to be included, 1366 questionnaires were analysed.

Anaesthetic questionnaires

Questionnaires were sent to consultant anaesthetists for further information on 1618 of the 1818 sample cases. No questionnaire was sent for the remaining 200 cases for the following reasons:

173	Name of appropriate consultant anaesthetist unobtainable or notified too late to send questionnaire
27	No anaesthetist involved *(local anaesthesia or sedation administered solely by the surgeon)*

Of the questionnaires distributed, 76.5% (1238/1618) were returned. After excluding 13 questionnaires which were returned incomplete or related to the wrong operation or patient, and three questionnaires which were returned too late to be included, 1222 questionnaires were analysed.

Table G6
Distribution and return of questionnaires by NHS region

SQ = Surgical Questionnaire AQ = Anaesthetic Questionnaire	No. of Qs distributed		No. of Qs returned		% return rate		No. of Qs analysed		No. hospitals represented	
	SQ	AQ	SQ	AQ	SQ	AQ	SQ	AQ	SQ	AQ
Anglia & Oxford	142	126	105	103	73.9	81.7	102	102	20	21
North Thames	220	193	151	124	68.6	64.2	151	121	41	37
North West	239	223	180	168	75.6	75.3	178	168	37	35
Northern & Yorkshire	239	214	193	180	80.8	84.1	189	177	35	35
South & West	221	191	179	169	80.6	88.5	177	168	31	31
South Thames	197	171	148	127	75.1	74.3	144	124	38	35
Trent	180	162	140	118	77.8	72.8	140	116	19	20
West Midlands	163	139	121	103	74.2	74.1	119	101	26	23
Wales	116	103	87	75	75.0	72.8	86	74	18	18
Northern Ireland	62	57	51	46	82.3	80.7	51	46	15	16
Guernsey	4	4	4	4	100.0	100.0	4	4	1	1
Jersey	2	2	2	2	100.0	100.0	2	2	1	1
Defence Medical Services	3	3	3	3	100.0	100.0	3	3	3	3
Independent sector	31	30	20	16	64.5	53.3	20	16	12	10
Total	**1818**	**1618**	**1384**	**1238**	**76.1**	**76.5**	**1366**	**1222**	**297**	**286**

It is pleasing to note that in the NHS, several regions/authorities achieved return rates of 80% or higher; there remains considerable room for improvement in the other regions and particularly in the independent sector.

Table G7
Distribution and return of surgical questionnaires by specialty

	Number of cases in sample	Number of questionnaires returned	% questionnaires returned	Number of questionnaires analysed
Cardiothoracic	130	87	66.9	85
General *(including colorectal)*	626	476	76.0	474
Gynaecology	76	65	85.5	63
Neurosurgery	82	58	70.7	58
Ophthalmology	14	11	78.6	11
Oral/maxillofacial	8	7	87.5	7
Orthopaedic	439	327	74.5	320
Otorhinolaryngology	21	19	90.5	19
Plastic	13	11	84.6	11
Urology	111	82	73.9	80
Vascular	298	241	80.9	238
Total	**1818**	**1384**	**76.1**	**1366**

NB: Laparotomies were included in "General" where the surgical questionnaire was not returned

The return rate of questionnaires for neurosurgery is still low in comparison with other specialties. Nevertheless, the return rate for that specialty does represent a substantial improvement compared with the last NCEPOD report[6] (1993/94 - *60.8%*). The return rate for urology has reduced in this report (1993/94 - *84.7%*).

Table G8
Reasons for the non-return of questionnaires

Surgical Questionnaires	Anaesthetic Questionnaires	
323	212	No reason given
78	125	Medical notes lost or unavailable
14	22	Surgeon/anaesthetist no longer working at the hospital or on sick-leave
3	3	Consultant did not wish to participate
16	18	Other
434	**380**	**Total**

Non-availability of notes remains a problem; it was the stated reason for inability to return 18% (78/434) of the missing surgical questionnaires and 33% (125/380) of the missing anaesthetic questionnaires.

Anaesthesia

Anaesthesia

ADVISORS

We are very grateful to the following consultant anaesthetist advisors who gave their time unstintingly to the consideration of anaesthetic questionnaires and guided the anaesthetist coordinators at 12 meetings over a period of more than one year.

Dr C Gillbe	(North Thames)
Dr S J Harris	(Anglia & Oxford)
Dr R Kishen	(North West)
Dr F J Pickford	(Wales)
Dr K N Robinson	(Anglia & Oxford)

METHOD

Questionnaires about anaesthesia were analysed for 1222 cases. The detailed sample was based on the first postoperative death reported for each consultant surgeon or gynaecologist, on the day of surgery or within the next three calendar days.

All questionnaires were reviewed by the coordinators. They considered that 801 of them should be examined in detail by the advisors, whose opinions form the basis for this report, although the coordinators are responsible for the contents.

Material in italics is taken directly and summarised from the questionnaires completed by practising clinicians. This information has not been altered. These vignettes are examples and serve to illustrate relevant points. There are also a number of tables giving additional details. The intention is not so much to comment specifically as to provide more information that would be helpful to the reader. For instance when a patient was not seen preoperatively by an anaesthetist, was this because of the urgency of the case, poor organisation, or the anaesthetist's unwillingness to make a preoperative visit?

Detailed study of the anaesthetic questionnaires by the coordinators and their advisors revealed, as before, much of which anaesthetists may justly be proud: these examples are indicated by ◆.

KEY POINTS

Five issues emerged as the focus of discussion in the advisors' meetings. They are therefore presented in some detail. They are summarised below with the page references.

SHOs WORKING ALONE [pages 31 to 35]
Everyone needs to pay even more attention to all aspects of training, experience and responsibility of SHOs, particularly but not only, in District General Hospitals.

DEATHS IN PATIENTS AGED 90 YEARS OR OVER [pages 38 to 42]
The special requirements for anaesthesia in the elderly must be remembered.

AORTIC STENOSIS [pages 48 to 49]
The well recognised risks of anaesthesia in this condition need to be re-emphasised.

PROBLEMS IN OBTAINING BLOOD PRODUCTS [page 58]
Organisational problems in the provision of blood and blood products persist.

ICU AND HDU BEDS [page 64]
The provision for ICU and HDU care was still inadequate.

Proxy anaesthetists

Table A1 (q1)
If you were not involved in any way with this anaesthetic and have filled out this questionnaire on behalf of someone else (i.e. proxy for), please indicate your position.

Chairman of Division	21
College Tutor	58
Duty consultant	156
Other consultant	85
Trainee	20
Other	5
Not applicable	877
Total	**1222**

1994/95	28% proxy
1993/94	27% proxy
1992/93	23% proxy

The National Confidential Enquiry into Perioperative Deaths depends on the efforts of consultants and others, often not directly involved with reported cases, to complete questionnaires and so maintain a satisfactory return rate. We are indebted to them.

Given the proportion of cases being undertaken by trainees and the rapidity with which many now rotate through training programmes, it seems unlikely that the percentage of proxy returns will decrease in the foreseeable future.

Surgical specialty

Table A2
Division of cases by specialty group

Cardiothoracic	68
General/colorectal	437
Gynaecology	49
Neurosurgery	49
Ophthalmology	3
Oral/maxillofacial	4
Orthopaedic	295
Otorhinolaryngology	16
Plastic	8
Urology	76
Vascular	217
Total	**1222**

This table shows the breakdown by surgical specialty of those cases where anaesthetic questionnaires were returned (table G7, page 19 relates to cases where surgical questionnaires were returned). Most cases of death within three days of surgery were in general/colorectal, vascular and orthopaedic surgery.

Table A3 (q44)
Specialty group by time of start of anaesthetic for final operation before death

	Weekday "in hours"	%	Weekday "out of hours"*	%	Weekday (time not stated)	%	Saturday or Sunday	%	Total
Cardiothoracic	55	81	4	6	1	1	8	12	68
General/colorectal	192	44	126	29	15	3	104	24	437
Gynaecology	41	84	-		5	10	3	6	49
Neurosurgery	26	53	11	22	2	4	10	20	49
Ophthalmology	2	67	-		-		1	33	3
Oral/maxillofacial	3	75	-		-		1	25	4
Orthopaedic	187	63	17	6	16	5	75	25	295
Otorhinolaryngology	14	88	2	13	-		-		16
Plastic	7	88	-		-		1	13	8
Urology	64	84	6	8	3	4	3	4	76
Vascular	102	47	66	30	4	2	45	21	217
Total	**693**	**57**	**232**	**19**	**46**	**4**	**251**	**21**	**1222**

Hospital

Table A4 (q2)
In what type of hospital did the anaesthetic take place?

		%
District General or equivalent	888	73
University/teaching	267	22
Surgical specialty	40	3
Other acute/partly acute	7	<1
Defence Medical	3	<1
Independent	17	1
Total	**1222**	

The anaesthetist(s)

Table A5 (q3)
Grade of most senior anaesthetist present at the start of this anaesthetic

		%
Consultant	640	52
Associate specialist	29	2
Clinical assistant	24	2
Senior registrar	169	14
Staff grade	42	3
Registrar	156	13
Senior house officer	160	13
Not answered	2	<1
Total	**1222**	

[see also surgical overall analysis, tables S42-S47 pages 96 to 98]

---

* see glossary, appendix B

The pie charts below show the percentage of cases anaesthetised according to the grade of the most senior anaesthetist present at the start of the anaesthetic, subdivided by surgical specialty and whether the case took place in routine hours. We have excluded specialties in which fewer than 49 questionnaires were returned and questionnaires where time of start was not recorded. Associate specialists, clinical assistants and staff grade doctors are included in the category 'other'.

Figure A1
Most senior anaesthetist present at start of anaesthetic

Cardiothoracic

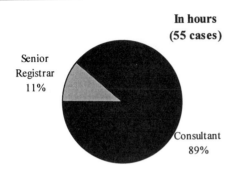

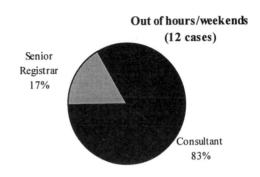

General/colorectal

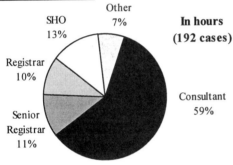

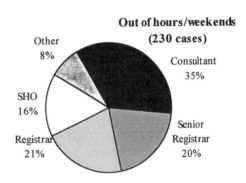

Gynaecology

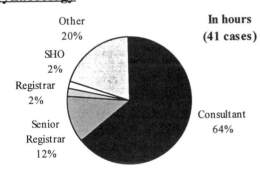

In hours

(41 cases)

Out of hours/weekends

Three cases

(continued overleaf)

Neurosurgery

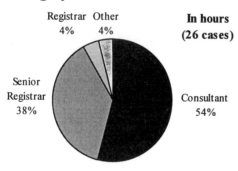

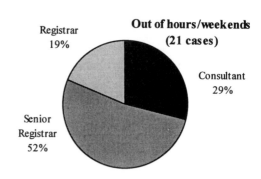

Orthopaedic

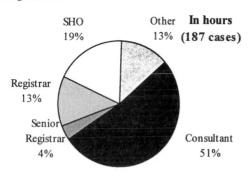

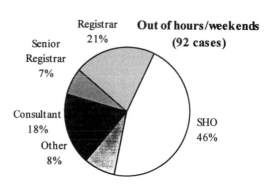

Vascular

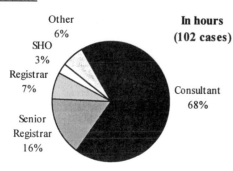

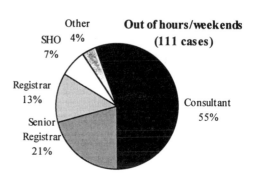

It is evident that consultant and senior registrar anaesthetists maintain a high level of involvement both in- and out-of-hours for cardiothoracic and vascular surgery. By contrast, there is a marked difference in neurosurgery and orthopaedic cases between consultant presence in- and out-of-hours.

To what extent are these variations in the allocation of staff justifiable in terms of the complexity of anaesthesia and surgery and the needs of patients?

Table A6 (qs 3 and 26)
Most senior anaesthetist present at start of anaesthetic by classification of operation[*]

	Emergency	%	Urgent	%	Scheduled	%	Elective	%	Not answered	Total
Consultant	187	29	191	30	167	26	84	13	11	640
Associate specialist	3	10	14	48	5	17	7	24	-	29
Senior registrar	66	39	71	42	21	12	7	4	4	169
Clinical assistant	2	8	12	50	8	33	2	8	-	24
Staff grade	5	12	17	40	13	31	7	17	-	42
Registrar	41	26	85	54	25	16	4	3	1	156
SHO	11	7	112	70	28	18	6	4	3	160
Not answered	1		1		-		-			2
Total	**316**	26	**503**	41	**267**	22	**117**	10	19	**1222**

Figure A2
Classification of operation for each grade of anasthetist as a percentage of the total number of cases for that grade

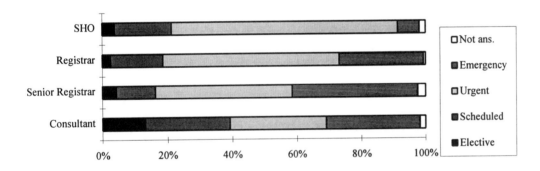

This illustrates the case mix that each grade undertook in the sample. The workload of SHOs was biased to urgent cases and that of senior registrars to urgent and emergency cases.

---

[*] see glossary, appendix B

Table A7 (q3)
Distribution of cases where most senior anaesthetist was an SHO or registrar

Region	SHO most senior				Registrar most senior				All cases	
	Number of cases		Number of hospitals		Number of cases		Number of hospitals		Number of cases	Number of hospitals
		%		%		%		%		
Anglia & Oxford	12	11.8	7	33.3	11	10.8	8	38.1	102	21
North Thames	3	2.5	3	8.1	19	15.7	16	43.2	121	37
North West	27	16.1	16	45.7	18	10.7	14	40.0	168	35
Northern & Yorkshire	25	14.1	15	42.9	20	11.3	14	40.0	177	35
Northern Ireland	4	8.7	3	18.8	8	17.4	4	25.0	46	16
South & West	23	13.7	13	41.9	21	12.5	13	41.9	168	31
South Thames	26	21.0	16	45.7	25	20.2	8	22.9	124	35
Trent	12	10.3	9	45.0	16	13.8	9	45.0	116	20
Wales	10	13.5	7	38.9	6	8.1	6	33.3	74	18
West Midlands	16	15.8	9	39.1	12	11.9	9	39.1	101	23
Other	1	4.0	1	6.7	-	-	-	-	25	15
Total	**159**	**13.0**	**99**	**34.6**	**156**	**12.8**	**111**	**38.8**	**1222**	**286**

These data need to be interpreted with care because the numbers are small. Selecting the apparently 'best' and the apparently 'worst' regions for comparison illustrates these difficulties. In North Thames only three of 121 cases were anaesthetised by SHOs; each was in a different hospital. In South Thames 26 of 124 patients were anaesthetised by SHOs. There are a number of ways in which this might be explained. For example, more senior grades may be more conscientious in covering SHOs in North Thames. The return rate of questionnaires from South Thames was 10% higher than that from North Thames; the latter may be failing to report many cases involving SHOs. It is possible that a more favourable balance between grades in North Thames allows their SHOs to have a supernumerary role. However, there is not a simple transfer of responsibilities between registrars and SHOs because there were fewer cases managed by registrars in North than in South Thames.

It is the policy of NCEPOD to aggregate data on a regional or national level so that individual trusts and hospitals cannot be identified. Nevertheless it was considered that since the data above appeared to show 'clustering' of SHO cases within regions, the administrative staff at NCEPOD should examine it in more detail to see if this was in fact the case. The following patterns were noted.

In the South & West region one hospital returned five cases where the SHO was the most senior anaesthetist out of a total of 23 for the whole region. Similarly in the North West one hospital had five of the 27; in Northern & Yorkshire a single hospital had five of the 25 and in West Midlands there was a hospital that had five of the 16 cases for the whole region.

SHOs working alone
[SHO the most senior anaesthetist present at the start of the anaesthetic]

In 159 cases (13% of the sample) an SHO was the most senior anaesthetist responsible for the anaesthetic. Half of them sought advice. None was in a specialist hospital.

Table A8 (qs 2, 3 and 12)

	Sought advice	Did not seek advice	Not answered	**Total**
DGH	66	65	9	**141**
Teaching hospital	8	7	3	**18**

A more senior anaesthetist came to help in 22 of the 66 cases (question 13) at District General Hospitals where SHOs sought advice.

Table A9 (qs 3 and 12)
Patients anaesthetised by SHOs, whose first UK full-time anaesthetic post was in 1994 and who did not seek advice

Operation	Day	Time	Age	Sex	Operation	ASA	Grade of surgeon	Comments
Laparotomy and gastrojejunostomy	Tues.	11.05	84	F	Scheduled	4	Consultant	Known to have severe IHD.
Dynamic hip screw (fracture neck of femur)	Sun.	11.30	90	F	Urgent	3	Registrar	MI one year previously, LVF, systolic aortic murmur.
Total hip replacement, MUA Colles fracture	Fri.	10.00	84	F	Urgent	2	Registrar	Developed bronchopneumonia postoperatively.
Resuture abdomen (hysterectomy)	Sun.	11.20	48	F	Urgent	?	Consultant	Massive pulmonary embolism.
Revision of total hip replacement	Tues.	13.46	87	F	Scheduled	2	Consultant	LVF postoperatively.
Hip hemiarthroplasty	Sat.	19.00	83	M	Urgent	2	Registrar	CCF, Bronchopneumonia postoperatively.
Laparotomy	Tues.	11.45	72	M	Urgent	3	Consultant	IDDM, IHD.

We are concerned about the training of these SHOs, none of whom had any qualification in anaesthesia and all of whom would have had less than 15 months experience in anaesthesia in the UK. These data are included, not to criticise their management, but to ask if their training might not have benefited from discussion with more experienced colleagues. The SHO responsible for the first case, who qualified in 1984, may have had previous overseas experience in anaesthesia. For the last two cases the anaesthetists were non-UK European nationals who graduated in 1991 and 1992, the remaining cases were all done by UK graduates. All the patients were in District General Hospitals.

ASA status and solo SHOs
[ASA grade of patients anaesthetised by solo SHOs]

Four patients, graded ASA 5, were anaesthetised by solo SHOs.

An 86-year-old resident of a nursing home was admitted with a comminuted proximal femoral fracture. She was demented, doubly incontinent, had asthma, ischaemic heart disease, peripheral vascular disease and poor renal function. Following fixation of the fracture, in a confused state, she removed her drain and tampered with her wound which became infected. Eighteen days after the initial operation she was taken to theatre at 23.00 hrs for debridement of the wound. An SHO with no qualification in anaesthesia who had sought advice from a registrar, gave her a short general anaesthetic during which it was noted that she needed frequent boluses of ephedrine. She died the following day.

The other three cases were laparotomies at which extensive ischaemic bowel was found.

An SHO who held no anaesthetic qualifications, anaesthetised an 85-year-old man for laparotomy. The patient, who had been admitted the previous evening, was found to have total superior mesenteric artery occlusion. The surgeon noted that having deemed the patient not suitable for further intervention, he was allowed to die with good analgesia and dignity.

An 87-year-old woman was admitted to hospital at 20.00 hrs. She had a cardiorespiratory arrest and was intubated. Recovering, she then extubated herself, but this was followed by another arrest, at which time she aspirated stomach contents into her lungs. Her trachea was reintubated and she was taken to theatre shortly afterwards at 01.00 hrs. An SHO, whose first anaesthetic post was seven years previously and who held the DA, sought advice from a consultant and received help from a registrar. The surgical registrar who had been two months in the grade but did not consult anyone, explored the right groin, found ischaemic bowel associated with an inguinal hernia and carried out a resection and anastomosis. Saturations of 92-93% were charted during the anaesthesia but the inspired oxygen was not recorded. Postoperatively she was taken to the ICU and her lungs ventilated. She died just over 24 hours later from respiratory failure and persistent hypotension. There is no indication as to what advice the consultant gave in this case.

A 64-year-old man noted in the clinical summary on the anaesthetic chart to be "in extremis, COAD all his life, on home O_2 therapy" was anaesthetised by an SHO who had passed the Part II FRCA and was experienced at that grade. He was taken to theatre at 20.00 hrs for an exploratory open-and-close laparotomy at which extensive infarcted large and small bowel was found. Postoperatively the patient's lungs were ventilated in the recovery area, he was given appropriate analgesia, and died seven hours later. The duty consultant who was contacted by the SHO and who completed the questionnaire, noted that it was apparent that the patient would not survive with or without surgery. He/she concludes "I did not attend this case. The SHO was very experienced and since the patient was ASA 5 I felt I would not be able to contribute anything extra to the anaesthetic management".

These ASA 5 patients had a low probability of survival whatever level of expertise was devoted to their care. Should these situations be regarded as part of the learning process of trainee doctors and therefore be precisely the type of case with which the consultant should be involved both for teaching and for trainee support?

A further 36 patients graded ASA 4 were anaesthetised by solo SHOs. Two received arterial embolectomies where the SHO provided sedation for the procedure which was performed by the surgeon under local anaesthesia. Again, in four instances questions need to be asked.

An 86-year-old woman was anaesthetised on a Sunday by an SHO who did not consult anyone more senior for advice. The patient was graded as ASA 4. She had asthma, emphysema, ECG signs of ischaemia and previous myocardial infarct. She was mentally confused. She had ankle oedema and peripheral vascular disease. She took oral hypoglycaemic drugs and had a possible chest infection. Management before operation was cursory: a few puffs of salbutamol were administered, there was no assessment of her cardiac failure and a sliding scale for insulin was not used to determine the appropriate dose. Her arterial blood pressure was 90/45 mmHg before a spinal anaesthetic was given by the SHO; the operation (hemiarthroplasty) was done on the same day as admission. The patient became breathless in the recovery room: again she was given salbutamol. More than four litres of intravenous fluids were given over less than five hours together with two units of blood. Pulmonary oedema was diagnosed in the ward where she died on the same day.

Is this standard of care acceptable? What was the explanation for such a precipitate action?

A 41-year-old man, ASA 4, was anaesthetised by an SHO who received advice but no actual help from a consultant anaesthetist. The anaesthetist was without qualification in anaesthesia although his/her first job in anaesthesia was in 1977. The SHO surgeon of five years' standing claimed to have done ten of these procedures (below knee amputation) in the last 12 months. The operation was done at 18.00 hrs on a Friday evening and was the third in a series: the patient had been in hospital for 24 days and had insulin-dependent diabetes which was out of control. Peripheral vascular disease, peripheral neuropathy, blindness and hypothyroid myopathy were known complicating conditions and he was on continuous peritoneal dialysis. He was anaemic with a leucocytosis and a severe electrolyte disturbance (potassium 6.8 and creatinine 963 micro mol.litre^{-1}). A spinal anaesthetic resulted in hypotension and oxygen saturations of 80-90% unresponsive to ephedrine. General anaesthesia was added (propofol and laryngeal mask airway) because the patient was distressed. The oxygen saturations improved to 93-95% in the recovery room where he remained for 15 minutes before going to the ward. Cardiac arrest supervened there within 24 hours.

All the above diagnoses were confirmed at postmortem examination. How could this management be justified?

In the two other cases the patients were over 90 and are therefore discussed elsewhere (pages 39 and 42).

Table A9 (qs 3, 5 and 12)
Time of start of anaesthesia, by specialty group, where the most senior anaesthetist was an SHO, without any qualification in anaesthesia

	Weekday - in hours		Weekday - out of hours[*] and Saturday/Sunday		Weekday - time not stated		Total	
		Sought advice		*Sought advice*		*Sought advice*		*Sought advice*
General/colorectal	10	7	10	3	-	-	20	10
Gynaecology	-	-	1	-	-	-	1	-
Orthopaedic	13	8	18	10	3	2	34	20
Urology	-	-	-	-	1	-	1	1
Vascular	3	2	3	2	-	-	6	4
Total	**26**	*17*	**32**	*15*	**4**	*2*	**62**	*34*

An SHO who has yet to pass any anaesthetic examination needs support and guidance from more senior staff.

---

[*] see glossary, appendix B

Some may have had extensive overseas experience but they too will need help if they are to adapt to practice in the UK. It is not reassuring that only three of 10 SHOs, who had yet to pass an examination in the UK, sought advice when dealing with general/colorectal cases outside normal working hours.

An SHO, working within an appropriately structured anaesthetic training programme, would be expected (in 1994/95) to be within the first two or three years of training and to be working towards obtaining Parts I and II of the FRCA. To what extent were the SHOs working alone of apparently greater ability than this? Eight SHOs held the FRCA; one worked in a teaching hospital and the other seven in District General Hospitals.

Taking the year in which the SHOs started in their first full-time anaesthetic post as an indicator of their experience in the specialty, there would appear to be differences between teaching and District General Hospitals.

Table A10 (qs 3 and 5)
SHOs working alone by year of their first anaesthetic post

	Teaching	DGH	Total
1960-1969	0	1	1
1970-1979	0	6	6
1980-1989	1	21	22
1990	1	5	6
1991	3	7	10
1992	9	23	32
1993	1	35	36
1994	0	31	31
Not answered	3	12	15
Total	18	141	159

The District General Hospital numbers are, not surprisingly, much greater. However, there do appear to be problems both with the responsibilities given to comparatively inexperienced anaesthetists and also with other SHOs stuck at this grade.

The teaching hospital numbers would seem to confirm that these SHOs were within appropriate training programmes. The numbers are small since SHOs were rarely working alone and there were no SHOs of very limited experience undertaking single-handed anaesthesia for cases reported to NCEPOD. This might be the result of SHOs starting their training outside teaching hospitals or the much closer supervision of those who do in fact begin their training there.

However, in five of the seven cases in teaching hospitals, where SHOs did not seek advice a question needs to be asked about delivery of care. Consultant opinion or presence might not have made any difference to the outcome but at least the attempt to deliver high quality of care would be apparent.

A 79-year-old patient was to have fixation of a fractured neck of femur. Her preoperative PaO$_2$ was 7 kPa breathing air and she was thought to have an upper lobe pneumonia. She had renal impairment and left ventricular failure and was graded ASA 4. The operation was carried out under spinal anaesthesia and ephedrine, salbutamol and ketamine were all given during the procedure. Four units of blood were needed postoperatively. She died from pneumonia on the third postoperative day.

An 86-year-old patient, ASA 3, had a dynamic hip screw for a fixation of a hip fracture. Preoperatively the patient had a low albumin, a chest infection and chronic cardiac failure. Steady deterioration occurred after discharge from the recovery room to the ward and the patient died on the third postoperative day.

A psychiatric patient aged 78 with epilepsy after a previous operation to clip a cerebral aneurysm needed a dynamic hip screw because of a femoral fracture. The systolic blood pressure remained between 80 and 90mmHg despite ephedrine and 2.5L of IV fluids during general anaesthesia and intermittent positive pressure ventilation of the lungs. Postoperatively the patient deteriorated and died on the second postoperative day.

A 76-year-old patient, ASA 4, who had had a myocardial infarct six months previously was admitted with a bowel obstruction and was taken to theatre at 02.00 hrs by an SHO who had not sought advice, but held the FRCA. The systolic blood pressure remained around 80mmHg during the combined general/epidural anaesthetic. Postoperatively the patient's lungs were ventilated in the recovery room since there was no ICU bed. She returned to the ward and died two days later of a further myocardial infarction.

An 83-year-old woman with insulin dependent diabetes mellitus, polyarthritis and severe dementia required a dynamic hip screw for a fractured neck of femur. On a Sunday morning, she was anaesthetised by an anaesthetic SHO who had Part II of the FRCA and two years of anaesthetic experience. General anaesthesia was induced who had midazolam 5mg and etomidate 5mg, maintained with fentanyl 250micrograms and isoflurane 0.6-1% and further analgesia was provided by a three-in-one block using 20ml 0.25% bupivacaine. The anaesthetist prescribed intravenous insulin by sliding scale until the following morning when this was stopped and normal insulin therapy resumed. Twenty-eight hours later she inhaled her vomit, became cyanosed and died.

In all these cases advice should have been sought. Was the fact that this did not happen the fault of the trainee or the trainer?

Interpretation

- There were wide variations between regions, and probably between hospitals, in the extent to which SHO anaesthetists were taking solo responsibility for cases reported to NCEPOD.
- In some District General Hospitals very inexperienced SHOs undertook anaesthesia for patients with serious anaesthetic risk factors.
- Both trainers and trainees have responsibility in ensuring that more senior advice and/or involvement takes place when sick patients are anaesthetised by SHOs. Departments must ensure that instructions on this are unambiguous and in writing. On-call consultants must maintain compliance.
- SHOs apparently stuck in the grade for many years continued to be employed in District General Hospitals. They should be transferred to a more appropriate grade or at least counselled about their career.
- The Royal College of Anaesthetists should make recommendations about the proportion of time that SHOs should spend in out-of-hours cover as part of their training.

ANALYSIS OF THE WHOLE SAMPLE (CONTINUED)

Table A11 (q 12)
Did the anaesthetist (of whatever grade) seek advice at any time from another anaesthetist (not mentioned in question 3)?

Yes	299
No	885
Not answered	21
Not known/not recorded	17
Total	**1222**

Table A12 (qs 3 and 12)
Grade of most senior anaesthetist and whether advice sought

	Advice sought	Advice not sought	Not known/not answered	**Total**
Senior house officer	75	73	12	**160**
Registrar	85	65	6	**156**
Senior registrar	51	109	9	**169**
Consultant	61	569	10	**640**
Staff grade	13	28	1	**42**
Associate specialist	8	21	-	**29**
Clinical assistant	4	20	-	**24**
Not answered	2	-	-	**2**
Total	**299**	**885**	**38**	**1222**

Table A13 (qs 3 and 12)
Most senior anaesthetist from whom advice was sought, by grade of most senior anaesthetist present at start of anaesthetic

	Gave advice						
	SHO	Registrar	Senior registrar	Consultant	Staff grade	Other/ grade not specified	**Total**
Sought advice							
Senior house officer	1	16	7	49	1	1	**75**
Registrar	-	-	10	73	-	2	**85**
Senior registrar	-	1	1	49	-	-	**51**
Consultant	2	3	2	53	1	-	**61**
Staff grade	-	-	-	13	-	-	**13**
Associate specialist	1	-	1	6	-	-	**8**
Clinical assistant	-	1	1	2	-	-	**4**
Grade not specified	1	-	-	1	-	-	**2**
Other	-	-	-	2	-	-	**2**
Total	**5**	**21**	**22**	**248**	**2**	**3**	**299**

◆ That the anaesthetists responsible for these patients sought advice in almost a quarter of the cases and that this included 53 cases where consultants sought advice from other consultants, must be to the benefit of those patients.

The patient

Figure A3 (q15)
Age of patient at time of operation

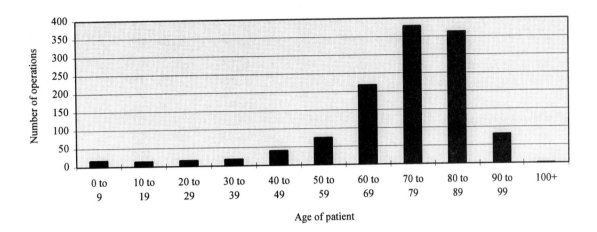

Deaths in patients 90 years or over

A sub-set of patients aged 90 years or over was identified for closer review. Patients of extreme old age have a high anaesthetic risk. They are more likely than younger patients to have degenerative changes in organ systems or coexistent disease. Moreover, their life expectancy is low (UK figures for 1993-95 are for males 3.6 years, females 4.4 years, Office for National Statistics). Thus, death may occur coincidentally with surgery or surgery may take place during the process of their dying.

Table A14
Surgical specialty group

Orthopaedic	60
General	11
Colorectal	6
Vascular	3
Urology	2
Total	**82**

Eighty-two (6.7%) of 1222 patients in this report were aged 90 years or over. Sixty (73.2%) of these were undergoing orthopaedic surgery and these accounted for one fifth of the total orthopaedic deaths returned for review. Fifty-three (88.3%)of the 60 orthopaedic cases were undergoing surgery after fractured neck of femur. Some would therefore assert that anaesthesia for orthopaedic surgery should be a priority.

Grade of anaesthetists for the 90+

Figure A4
Grade of most senior anaesthetist: comparison between 90+ age group and whole sample

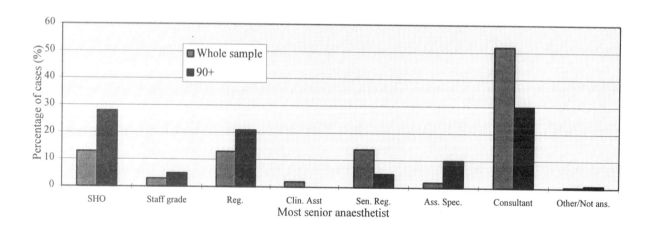

The most junior training grades, SHOs and registrars, anaesthetised almost 50% of the patients over 90 but only 26% of the whole sample. Ten (43%) of the 23 SHOs and five (28%) of the 18 registrars sought advice.

◆ In 80% of occasions when advice was sought the trainee received help (that is, someone came to assist).

Ten of the 23 SHOs had yet to pass an examination in anaesthesia and, of these, six did not seek advice from colleagues with more experience. In these six cases the patient was undergoing orthopaedic surgery. In most of the cases anaesthetised by junior anaesthetists in training grades the technique of anaesthesia seemed appropriate and did not affect the outcome.

An SHO who qualified 17 years earlier and had four years of anaesthetic experience but no higher anaesthetic qualification anaesthetised a 93-year-old, but otherwise fit, woman for a dynamic hip screw. General anaesthesia included thiopentone 350mg and fentanyl 100micrograms. Fluid therapy on the day before and the day of surgery was mainly dextrose saline. The intravenous infusion was discontinued on the morning of the first postoperative day. The patient subsequently drank little. On the second postoperative morning her serum sodium was 122m mol.litre^{-1}. She became confused and was given chlorpromazine 25mg and haloperidol 2mg before her death two hours later.

There was no consultation by this trainee who failed to recognise the sensitivity of the elderly to anaesthetic drugs. The management after operation may not have been under the anaesthetist's control but it was determinant in her death. Was this appropriate postoperative care for the elderly?

Table A15 (qs 3 and 26)
Classification of operation and most senior anaesthetist

	Emergency	Urgent	%	Scheduled	Elective	Not answered	Total
Consultant	-	20	*29.9*	2	3	1	**26**
Associate specialist	-	7	*10.4*	1	-	-	**8**
Senior registrar	-	3	*4.5*	-	-	-	**3**
Registrar	-	14	*20.9*	4	-	-	**18**
Staff grade	-	3	*4.5*	-	-	-	**3**
SHO	-	19	*28.4*	4	-	-	**23**
Not answered	-	1	*1.5*	-	-	-	**1**
Total	**-**	**67**	*100*	**11**	**3**	**1**	**82**

Table A16 (qs 3 and 44)
Grade of most senior anaesthetist and time of day

	Weekday in hours	Weekday out of hours*	Weekday time not stated	Weekend	Total
Consultant	21	1	1	3	**26**
Associate specialist	4	2	1	1	**8**
Senior registrar	2			1	**3**
Registrar	5	8		5	**18**
Staff grade	2		1		**3**
SHO	11	5	2	5	**23**
Not answered				1	**1**
Total	**45**	**16**	**5**	**16**	**82**

The percentage of patients anaesthetised by SHOs/registrars was:

Out-of-hours	72%
In-hours	36%

The majority of patients (54.9%) were anaesthetised during weekdays in-hours and of these 60% were anaesthetised by senior grades (consultant, senior registrar or associate specialist), 35.5% were anaesthetised by SHOs and registrars. Thirty-nine percent of patients were anaesthetised out of hours (weekdays after 18.00 hrs or weekends). Of these 71.9% were anaesthetised by SHOs and registrars. These grades anaesthetised 36.5% of the out-of-hours cases in the whole sample.

---

* see glossary, appendix B

Asa status of the 90+

Table A17 (q35)
ASA status

1	1
2	13
3	35
4	24
5	2
Not known	7
Total	**82**

Seventy-two percent of patients were classified as ASA 3 or 4. The two ASA 5 patients are described below.

A 91-year-old woman was assessed before operation by an anaesthetic SHO and registrar. She had peritonitis with a differential diagnosis of either mesenteric infarction or perforated diverticulum. Other coexisting conditions were previous myocardial infarction, chronic cardiac failure and angina. She was clinically unwell and assessed as ASA 5. There was discussion with a consultant anaesthetist and she underwent surgery at 06.00 hrs. A diagnostic laparotomy performed by a locum surgical senior registrar confirmed small bowel infarction and she died in recovery at 07.00 hrs. No surgical questionnaire was received.

Did the need to make a diagnosis take precedence over everything else?

A 99-year-old 'frail' woman was assessed before operation (Richard's screw and plate) by a consultant anaesthetist. She had ECG evidence of right bundle branch block and a bradycardia of 30/min. She had been on metoprolol until two days preoperatively. She was assessed as ASA 5. Intravenous atropine caused her heart rate to increase to 55/min. Anaesthesia was induced with thiopentone 50mg, suxamethonium 50mg and ketorolac 10mg. The patient rapidly became hypotensive and unresponsive to ephedrine 6mg and adrenaline 2mg. She died 10 minutes after induction.

If the patient had been younger would the management have been different?

Clinical management

As with previous NCEPOD reports, there were cases where fluid management could be questioned.

A 97-year-old woman was admitted with a fractured neck of femur. She was confused and had ischaemic heart disease, hypertension, non-insulin-dependent diabetes mellitus and mild renal impairment with a plasma urea of $12.5m\ mol.litre^{-1}$ and creatinine of 130micro $mol.litre^{-1}$. Her plasma sodium was $132m\ mol.litre^{-1}$. Surgery was 12 hours after admission during which time she received 1000ml of dextrose saline and had no measurable urine output, but was incontinent once. The systolic arterial pressure during general anaesthesia was less than 100mmHg for the final hour of her surgery which lasted a total of 1 hour 20 minutes. On the day of operation she had a total of 3550ml of fluid intravenously and no urine output. On the first postoperative day a urinary catheter was passed. On this day her total fluid intake was 2200ml and urine output 147ml. She died on the second postoperative morning with pulmonary oedema.

All doctors who prescribe intravenous fluids should understand the implications of fluid overload. Is basic fluid management not taught in medical schools?

There were several occasions when the drug choice and dosage seemed to be inappropriate for the age and condition of the patient.

A 95-year-old patient was admitted with an acute abdomen as a result of perforated diverticular disease. General anaesthesia was induced with propofol 100mg and fentanyl 100 micrograms and maintained with nitrous oxide and isoflurane 0.5-0.75%. An epidural was inserted and she received 9ml of 0.5% bupivacaine at the start of surgery. The systolic arterial pressure decreased to less than 100mmHg for 45 minutes, despite 24mg of ephedrine and 3000ml of fluid intravenously. At the end of surgery she received doxapram 20mg and the epidural was continued with a fentanyl and bupivacaine solution. At 23.00 hrs, after four hours in the recovery room she was returned to the general ward. At 06.30 hrs on the following morning she required naloxone. In the 24 hours postoperatively she developed an acutely ischaemic leg and the decision to do nothing further was made. Twenty-four hours after surgery the epidural catheter "fell out" and an infusion of subcutaneous diamorphine was started. She died 36 hours later.

A 97-year-old patient with a fractured neck of femur and (echocardiographically confirmed) aortic stenosis with a gradient of 95mmHg, was given papaveretum 20mg and prochlorperazine 12.5mg im. before surgery. On arrival in theatre she was hypotensive with respiratory depression, rigidity and tremor. She was given procyclidine to "excellent effect". Anaesthesia was induced in theatre with thiopentone 25mg, midazolam 5mg and alfentanil 250micrograms and maintained with nitrous oxide and isoflurane. This was supplemented with a 3-in-1 block using 20ml of 0.25% bupivacaine. Controlled ventilation of the lungs was facilitated by atracurium 35mg. During her operation (40 minutes) she was hypotensive and this was unresponsive to methoxamine. She remained hypotensive, refractory to methoxamine in recovery, developed tachypnoea with hypoxemia and died two hours later.

Postoperative care of the 90+.

Forty-two (51%) patients died on the day of surgery or the first postoperative day. Five patients died in theatre and three of these coincided with the use of orthopaedic cement. Recognising that there may be good surgical indications for the use of cement with prostheses, anaesthetists need to be even more aware of the risks of hypotension when other risk factors co-exist. These other risk factors are hypovolaemia, osteoporosis, advanced age, long-stem femoral component, previously undisturbed intramedullary canal and underlying malignant disease.

Table A18 (qs 65, 71 and 80)
Location of postoperative care in patients aged over 90 years, compared with whole sample

	90+ years		Whole sample	
Died in theatre	5		149	
Died in recovery	9		50	
ICU care before death	5	6%	460	38%
HDU care before death	4	5%	31	3%
None of the above	59		532	
Total	**82**		**1222**	

Should advanced age exclude a patient from ICU care?

The small total number admitted to ICU and HDU may not be surprising in view of the over-subscription for and under-provision of these facilities. However, if these high risk patients were considered suitable for operations they did have the right to expect appropriate preoperative and postoperative care.

A 90-year-old patient underwent surgery for oversewing a perforated duodenal ulcer. Preoperatively she was unwell with fast atrial fibrillation and hypotension with minimal urine output. Her serum creatinine was 265micro mol.litre^{-1}, urea 38.3m mol.litre^{-1} and plasma potassium 6.3m mol.litre^{-1} She received 600ml of fluid and 0.3mg of digoxin before operation. Peroperatively a CVP was inserted and she received 100ml of fluid and 1 unit of blood. Postoperatively the patient was unresponsive to stimulation. The anaesthetic SHO and surgical registrar made the decision to make no attempt to resuscitate her. She was returned to the general ward still hypotensive and in fast atrial fibrillation with no urine output. She received normal saline 1000ml iv over 10 hours and was prescribed a further 1000ml over eight hours. She died 14 hours after her surgery.

Were the decisions made in the patient's best interests and by the most appropriate staff?

Interpretation

- Consultant anaesthetists and surgeons need to discuss plans before operation and to decide best practice.
- It may be appropriate for a junior trainee to anaesthetise the very elderly for straightforward surgery but consultation with more experienced colleagues could result in improved management strategies.
- There is a high incidence of coexistent disease. Thorough preoperative assessment and preparation is an absolute prerequisite for surgery.
- Anaesthesia should be appropriate for the age and frailty of these patients.
- Multidisciplinary planning should extend into the postoperative period.

ANALYSIS OF THE WHOLE SAMPLE (CONTINUED)

Table A19 (qs 18 and 19)
Number of calendar days between operation and death

Same day	345
Next day	398
2 days	273
3 days	206
Total	**1222**

Table A20 (q26) and Figure A5
Classification of operation[*] (last before death)

Emergency	316	*25.9%*
Urgent	503	*41.2%*
Scheduled	267	*21.8%*
Elective	117	*9.6%*
Not answered	19	*1.5%*
Total	**1222**	

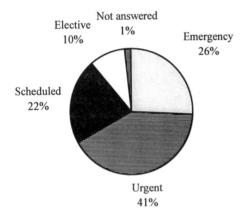

Comparison with previous years

	1992/93	1993/94	1994/95
Emergency	25%	15%	*26%*
Urgent	35%	42%	*41%*
Scheduled	30%	30%	*22%*
Elective	9%	12%	*10%*

---

[*] see glossary, appendix B

Table A21 (q26)
Classification of final operation/surgical specialty

	Elective	%	Scheduled	%	Urgent	%	Emergency	%	Not answered	Total
Cardiothoracic	9	13	31	46	14	21	13	19	1	**68**
General/colorectal	14	3	58	13	235	54	120	27	10	**437**
Gynaecology	11	22	30	61	5	10	3	6	-	**49**
Neurosurgery	5	10	5	10	13	27	26	53	-	**49**
Ophthalmology	2	67	-		1	33	-		-	**3**
Oral/maxillofacial	-		3	75	-		1	25	-	**4**
Orthopaedic	40	14	66	22	178	60	9	3	2	**295**
Otorhinolaryngology	4	25	8	50	2	1	2	1	-	**16**
Plastic	1	13	4	50	3	38	-		-	**8**
Urology	24	32	33	43	13	17	6	8	-	**76**
Vascular	7	3	29	13	39	18	136	63	6	**217**
Total	**117**	*10*	**267**	*22*	**503**	*41*	**316**	*26*	**19**	**1222**

If the provision of out-of-hours anaesthesia is to move to a consultant-based service, then the table above suggests that there would need to be a marked increase in consultant numbers in those Trusts where vascular, general/colorectal or neurosurgical operations are carried out.

Table A22 (q29)
Was an anaesthetist consulted by the surgeon (as distinct from informed) before the operation?

		94/95	93/94	92/93
Yes	662	54.2%	49.7%	50.7%
No	514			
Not answered	15			
Not known/not recorded	31			
Total	**1222**			

Table A23 (q30)
Where did the anaesthetist assess the patient before the operation?

Ward	911
Outpatient department	6
Theatre suite	74
Accident and Emergency department	93
ICU/HDU	104
Other	10
Not assessed	4
Not answered	10
Not known/not recorded	10
Total	**1222**

Was this anaesthetist present at the start of the operation?

Yes	1143
No	58
Not answered	12
Not known/not recorded	5
Not assessed (see q30)	4
Total	**1222**

Table A24 (qs 26 and 30)
Classification of operation when the patient was assessed in the theatre suite

Emergency	50
Urgent	14
Scheduled	4
Elective	3
Not answered	3
Total	**74**

Elective and scheduled cases assessed in the theatre suite

	Age	Day of admission	Time of admission	Day of death	Operation	Complications
Elective	65	1 day preop	16.00	0	TURP	MI - Difficult intubation
Elective	72	1 day preop	18.00	2	Total knee replacement	MI
Elective	73	1 day preop	n/a	2	TURP	Mental debility and Bronchopneumonia
Scheduled	66	6 days preop	n/a	3	Aorto bifemoral graft	Cardiac arrest
Scheduled	83	3 days preop	09.00	3	Removal Denham pin	PE
Scheduled	84	on day of surgery	10.00	3	TURP	Renal failure. Pericarditis and pleurisy
Scheduled	86	6 days preop	n/a	0	Revision total hip	This case is described below

The 86-year-old woman had to have a revision of her artificial hip joint when the attempt to reduce its dislocation failed. She weighed 44 kg, had atrial fibrillation, was dyspnoeic at rest, was taking nifedipine and was in left heart failure. The consultant anaesthetist's technique for the manipulation was for her to breathe enflurane spontaneously through a laryngeal mask. This method was not altered when the operation became invasive. Her haemoglobin was 9.8 gm/100 ml at the start of the operation and she received three units of packed cells with three doses of frusemide during the procedure. The systolic blood pressure was around 80mmHg for one and a half hours when the oxygen saturations were between 92 and 85%. Cardiac arrest occurred in theatre from which she was resuscitated but she died four hours later in recovery whilst receiving IPPV and inotropes. The postmortem examination confirmed the diagnosis of recent myocardial infarction.

Is the standard of care for the patients listed above one which anaesthetists can condone?

Table A25 (q31a)
Which of the following investigations were done before the anaesthetic? (Including tests carried out in the referral hospital and available before the operation)

None		15
Haemoglobin		1168
Packed cell volume (haematocrit)		819
White cell count		1100
Sickle cell test (e.g. Sickledex)		21
Blood group +/- cross match		96
Coagulation screen		379
Plasma electrolytes	Na	1132
	K	1110
	Cl	389
	HCO_3	540
Blood urea		1079
Creatinine		992
Serum albumin		491
Bilirubin (total)		432
Glucose		628
Amylase		198
Urinalysis (ward or lab)		363
Blood gas analysis		297
Chest X-ray		860
Electrocardiography		1032
Respiratory function tests		59
Special cardiac investigation (e.g. cardiac catheterization)		92
Special neurological investigation (e.g. imaging)		47
Others relevant to anaesthesia*		84
Investigations not specified/ not known/not recorded		10

others (may be multiple) included:

abdominal X-ray/ultrasound	24
thyroid function test	13
calcium/serum calcium	10
CT scan	10
cervical spine/neck X-ray	9
cardiac enzymes	5
digoxin level	3
miscellaneous	14

Nine of the 15 patients without preoperative investigations had a ruptured abdominal aortic aneurysm, three had major trauma and one was to have an emergency pulmonary embolectomy. These 13 patients went directly to theatre. For two (MUA shoulder and laparotomy for perforated duodenal ulcer) no reason was given for the lack of preoperative investigations.

Table A26 (q32)
Coexisting medical diagnoses

None	108
Not answered	24
Not known/not recorded	4
Respiratory	380
Cardiac	702
Neurological	257
Endocrine	178
Alimentary	219
Renal	170
Hepatic	72
Musculoskeletal	159
Vascular	183
Haematological	119
Genetic abnormality	5
Obesity	64
Sepsis	125
Others*	88

* others (may be multiple) includes:

malignancy	52
cachexia	14
eye	11
other (miscellaneous)	11

Aortic Stenosis

Aortic stenosis is a known predictor of increased operative risk. Ten patients in this sample were reported to have aortic stenosis, mild to severe.

Diagnosis of aortic stenosis

The diagnosis was missed preoperatively in five patients. Two patients were undergoing emergency abdominal aortic aneurysm repair. In the other three cases the preoperative diagnosis may have affected the patient management. One of these is described below.

A 54-year-old woman had undergone four uneventful general anaesthetics for laryngoscopies in the previous six years. She was scheduled for laryngectomy for a carcinoma of the larynx which was undertaken at a district general hospital with both ICU and HDU facilities. The patient was being treated for chronic heart failure with digoxin and diuretics. During her preoperative assessment a consultant anaesthetist noted the history of dyspnoea on exertion, a pan-systolic murmur on auscultation, cardiomegaly on the chest X-ray and left ventricular hypertrophy with ST segment depression on the ECG, but failed to recognise that aortic stenosis was present. General anaesthesia was induced with etomidate and maintained with fentanyl 200mg and isoflurane 1%. Preoperative arterial pressure was recorded as 120/70mmHg. Peroperative monitoring included intra-arterial pressure. The systolic arterial pressure decreased to between 75 to 100mmHg throughout the three hours of surgery. Ephedrine to a total of 12micrograms was given during the first 15 minutes of surgery when the systolic arterial pressure further decreased, to 60mmHg, but subsequently no attempt was made to correct it. Peroperative blood loss was 250ml and her total intravenous fluid intake on the day of surgery was 2000ml. Postoperatively she returned to the general ward. At 02.00 hrs, nine hours after surgery, the medical staff noted that she had been hypotensive since her return from theatre with an arterial pressure of 80/50mmHg. Her pulse rate was then 95/min, she had basal crepitations and had not passed urine. She was given 500ml of gelofusine over one hour. At 04.30 hrs she was distressed and in pulmonary oedema. At 05.00 hrs she suffered a cardiac arrest and died. Her postmortem examination reported gross left ventricular hypertrophy and severe aortic stenosis with almost complete obstruction. There was no evidence of residual tumour.

This patient had a surgically correctable valvular heart condition.

Peroperative management of patients with aortic stenosis

An anaesthetic which predisposes to hypotension is inappropriate in patients with aortic stenosis and particularly when the aortic stenosis is associated with angina. A low diastolic arterial pressure impairs myocardial perfusion. Many anaesthetists are wary of spinal anaesthesia.

A 71-year-old man was scheduled for bilateral knee replacement to be performed by two surgeons simultaneously at a district general hospital with ICU and HDU facilities. He had a history of angina and one year previously had an angiogram which had shown ischaemic heart disease and mild aortic stenosis. His preoperative ECG showed ST segment depression. He received spinal anaesthesia using 2.5ml plain bupivacaine. Before anaesthesia his blood pressure, which was monitored non-invasively, was 96/46mmHg. During surgery the systolic arterial pressure was between 86-108mmHg, the measured blood loss was 1500ml and replacement fluid was 2000ml of clear fluid and two units of packed red blood cells. Postoperatively he was returned to the general ward and during the first 36 hours he was noted to be "hypotensive but well". At 36 hours postoperatively he became rapidly breathless and suffered a fatal cardiac arrest. A postmortem examination reported severe coronary atheroma with acute myocardial ischaemia and moderate to severe aortic stenosis.

Would a reassessment of his valve disease have affected his perioperative management?

Postoperative care of patients with aortic stenosis

The severity of a patient's medical condition warrants increased care as much as the extent of the surgery.

An 84-year-old man with known aortic stenosis and with shortness of breath on exertion was scheduled for a gastrectomy. He was monitored invasively peroperatively; postoperatively he was nursed on the intensive care unit overnight. He made an uneventful early recovery. Six days later he developed a deep wound dehiscence. An SHO anaesthetist without anaesthetic qualifications and without consulting a senior anaesthetist returned with him to theatre. General anaesthesia was induced with propofol to a total of 200mg and maintained on a laryngeal mask airway with isoflurane 0.6-2.0%. Analgesia was provided by alfentanil and morphine. There was a short period of hypotension after induction. He was returned to the general ward where 18 hours later he had a cardiac arrest and died. A postmortem examination reported severe atheroma with a recent myocardial infarction and mild aortic stenosis.

This patient received excellent anaesthetic care during his <u>first</u> operation but would the outcome have been different if the SHO had asked for help during the second operation?

Interpretation

- A patient with an ejection systolic murmur in association with evidence of left ventricular hypertrophy or myocardial ischaemia requires referral to a cardiologist preoperatively for assessment of the aortic valve.
- If there is significant aortic stenosis then consultation between the specialties should agree the sequence and extent of surgical interventions.
- Anaesthetists need to be aware of the high risks of aortic stenosis associated with hypotension in the perioperative period.

ANALYSIS OF THE WHOLE SAMPLE (CONTINUED)

Table A27 (q35) and Figure A6
ASA status

ASA 1	14
ASA 2	148
ASA 3	354
ASA 4	383
ASA 5	247
Not answered	76
Total	**1222**

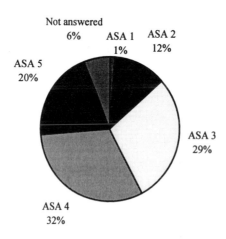

Table A28 (q35)
ASA status/surgical specialty

	ASA 1	%	ASA 2	%	ASA 3	%	ASA 4	%	ASA 5	%	Not ans.	Total
Cardiothoracic	-		5	7	20	29	28	41	8	12	7	**68**
General/colorectal	2	<1	38	9	126	29	158	36	98	22	15	**437**
Gynaecology	2	4	9	18	21	43	12	24	2	4	3	**49**
Neurosurgery	2	4	1	2	7	14	15	31	20	41	4	**49**
Ophthalmology	-		-		2	67	-		-		1	**3**
Oral/maxillofacial	-		-		2	50	1	25	1	25	-	**4**
Orthopaedic	4	1	68	23	109	37	83	28	9	3	22	**295**
Otolaryngology	1	6	1	6	6	38	4	25	-		4	**16**
Plastic	-		2	25	2	25	3	38	-		1	**8**
Urology	3	4	16	21	30	39	19	25	4	5	4	**76**
Vascular	-		8	4	29	13	60	28	105	48	15	**217**
Total	**14**	*1*	**148**	*12*	**354**	*29*	**383**	*31*	**247**	*20*	**76**	**1222**

There was a startling apparent increase in the proportion of ASA 5 patients in this year's sample. Whatever the demerits of the ASA classification one would expect early deaths to contain a higher proportion of ASA 5 patients than any sample which included 30-day deaths; it does.

Table A29 (qs 26 and 35)
Classification of final operation by ASA status

	Elective	%	Scheduled	%	Urgent	%	Emergency	%	Not ans.	Total
ASA 1	6	43	5	36	2	14	1	7	-	14
ASA 2	42	28	55	37	45	30	4	3	2	148
ASA 3	44	12	121	34	164	46	19	5	6	354
ASA 4	17	4	65	17	205	54	93	24	3	383
ASA 5	-		1	<1	57	23	184	74	5	247
Not answered	8	11	20	26	30	39	15	20	3	76
Total	**117**	*10*	**267**	*22*	**503**	*41*	**316**	*26*	**19**	**1222**

Table A30 (qs 3 and 35)
Most senior anaesthetist present at start of anaesthetic by ASA status

	ASA 1	%	ASA 2	%	ASA 3	%	ASA 4	%	ASA 5	%	Not ans.	Total
Consultant	7	1	73	11	167	26	210	33	142	22	41	640
Assoc. specialist	1	3	3	10	11	38	8	28	3	10	3	29
Senior registrar	-		8	5	30	18	59	36	61	37	8	166
Clinical assistant	1	4	6	25	9	38	3	13	3	13	2	24
Staff grade	-		9	21	13	31	13	31	4	10	3	42
Registrar	1	1	11	7	55	35	53	34	27	17	9	156
SHO	4	3	38	24	67	42	36	23	4	3	10	159
Other	-		-		1		1		2		-	4
Not answered	-		-		1		-		1		-	2
Total	**14**	*1*	**148**	*12*	**354**	*29*	**383**	*31*	**247**	*20*	**76**	**1222**

Table A31 (qs 2, 3 and 35) and Figure A7
Hospital type where ASA status of patient was 4 or 5 and the most senior anaesthetist was a consultant or senior registrar

	Consultant	Senior registrar
District General	261	41
University/teaching	72	73
Surgical specialty	11	9
Other NHS	3	-
Independent	5	-
Total	**352**	**123**

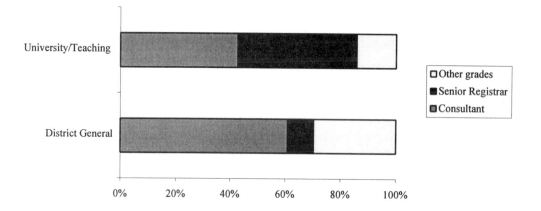

In District General Hospitals 70% of ASA 4 or 5 patients were anaesthetised by a consultant or senior registrar, 61% of them by a consultant. In university/teaching hospitals 86% of ASA 4 or 5 patients were anaesthetised by a consultant or senior registrar, 42% of them by a consultant.

The difference in proportions, senior registrar to consultant, between these two categories of hospitals reflects the distribution of senior registrars in training.

◆ This high proportion of seriously ill patients being anaesthetised by the most senior grades represents good practice.

Table A32 (q38)
Did the patient receive intravenous fluid therapy in the 12 hours before induction?

Yes	795
No	412
Not answered	8
Not known/not recorded	7
Total	**1222**

Table A33 (q38)
Patients who received intravenous fluid therapy in the 12 hours before induction

	Emergency	%	Urgent	%	Scheduled	%	Elective	%	Not answered	Total
General/colorectal	114	95.0	227	96.6	21	36.2	1	7.1	9	**372**
Orthopaedic	8	88.9	112	62.9	35	53.0	3	7.5	1	**159**
Vascular	118	86.8	31	79.5	9	31.0	2	28.6	6	**166**
All specialties	**276**	**87.3**	**404**	**80.3**	**89**	**33.3**	**10**	**8.5**	**16**	**795**

Table A34 (q40a)
Were premedicant drugs prescribed?

		1994/95	1993/94	1992/93
Yes	299	*24.5%*	*31.2%*	*34.8%*
No	916			
Not answered	7			
Total	**1222**			

Atropine	15
Chloral hydrate	3
Diazepam	29
Droperidol	3
Fentanyl	5
Hyoscine	19
Lorazepam	22
Ketamine	3
Metoclopramide	81
Midazolam	7
Morphine	38
Papaveretum	18
Pethidine	23
Prochlorperazine	11
Temazepam	134
Promethazine	14
Trimeprazine	2
Non-steroidal analgesics	8
Other	15
Premed given but drug not recorded	4

In 1992/93,[5] a report on 30-day deaths, of the patients receiving premedicant drugs 34.4% received opioids and 59.3% benzodiazepines. In this sample of three-day deaths, of the patients receiving premedicant drugs 28.1% received opioids and 64.2% benzodiazepines.

Table A35 (q41a)
Was non-invasive monitoring established just before the induction of anaesthesia?

Yes	1145
No	49
Not answered	10
Not known/not recorded	18
Total	**1222**

ECG	1052
BP	913
Pulse oximetry	1115
Capnography	272
Inspired oxygen	377
Temperature	59
Other*	10

Other includes:

Urinary catheter	5
Blood loss	2
Precordial stethoscope	2
ECG	1

Cases in which non invasive monitoring was not established before induction of anaesthesia:

Intubated on arrival in theatres	15
Full invasive monitoring	7
Proxy anaesthetist responding to the questionnaire	9

Of the remaining 18 patients that were reported as having no non-invasive monitoring preoperatively the grades of the most senior anaesthetist were:

Consultant	14
Senior registrar	2
Staff grade	1
Clinical assistant	1

Is experience a substitute for patient monitoring?

Table A36 (q42a)
Was invasive monitoring established before induction of anaesthesia e.g. CVP, arterial line?

Yes	393
No	805
Not answered	18
Not known/not recorded	6

CVP	287
Arterial line	299
Pulmonary arterial line	46
Blood gas analysis	152
Other	11

Table A37 (q52a)
Were monitoring devices used during the management of this anaesthetic?

Yes	1218
No	-
Not answered	2
Not known/not recorded	2
Total	**1222**

	Anaesthetic Room	Operating Room
ECG	761	1214
Pulse oximeter	824	1217
Indirect BP	665	1104
Pulse meter	153	305
Oesophageal or precordial (chest wall) stethoscope	20	37
Fresh gas O_2 analyser	207	754
Inspired gas O_2 analyser	176	907
Inspired anaesthetic vapour analyser	78	665
Expired CO_2 analyser	196	1069
Airway pressure gauge	169	975
Ventilation volume	97	774
Ventilation disconnect device	150	973
Peripheral nerve stimulator	24	283
Temperature	18	198
Urine output	122	624
CVP	151	524
Direct arterial BP (invasive)	127	446
Pulmonary arterial pressure	19	72
Intracranial pressure	-	3
EEG/CFAM/evoked responses	-	-
Other	-	16
Anaesthetic room not used	338	-
Operating theatre not used	-	-
Not answered	34	1
Not known/not recorded	10	-

One patient was recorded as having no pulse oximetry. This was a patient undergoing repair of a ruptured aortic aneurysm and the oximeter was not sensing the pulse.

For the four patients who had no ECG monitoring in theatre, the grades of anaesthetist were:

Age	Anaesthetist	Monitoring	Operation
43	Consultant	Pulse oximetry, CVP and direct arterial BP.	Extensive burns of limbs and chest.
80	Consultant	Pulse oximetry only.	Diagnostic D&C and hysteroscopy (grade IV angina).
83	Consultant	Pulse oximetry and indirect BP.	Laparotomy for ovarian carcinoma.
91	SHO	Pulse oximetry only.	MUA of a dislocated shoulder.

Capnography was not widely used in the anaesthetic room. Some anaesthetists commented (question 53) that this equipment was not available for them in this location.

Pulmonary artery pressure was monitored in 38 patients undergoing laparotomy (many with abdominal sepsis), 18 patients undergoing cardiac surgery (34% of all cardiac surgery) and nine patients undergoing abdominal aortic aneurysm repair (6.6% of all abdominal aortic aneurysms). Should pulmonary artery pressure be monitored more frequently? (See NCEPOD report, 1993/94[6]).

Table A38 (q53)
Did anything hinder full monitoring?

Yes	67
No	1131
Not answered	17
Not known/not recorded	7
Total	**1222**

Non-availability of monitors	12
Problems with SaO_2 (vasoconstriction)	6
Problems with CVP line	4
Miscellaneous	31
Not stated	14

Table A39 (q48)
Was there a trained anaesthetist's assistant (ie ODA, SODA, anaesthetic nurse) present for this case?

Yes	1207
No	10
Not answered	2
Not known/not recorded	3
Total	**1222**

Table A40 (q48)
Regional distribution of cases where no trained anaesthetist's assistant was present

	No trained assistant	All cases
Anglia & Oxford	-	102
North Thames	-	121
North West	-	168
Northern & Yorkshire	1	177
Northern Ireland	7	46
South & West	-	168
South Thames	1	124
Trent	-	116
Wales	-	74
West Midlands	-	101
Other (non-NHS)	1	25
Total	**10**	**1222**

Table A41 (q51a)
Did the patient receive intravenous fluids during the operation?

Yes	1155
No	40
Not answered	9
Not known/not recorded	18
Total	**1222**

Dextrose 5%	39	
Dextrose 4% saline 0.18%	112	
Dextrose 10%	10	
Saline 0.9%	351	
Hartmann's (compound sodium lactate)	733	
Other	27	*(includes 14 NaHCO$_3$)*

Modified gelatin (Gelofusine, Haemaccel)	665	
Human albumin solution	84	
Starch (HES)	102	
Dextran	19	
Mannitol	59	
Other	1	

Whole blood	305	
Platelets	68	
Fresh frozen plasma	166	
Other component	142	*(includes 133 red cell components)*

Problems in obtaining blood products

Most anaesthetists have encountered the frustration and anxiety arising out of organisational difficulties in obtaining blood and blood products when they are urgently needed. Organisational difficulties were commented upon in seven cases.

A 79-year-old patient with ischaemic heart disease was scheduled for a cystoscopy and trans-rectal prostatic needle biopsy. He had a preoperative haemoglobin of 9.0 gm/dl. The anaesthetist requested that blood be cross-matched. However, the surgical team did not arrange this.

Delays were experienced in six cases in obtaining blood or blood products when they were required. The operations were; ruptured abdominal aortic aneurysm (4), laparotomy (1) and splenectomy (1).

The distance of a hospital from central transfusion services was a factor in two cases; in one there was a three-hour delay for platelets to come from another town when the patient's platelet count was $20x10^9$/L. In the other, blood products were delayed after they were ordered from the regional centre 60 miles away. Centralised blood transfusion services should include provision for rapid transportation of urgently required blood products.

Poor local organisation was responsible when a consultant surgeon and anaesthetic senior registrar had a 30-minute delay during an urgent laparotomy before a haematology registrar was contacted, then a subsequent 20-minute delay before the laboratory technician was permitted to defrost some fresh frozen plasma.

Postoperative coagulopathy was implicated in the deaths of five patients who had large blood losses. In three of these cases, with measured blood losses of 4,000, 7,000 and 8,000 ml, there was no record of replacement of clotting factors. One patient received 17 units of blood, 300 ml of fresh frozen plasma and no platelets. In another, a 68-year-old patient underwent a nephrectomy and removal of L2 vertebral body. Overnight concealed blood loss was unrecognised by the attending ICU medical staff. The next morning, when the haemoglobin was 2.0gm/dl, the patient underwent re-exploration at which time blood was replaced but clotting factors were not. This patient subsequently died with a coagulopathy and uncontrolled bleeding.

INTERPRETATION

- Organisational delays in the transport of urgently required blood or blood products to patients in theatre are unacceptable.
- It is recommended that anaesthetic departments, haematology departments and the regional blood transfusion service co-operate to produce written agreed procedures for the rapid procurement of blood and blood products when they are urgently required. These should be circulated to all members of the anaesthetic, operating and surgical departments.
- Anaesthetic departments should have written protocols about the replacement of clotting factors.

ANALYSIS OF THE WHOLE SAMPLE (CONTINUED)

Table A42 (q55)
What type of anaesthetic was used?

General alone	936
Local infiltration alone	-
Regional alone	55
General and regional	137
General and local infiltration	35
Sedation alone	3
Sedation and local infiltration	4
Sedation and regional	44
Not answered	2
No anaesthetic given	5
Not known/not recorded	1
Total	**1222**

Table A43 (q57)
How was the airway established during anaesthesia?

Face mask (with or without oral airway)	23
Laryngeal mask	75
Orotracheal intubation	909
Nasotracheal intubation	16
Endobronchial intubation	23
Tracheostomy	11
Patient already intubated prior to arrival in theatre suite	99
Other	3
Not known/not recorded	2
Total	**1108**

Table A44 (q59)
Were there any problems with airway maintenance or ventilation?

Yes	44
No	1057
Not answered	2
Not known/not recorded	5
Total	***1108**

* general anaesthesia with or without regional or local anaesthesia

The problems were:

14/44 had "parenchymal lung" problems which included: ARDS, infection, infiltration, trauma, pulmonary oedema and hypoxia of undisclosed origin.

3/44 had "mechanical" problems: tension pneumothorax, hypoxia with an open chest and breathing with 'small tidal volumes'.

6/44 had "airway" problems which included: tracheal oedema, blood, vomit, sputum and bronchospasm.

15/44 had "tube related" problems which included: difficult intubation, malposition of the tube during anaesthesia and inadequate airway with the LMA (2 cases)

3/44 were "miscellaneous": precautions for a rheumatoid neck, oesophageal intubation and hypoxia with hypotension during spinal anaesthesia.

3/44 the cause was not stated

Table A45 (q60)
If the anaesthetic included a regional technique, which method was used?

Epidural - caudal	5
Epidural - lumbar	51
Epidural - thoracic	32
Interpleural	-
Intravenous regional	2
Cranial or peripheral nerve blocks	17
Plexus block (e.g. brachial, 3 in 1 block)	28
Subarachnoid (spinal)	98
Surface (e.g. for bronchoscopy)	2
Not answered	6
Total	**236**

Table A46 (q61)
Which agent was used?

Local	221
Narcotic	42
Other	5
Not answered	10
Total	**236**

Table A47 (q62)
Which sedative drugs were given for this procedure (excluding premedication)?

Inhalant	3
Narcotic analgesic	11
Benzodiazepine	32
Sub-anaesthetic doses of IV anaesthetic drugs	18
Other	3
Not answered	1
Total cases	***51**

* sedation with or without regional or local anaesthesia

Table A48 (q63)
Was oxygen given?

Yes	90
No	4
Not answered	10
Not known/not recorded	2
Total	**106**

Routine	72
Otherwise indicated	23
Not answered	2

Table A49 (q64)
Which special care areas exist in the hospital in which the operation took place?

None	4
Not answered	37
Recovery area/room	1138
High dependency unit	332
Intensive care unit	1007
Other*	5
Total	**1222**

* Other includes one each of the following: specialised ICU only, renal high care ward, monitored beds on selected wards, ability to 'special' patient on ward - 1:1 nursing, assessment unit.

Of the four questionnaires that claimed their hospital had no special care facilities, there were other questionnaires received from three of the hospitals that indicated that these facilities were available. It is probable therefore that these represent erroneous information rather than the true state of affairs.

Careful cross-referencing of the questionnaires by hospital, carried out by the administrative staff at NCEPOD, suggests that for the 326 hospitals from which information was returned, 98% had a recovery area, 48% had an HDU and 85% an ICU.

Table A50 (q64)
Availability of essential services/surgical specialty of procedure

	Adult HDU	%	Adult ICU	%	None	Total
Cardiothoracic	48	71	63	93	1	68
General/colorectal	114	26	380	87	-	437
Gynaecology	10	20	37	76	-	49
Neurosurgery	15	31	46	93	-	49
Orthopaedic	66	22	214	73	1	295
Urology	17	22	59	78	-	76
Vascular	49	23	187	86	2	217
Other specialties	12		21			
Total	**331**	27	**1007**	82	4	1222

Table A51 (q65)
Where did the patient go on leaving theatre?

Recovery area/room	676
High dependency unit	11
Intensive care unit	315
Specialised ICU	48
Ward	17
Another hospital	4
Other*	1
Not known/not recorded	1
Died in theatre	149
Total	**1222**

* This was described as "non-equipped recovery area without trained staff."

Of the 17 patients who returned directly to the ward the reasons were:

5/17 recovery facilities were not available 24 hours a day. All involved general anaesthesia and the operations were: laparotomy (2), fixation of fractured femur (2) and burr holes (1).

2/17 patients were deemed not for resuscitation and returned to the ward directly from theatre.
10/17 no reason stated. Seven cases involved general anaesthesia, three cases involved regional anaesthesia.

It is unacceptable to undertake anaesthesia when no specialised recovery service is available. Hospital managers must be made aware of their responsibility to make provision for this essential facility wherever and whenever anaesthesia is given.

Table A52 (q71)
Where did this patient go next (i.e. after the recovery room)?

Not applicable - recovery room not used	546
Ward	548
High dependency unit	26
Intensive care unit	27
Specialised ICU	8
Home	1
Another hospital	3
Died in recovery area	50
Other	1
Not answered	12
Total	**1222**

Table A53 (q69)
Were monitoring devices used during the management of this patient in the recovery room?

Yes	643
No	5
Not answered	26
Not known/not recorded	2
Not applicable - recovery room not used	546
Total	**1222**

ECG	410
Pulse oximeter	623
Indirect BP	608
Pulse meter	118
Oesophageal or precordial (chest wall) stethoscope	4
Inspired gas O_2 analyser	17
Expired CO_2 analyser	15
Airway pressure gauge	21
Ventilation volume	16
Ventilator disconnect device	22
Peripheral nerve stimulator	7
Temperature	76
Urine output	166
CVP	73
Direct arterial BP (invasive)	35
Blood gas analysis	31
Pulmonary arterial pressure	5
Intracranial pressure	1
Cardiac output	3
Other*	3
Not specified	1

* Other includes three patients whose blood sugar was determined.

◆ Ninety-seven percent of these patients received pulse oximetry monitoring in the recovery room.

Table A54 (q68)
Were you unable at any time to transfer the patient into an ICU, HDU, etc?

Yes	73
No	958
Not answered	36
Not known/not recorded	6
Not applicable - died in theatre	149
Total	**1222**

Reasons (may be multiple):

Closed at night	1
Closed at weekend	1
Understaffing	12
Lack of beds	45
No ICU or HDU in hospital	16
Other	8
Not specified	2

Table A55
Distribution of cases where unable to transfer the patient into an ICU, HDU etc.

	Unable to transfer	All cases
Anglia & Oxford	4	102
North Thames	7	121
North West	15	168
Northern & Yorkshire	7	177
Northern Ireland	2	46
South & West	13	168
South Thames	8	124
Trent	4	116
Wales	2	74
West Midlands	11	101
Miscellaneous	-	25
Total	**73**	**1222**

This information relates to 1994/95. The problems of underprovision of ICU and HDU beds, highlighted in previous NCEPOD reports, persist.

Table A56 (q73)
Did any of the following events, which required specific treatment, occur during anaesthesia or immediate recovery (ie the first few hours after the end of the operation)?

Yes	586
No	607
Not answered	24
Not known/not recorded	5
Total	**1222**

Air embolus	2
Airway obstruction	6
Anaphylaxis	1
Arrhythmia	93
Bradycardia *(to or less than 50% of resting)*	92
Bronchospasm	8
Cardiac arrest *(unintended)*	*167
Convulsions	2
Disconnection of breathing system	-
Hyperpyrexia *(greater than 40°C or very rapid increase in temperature)*	2
Hypertension *(increase of more than 50% resting systolic)*	18
Hypotension *(decrease of more than 50% resting systolic)*	353
Hypoxaemia	92
Misplaced tracheal tube	5
Pneumothorax	6
Pulmonary aspiration	12
Pulmonary oedema	28
Respiratory arrest *(unintended)*	17
Tachycardia *(increase of 50% or more)*	52
Unintentional delayed recovery of consciousness	21
Ventilatory inadequacy	52
Total spinal	2
Wrong dose or overdose of drug	2
Other	23

* Cardiac arrest - surgical specialty

Vascular	58
Orthopaedic	38
General/colorectal	34
Cardiothoracic	17
Urology	11
Gynaecology	6
Otorhinolaryngology	3
Total	**167**

Table A57 (q75a)
What were the complications or events after this operation?

Ventilatory problems	335
Cardiac problems	560
Hepatic failure	18
Septicaemia	165
Renal failure	233
Central nervous system failure	124
Progress of surgical condition	184
Electrolyte imbalance	97
Haematological disorder/coagulopathy	141
Other	41
Not applicable (died in theatre)	149
Not answered/"none"	165
Not known/not recorded	2
Total	**1222**

Table A58 (q76)
Were drugs given for pain in the first 48 hours after operation?

Yes	863
No	165
Not answered	37
Not known/not recorded	8
Not applicable - died in theatre	149
Total	**1222**

Drug type (may be multiple):

Opiate/opioid	812
Local analgesic	81
Non-steroidal analgesic	69
General (inhaled) anaesthetic	6
Other	47
Not specified	1

Method/route (may be multiple):

Intramuscular injection	334
Oral	86
Rectal	28
Continuous intravenous infusion	341
Patient-controlled analgesia	77
Continuous epidural	67
Patient-controlled epidural analgesia	1
Inhaled	2
Other	1
Not specified	4

Table A59 (q77)
Did complications occur as a result of these analgesic methods?

Yes	32
No	815
Not answered	11
Not known/not recorded	5
Not applicable (e.g. no analgesia given)	359
Total	**1222**

The causes of complications were:
  5/32 Respiratory depression - iv opioid 3, sc opiate 1, iv + epidural opioid 1
  4/32 Hypotension - epidural 4
  2/32 Excessive sedation - iv opioid 1, im opioid 1
  2/32 Confusion - iv opioid 1, im opioid 1
  2/32 Gastro-intestinal bleeding - NSAID 2
  13/32 Not specified - iv opioid 2, im opioid ± NSAID 7, im NSAID 1, epidural 3
  4/32 Others - histamine reaction 1, poor pain control 1, cardiovascular deterioration 1, NSAID induced renal failure 1

Only three of these patients were nursed on the ICU/HDU, two with patient-controlled analgesia and one with a continuous opioid infusion for pain control. The remaining 29 were nursed on a general ward including all the patients who were given epidural analgesia.

Nine patients had epidural analgesia with opioid and bupivacaine; of these, three also had concurrent intravenous opioids.

Eight patients had either patient-controlled analgesia (4) or continuous opioid analgesia (4) as their main method for analgesia.

Information on pain services and the supervision of these patients on the wards was limited. Nevertheless, there was some evidence of administration of excessive analgesia.

Table A60 (q78)
Were other sedative/hypnotic or other drugs given?

Yes	326
No	644
Not answered	96
Not known/not recorded	7
Not applicable - died in theatre	149
Total	**1222**

Propofol	140
Midazolam	133
Other benzodiazepine	19
Other	46
Not specified/ details not known	5

Table A61 (q80)
Place of death

Theatre	151
Recovery area	53
Intensive care unit	426
High dependency unit	20
Ward	548
Home	2
Another hospital	8
Other*	12
Not answered	2
Total	**1222**

Other:

CCU	9
Toilet	1
Special respiratory unit	1
CT scanning unit	1

Table A62 (q82)
Do you have morbidity/mortality review meetings in your department?

Yes	1120
No	91
Not answered	11
Total	**1222**

For 91 cases the respondent stated that there were no morbidity/mortality review meetings in their hospital; 19 of these were in university/teaching hospitals.

Table A63 (q82a)
If yes, will this case be or has it been discussed at your departmental meeting?

Yes	471
No	624
Not answered	22
Not known/not recorded	3
Total	**1120**

Early deaths are traditionally, if inaccurately, ascribed to the effects of anaesthesia. It is particularly surprising that fewer than half of this sample were even considered at departmental meetings.

Table A64 (q83)
Has a consultant anaesthetist seen and agreed this form?

Yes	756
No	42
Not answered	359
Not known/not recorded	65
Total	**1222**

Positive points indicated by the symbol ◆ in the section about anaesthesia

For the total sample:

>   the anaesthetists responsible for these patients sought advice in almost a quarter of the cases which included 53 cases where consultants sought advice from other consultants.

>   a high proportion of seriously ill patients (ASA 4 and 5) were anaesthetised by the most senior grades (senior registrars and consultants).

>   ninety-seven percent of these patients received pulse oximetry monitoring in the recovery room.

For the patients aged over 90:

>   in 80% of occasions when advice was sought, the trainee received help (that is, someone came in to assist).

>   fifty-nine (72%) of the 82 patients received preoperative fluid therapy indicating a high level of awareness of the potential for dehydration in this population.

Surgery

Introduction

The method of collection for the surgical data has been described in the general data section (page 18). This report presents the data in a different manner from previous years. The overall or accumulated figures for all specialties for deaths occurring within three calendar days of a surgical procedure (limited to one death per surgeon, see page 18) are given here. Individual surgeons and departments can compare their own performance against these tables and identify areas where there is cause for local concern and scope for improvement. There are then commentaries for each specialty. The presentation for these specialty commentaries is not uniform since there were differing numbers of deaths between the surgical specialties and individual issues which required comment. In the anaesthetic section of this report, good practice is highlighted with a ◆; where appropriate this approach has been used for the surgical sections in this report.

Key points about surgical practice are given on page 75.

The individual questionnaires and accumulated data were reviewed by advisors whose interests are relevant to the specialties involved and who were recommended to NCEPOD from within the profession. These advisors are listed below with a record of their attendance at meetings. NCEPOD is grateful to them for their help and guidance in the production of this report.

Advisory group	Meetings held	Meetings attended
Cardiothoracic		
W J Brawn	2	1
C Forrester-Wood	2	2
M T Jones	2	1
K M Taylor	2	2
General/colorectal		
J Beynon	4	3
T G J Brightmore	4	4
D Cade	4	4
J Chamberlain	4	2
K R Gardiner	4	3
D Kumar	4	4
J MacFie	4	4
G Proud	4	4
J K Pye	4	3
P D Wright	4	1
Gynaecology		
S G Crocker	1	1
D H Oram	1	1
C J Richards	1	1
R E Robinson	1	1

(continued overleaf)

Advisory group	Meetings held	Meetings attended
Neurosurgery		
J R Bartlett	1	1
D G Hardy	1	1
J Jakubowski	1	1
Ophthalmology, Oral/maxillofacial, Otorhinolaryngology		
P Bacon	1	1
I C Martin	1	1
R G Mills	1	1
C M Milton	1	1
J M Olver	1	1
Orthopaedic		
J W Calderwood	3	2
S T Donell	3	1
S Frostick	3	3
B Parker	3	3
B A Taylor	3	2
Plastic		
J H Goldin	1	1
A G Leonard	1	1
Urology		
M C Bishop	2	2
I Eardley	2	2
G N A Sibley	2	2
Vascular		
J D Holdsworth	3	3
R W Marcuson	3	3
C W Jamieson	3	3

KEY POINTS

Ten issues emerged from discussion in the surgical advisors' meetings. There were three specialty issues and seven relating to general good practice. They are summarised below with the page reference where appropriate.

SPECIALTY ISSUES

Radical pelvic surgery [pages 113 to 119]
Deliberation about individual cases including multidisciplinary discussion should occur before embarking on this type of surgery.

Transfer to neurosurgical units [pages 78 and 124]
There are recent recommendations for the management of an urgent transfer of head-injured patients to neurosurgical units; these should be widely circulated and adopted.

Emergency vascular surgery [pages 134 to 137]
Thirty-six percent of emergency vascular procedures were performed by non-vascular surgeons. This should be remedied.

GENERAL ISSUES

Data collection [pages 20, 95 and 104]
Surgeons should aim to complete and return all NCEPOD surgical questionnaires in order to improve the overall current return rate of 76%.

Critical care services for paediatric surgery [page 91]
Wherever children with major injuries are admitted or major paediatric surgery is performed, there needs to be an adequate provision of dedicated paediatric critical care services (ICU/HDU).

Provision for ICU and HDU care [pages 91, 102 and 105]
There needs to be a commitment to continue resourcing essential services to support high risk surgery.

Communication between grades
Surgical trainees must at all times discuss cases with their consultants prior to surgery.

Communication between specialties
Patients should not undergo operative intervention until there has been appropriate appraisal of risks and a discussion between surgeons and anaesthetists.

Audit [page 94]
Audit should be applied more widely and effectively. This is particularly so in specialties where audit activity was low e.g. gynaecology (54%) and ophthalmology (36%).

Locums [pages 94 and 124]
Clinical directors and individual consultants ought to make efforts to assure themselves of the abilities of locums and keep appropriate records.

Overall analysis (surgery)

Table S1
Surgical questionnaires

Total questionnaires sent	1818
Total questionnaires returned	1384
Total questionnaires analysed	1366
Number of individual hospitals represented	293
Return rate	**76.1%**

Table S2
Surgical specialty of cases

	SQs sent	SQs returned	Return rate %	SQs analysed*
Cardiothoracic	130	87	66.9	85
General/colorectal	626	476	76.0	474
Gynaecology	76	65	85.5	63
Neurosurgery	82	58	70.7	58
Ophthalmology	14	11	78.6	11
Oral/maxillofacial	8	7	87.5	7
Orthopaedic	439	327	74.5	320
Otorhinolaryngology	21	19	90.5	19
Plastic	13	11	84.6	11
Urology	111	82	73.9	80
Vascular	298	241	80.9	238
Total	**1818**	**1384**	*76.1*	**1366**

* See explanation in general data section (page 18).

Table S3 (qs 3, 4 and 5)
Sex/age of patient at time of final operation

	Male	Female	Total
0 to 10*	17	6	**23**
11 to 20	10	3	**13**
21 to 30	18	4	**22**
31 to 40	9	15	**24**
41 to 50	29	24	**53**
51 to 60	50	36	**86**
61 to 70	166	92	**258**
71 to 80	246	197	**443**
81 to 90	135	242	**377**
91 to 100	13	52	**65**
101+	1	1	**2**
Total	**694**	**672**	**1366**

* i.e. day of birth to day preceding eleventh birthday

Table S4 (qs 3 and 4)
Specialty group by age of patient

	0 to 40		41 to 90		91 or older		Total
Cardiothoracic	12	*14%*	73	*86%*	-	-	85
General/colorectal	32	*7%*	434	*91%*	8	*2%*	474
Gynaecology	2	*3%*	61	*97%*	-		63
Neurosurgery	22	*38%*	36	*62%*	-		58
Ophthalmology	-		10	*91%*	1	*9%*	11
Oral/maxillofacial	2	*29%*	5	*71%*	-		7
Orthopaedic	7	*2%*	262	*82%*	51	*16%*	320
Otorhinolaryngology	2	*11%*	17	*89%*	-		19
Plastic	1	*9%*	10	*91%*	-		11
Urology	-		77	*96%*	3	*4%*	80
Vascular	2	*1%*	232	*97%*	4	*2%*	238
Total	**82**	*6%*	**1217**	*89%*	**67**	*5%*	**1366**

Deaths of patients aged 90 years or over. Of the 51 orthopaedic patients, 49 of these had surgery for fractured neck of femur and the other two were a case of dislocated shoulder, which was reduced under sedation only, and a manipulation of a dislocated prosthesis. Of the patients dying after general surgery, three patients had colonic pathology (requiring resection) and two had small bowel resections. The vascular patients who died had either amputations (2) or acute ischaemia of a limb (2); none followed ruptured aortic aneurysm surgery. All deaths in urology followed endoscopic surgery for bladder tumours; the ophthalmology case followed an evisceration. (See also the anaesthesia section, pages 38-42).

Eighty-two patients who died were under the age of 41; 32 of these died following general surgical or colorectal procedures, which included neonatal procedures, major abdominal trauma and malignancy. Patients under 40 who died following neurosurgical procedures mainly had acute head injuries and their sequelae, or bleeding intracranial aneurysms. The other deaths in younger patients were for a mixture of pathologies and procedures from which no theme could be extracted.

Table S5 (q8) (see glossary, appendix B)
Admission category

	Elective		Urgent		Emergency		Not answered	Total
Cardiothoracic	39	*46%*	13	*15%*	31	*36%*	2	85
General/colorectal	73	*15%*	34	*7%*	365	*77%*	2	474
Gynaecology	33	*52%*	10	*16%*	20	*32%*	-	63
Neurosurgery	5	*9%*	10	*17%*	42	*72%*	1	58
Ophthalmology	7	*64%*	-		4	*36%*	-	11
Oral/maxillofacial	2	*29%*	1	*14%*	4	*57%*	-	7
Orthopaedic	44	*14%*	13	*4%*	263	*82%*	-	320
Otorhinolaryngology	9	*47%*	2	*11%*	8	*42%*	-	19
Plastic	4	*36%*	1	*9%*	6	*55%*	-	11
Urology	56	*70%*	1	*1%*	23	*29%*	-	80
Vascular	31	*13%*	12	*5%*	195	*82%*	-	238
Total	**303**	*22%*	**97**	*7%*	**961**	*70%*	**5**	**1366**

The above table shows the high percentage of emergency admissions amongst patients who subsequently died within three days of operation. This high level of emergency admissions reflects the general trend for rising numbers of emergency admissions which have produced increased pressures on hospital beds, cancellations of elective work and the shortening of the average length of hospital stay.[8]

Table S6 (q9)
Specialty group where patient was admitted via the A & E department

Cardiothoracic	8	*9%*
General/colorectal	117	*25%*
Gynaecology	7	*11%*
Neurosurgery	6	*10%*
Ophthalmology	1	*9%*
Oral/maxillofacial	1	*14%*
Orthopaedic	231	*72%*
Otorhinolaryngology	3	*16%*
Plastic	3	*27%*
Urology	7	*9%*
Vascular	88	*37%*
Total	**472**	*35%*

Table S7 (q9)
Specialty group where patient was transferred as an in-patient from another hospital

Cardiothoracic	26	*31%*
General/colorectal	40	*8%*
Gynaecology	7	*11%*
Neurosurgery	45	*78%*
Ophthalmology	1	*9%*
Oral/maxillofacial	1	*14%*
Orthopaedic	23	*7%*
Otorhinolaryngology	3	*16%*
Plastic	4	*36%*
Urology	3	*4%*
Vascular	23	*10%*
Total	**176**	*13%*

There is a need for guidance about transfer of patients; 13% of these patients who died were transferred from another hospital. This percentage is much higher in neurosurgery (78% of patients were transferred). The Association of Anaesthetists of Great Britain and Ireland has recently published "Recommendations for the transfer of patients with acute head injuries to Neurosurgical units"[9] the summary of which states:

1. There should be a designated consultant in the referring hospital with overall responsibility for the transfer of patients with head injuries to the neurosurgical unit and one at the neurosurgical unit with overall responsibility for receiving the transfers.

2. Local guidelines on the transfer of patients with head injuries should be drawn up between the referring hospital trusts and the neurosurgical unit which should be consistent with established national guidelines. Details of the transfer of the responsibility for patient care should also be agreed.

3. Thorough resuscitation and stabilisation of the patient must be completed before transfer to avoid complications during the journey. A patient persistently hypotensive, despite resuscitation, must not be transported until all possible causes of the hypotension have been identified and the patient stabilised.

4. Only in exceptional circumstances should a patient with a significantly altered conscious level requiring transfer for neurosurgical care not be intubated.

5. Patients with head injuries should be accompanied by a doctor with at least two years experience in an appropriate specialty (usually anaesthesia). Ideally, they should be on a Specialist Register. They should be familiar with pathophysiology of head injury, the drugs and equipment they will use, working in the confines of an ambulance (or helicopter if appropriate) and have received supervised training in the transfer of patients with head injuries. They must have an adequately trained assistant. They must be provided with appropriate clothing for the transfer, medical indemnity and personal insurance.

6. The transfer team must be provided with a means of communication with their base hospital and the neurosurgical unit during the transfer - a portable phone may be suitable.

7. Education, training and audit are crucial to improving standards of transfer; appropriate time and funding should be provided.

Table S8 (q20)
ASA class

	ASA 1		ASA 2		ASA 3		ASA 4		ASA 5		Not answered	Total
Cardiothoracic	3	4%	15	18%	26	31%	28	33%	11	13%	2	85
General/colorectal	14	3%	67	14%	133	28%	189	40%	63	13%	8	474
Gynaecology	5	8%	17	27%	19	30%	13	21%	3	5%	6	63
Neurosurgery	2	4%	6	10%	9	16%	17	29%	24	41%	-	58
Ophthalmology	1	9%	5	45%	3	27%	1	9%	-		1	11
Oral/maxillofacial	-		1	14%	3	43%	1	14%	2	29%	-	7
Orthopaedic	19	6%	81	25%	112	35%	75	23%	6	2%	27	320
Otorhinolaryngology	2	11%	4	21%	6	32%	5	26%	1	5%	1	19
Plastic	4	36%	2	18%	1	9%	4	36%	-		-	11
Urology	1	1%	34	43%	30	37%	12	15%	3	4%	-	80
Vascular	6	3%	23	10%	57	24%	107	45%	44	18%	1	238
Total	**57**	**4%**	**255**	**19%**	**399**	**29%**	**452**	**33%**	**157**	**11%**	**46**	**1366**

Surgeons continue to use the ASA classification incorrectly. The authors suggest that surgeons and anaesthetists discuss the patient and, in collaboration, record a joint ASA classification agreed by both.

The distribution of the ASA classes, whilst approximately normal in most specialties, is skewed in some. For example, more urological patients were classed as relatively fitter than one might have anticipated and, less surprisingly, a similar proportion of neurosurgical patients were ASA 5. Urologists are, perhaps, so familiar with the elderly that they tend to minimise the risks of inevitable intercurrent disease.

Table S9 (q21)

Were there any coexisting problems (other than the main diagnosis) at the time of final surgery?

Yes	1075	*79%*
No	268	*20%*
Not answered	21	
Not known/not recorded	2	
Cardiac	604	*44%*
Respiratory	371	*27%*
Renal	168	*12%*
Malignancy	161	*12%*
Vascular	157	*11%*
Endocrine *(inc. diabetes mellitus)*	127	*9%*
Neurological	121	*9%*
Sepsis	120	*9%*
Haematological	111	*8%*
Gastrointestinal	104	*8%*
Musculoskeletal	84	*6%*
Psychiatric	63	*5%*
Alcohol-related problems	33	*2%*
Drug addiction	2	*<1%*
Genetic abnormality	4	*<1%*
Other	75	*5%*
Total cases *(answers may be multiple)*	**1366**	

Table S10 (q21)

Specialty group where no coexisting problems were indicated

Cardiothoracic	31	*36%*
General/colorectal	74	*16%*
Gynaecology	11	*17%*
Neurosurgery	34	*59%*
Ophthalmology	1	*9%*
Oral/maxillofacial	1	*14%*
Orthopaedic	33	*10%*
Otorhinolaryngology	4	*21%*
Plastic	3	*27%*
Urology	15	*19%*
Vascular	61	*26%*
Total	**268**	*20%*

Table S11 (q27)
Anticipated risk of death in relation to the proposed operation

	Not expected		Small but significant risk		Definite risk		Expected		Not answered	Total
Cardiothoracic	3	4%	21	25%	53	62%	8	9%	-	85
General/colorectal	46	10%	53	11%	322	68%	51	11%	2	474
Gynaecology	19	30%	18	29%	25	40%	1	1%	-	63
Neurosurgery	5	9%	9	16%	25	43%	18	31%	1	58
Ophthalmology	5	45%	4	36%	2	18%	-		-	11
Oral/maxillofacial	2	29%	3	43%	2	29%	-		-	7
Orthopaedic	46	14%	82	26%	180	56%	10	3%	2	320
Otorhinolaryngology	8	42%	6	32%	4	21%	-		1	19
Plastic	6	55%	2	18%	3	27%	-		-	11
Urology	31	39%	25	31%	21	26%	3	4%	-	80
Vascular	7	3%	18	8%	178	75%	34	14%	1	238
Total	**178**	13%	**241**	18%	**815**	60%	**125**	9%	**7**	**1366**

The figure of 13% for unexpected deaths is surprising given that the sample is of early postoperative deaths.

Table S12 (q28)
Classification of final operation (see glossary, appendix B)

	Elective		Scheduled		Urgent		Emergency		Not answered	Total
Cardiothoracic	21	25%	22	26%	18	21%	24	28%	-	85
General/colorectal	21	4%	58	12%	252	53%	142	30%	1	474
Gynaecology	14	22%	34	54%	11	18%	4	6%	-	63
Neurosurgery	2	3%	3	5%	16	28%	37	64%	-	58
Ophthalmology	8	73%	1	9%	2	18%	-		-	11
Oral/maxillofacial	1	14%	2	29%	3	43%	1	14%	-	7
Orthopaedic	42	13%	53	17%	209	65%	16	5%	-	320
Otorhinolaryngology	3	16%	10	53%	5	26%	1	5%	-	19
Plastic	-		7	64%	3	27%	1	9%	-	11
Urology	24	3-%	35	44%	13	16%	8	10%	-	80
Vascular	8	3%	23	10%	39	16%	168	71%	-	238
Total	**144**	11%	**248**	18%	**571**	42%	**402**	29%	**1**	**1366**

Seventy-one percent of patients who died underwent urgent or emergency operations. Further details are given in the relevant surgical specialty sections.

Table S13 (q39)
Were there any unanticipated intra-operative problems?

Yes	312
No	1032
Not answered	21
Not known / not recorded	1
Total	**1366**

Table S14 (q39)
Specialty group where unanticipated intra-operative problems occurred: number and percentage of deaths in each specialty

Cardiothoracic	40	*47%*
General/colorectal	102	*22%*
Gynaecology	17	*27%*
Neurosurgery	8	*14%*
Oral/maxillofacial	1	*14%*
Orthopaedic	46	*14%*
Otorhinolaryngology	1	*5%*
Plastic	2	*18%*
Urology	16	*20%*
Vascular	79	*33%*
Total	**312**	*23%*

Nearly a quarter of all cases presented unanticipated intraoperative problems. Is this a reflection of case selection, surgical ability or random chance?

Table S15
Grade of most senior operating surgeon where there were unanticipated intraoperative problems

	Consultant	Senior registrar	Registrar	SHO	Other/not stated	Total
Cardiothoracic	38	1	1	-	-	40
General/colorectal	71	11	15	-	5	102
Gynaecology	12	3	2	-	-	17
Neurosurgery	3	1	3	-	1	8
Oral/maxillofacial	1	-	-	-	-	1
Orthopaedic	17	6	8	4	11	46
Otorhinolaryngology	1	-	-	-	-	1
Plastic	1	1	-	-	-	2
Urology	13	-	3	-	-	16
Vascular	62	11	5	-	1	79
Total	**219**	**34**	**37**	**4**	**18**	**312**

Table S16 (q46)
The postoperative complications:

Not answered/"none"	86	
Not applicable - death in theatre	152	*11%*
Not known/not recorded	1	
Low cardiac output/other cardiac problems	487	*36%*
Cardiac arrest	349	*26%*
Respiratory distress	284	*21%*
Renal failure	240	*18%*
Haemorrhage/postoperative bleeding requiring transfusion	176	*13%*
Generalised sepsis	167	*12%*
Stroke or other neurological problems	68	*5%*
Persistent coma	59	*4%*
DVT and/or pulmonary embolus	43	*3%*
Peripheral ischaemia	42	*3%*
Other organ failure	32	*2%*
Hepatic failure	23	*2%*
Other	134	*10%*
Total cases *(answers may be multiple)*	**1366**	

Table S17 (qs 30 and 48)
Calendar days from operation to death
(ie not 24-hour periods)

	Same day		Next day		2 days		3 days		Total
Cardiothoracic	43	*51%*	18	*21%*	12	*14%*	12	*14%*	**85**
General/colorectal	118	*25%*	166	*35%*	105	*22%*	85	*18%*	**474**
Gynaecology	12	*19%*	23	*37%*	19	*30%*	9	*14%*	**63**
Neurosurgery	3	*5%*	21	*36%*	21	*36%*	13	*23%*	**58**
Ophthalmology	2	*18%*	6	*55%*	2	*18%*	1	*9%*	**11**
Oral/maxillofacial	2	*29%*	2	*29%*	1	*14%*	2	*28%*	**7**
Orthopaedic	82	*26%*	97	*30%*	79	*25%*	62	*19%*	**320**
Otorhinolaryngology	3	*16%*	6	*32%*	7	*37%*	3	*16%*	**19**
Plastic	2	*18%*	3	*27%*	3	*27%*	3	*27%*	**11**
Urology	18	*23%*	28	*35%*	21	*26%*	13	*16%*	**80**
Vascular	95	*40%*	76	*32%*	41	*17%*	26	*11%*	**238**
Total	**380**	*28%*	**446**	*32%*	**311**	*23%*	**229**	*17%*	**1366**

Table S18 (q13)
Was there any delay in either the referral or the admission of this patient?

	Yes		No	Not answered	Total
Cardiothoracic	6	7%	77	2	85
General/colorectal	41	9%	414	19	474
Gynaecology	8	13%	53	2	63
Neurosurgery	6	10%	52	-	58
Ophthalmology	1	9%	9	1	11
Oral/maxillofacial	1	14%	5	1	7
Orthopaedic	22	7%	272	26	320
Otorhinolaryngology	-		17	2	19
Plastic	-		11	-	11
Urology	9	11%	64	7	80
Vascular	21	9%	210	7	238
Total	**115**	*8%*	**1184**	**67**	**1366**

See individual sections for comments on this.

Table S19 (q29)
Were there any delays (between admission and surgery) due to factors other than clinical?

	Yes		No	Not answered	Total
Cardiothoracic	9	11%	76	-	85
General/colorectal	21	4%	447	6	474
Gynaecology	2	3%	61	-	63
Neurosurgery	3	5%	53	2	58
Ophthalmology	-		11	-	11
Oral/maxillofacial	-		7	-	7
Orthopaedic	30	9%	285	5	320
Otorhinolaryngology	-		18	1	19
Plastic	-		11	-	11
Urology	1	1%	78	1	80
Vascular	18	8%	216	4	238
Total	**84**	*6%*	**1263**	**19**	**1366**

In orthopaedic surgery the delays were caused by a lack of theatre space in 19 cases and another two were due to the absence of medical or nursing staff. The remaining delays in orthopaedic surgery were due to miscellaneous problems.

In general and colorectal surgery seven of the 21 delays were because there was no theatre; three delays were due to the patient refusing operation and three were due to delay in referral to the appropriate specialty after admission; the remainder were as a result of miscellaneous factors.

Of the 18 vascular cases, three were delayed due to a lack of intensive care beds, three were delayed because of problems with appropriate medical staff and on two occasions there was no operating theatre available. The rest were due to miscellaneous causes.

In cardiothoracic surgery the main delays were the result of long waiting lists and heavy workload together with a lack of intensive care beds.

Table S20 (q47)
Was there any shortage of personnel in this case?

	Yes		No	Not answered	Total
Cardiothoracic	-		77	8	85
General/colorectal	2	<1%	458	14	474
Gynaecology	2	3%	59	2	63
Neurosurgery	-		57	1	58
Ophthalmology	1	9%	10	-	11
Oral/maxillofacial	-		7	-	7
Orthopaedic	3	1%	304	13	320
Otorhinolaryngology	-		18	1	19
Plastic	-		11	-	11
Urology	-		77	3	80
Vascular	3	1%	212	23	238
Total	**11**	*1%*	**1290**	**65**	**1366**

These are very small numbers and where there were shortages these were a mixture of lack of nursing staff, surgeons and anaesthetists.

Table S21 (qs 30 and 31)
Specialty group by time of start of final operation before death

	Weekday "in hours"		Weekday "out of hours"*		Weekday (time not stated)		Saturday or Sunday		Total
Cardiothoracic	68	80%	8	10%	2	2%	7	8%	85
General/colorectal	210	44%	126	27%	20	4%	118	25%	474
Gynaecology	50	79%	1	1%	6	10%	6	10%	63
Neurosurgery	26	45%	19	33%	2	3%	11	19%	58
Ophthalmology	8	73%	1	9%	1	9%	1	9%	11
Oral/maxillofacial	4	57%	-		-		3	43%	7
Orthopaedic	189	59%	20	6%	34	11%	77	24%	320
Otorhinolaryngology	15	79%	3	16%	1	5%	-	-	19
Plastic	7	64%	2	18%	2	18%	-	-	11
Urology	62	78%	8	10%	6	7%	4	5%	80
Vascular	92	39%	70	29%	15	6%	61	26%	238
Total	**731**	*54%*	**258**	*19%*	**89**	*6%*	**288**	*21%*	**1366**

An analysis of times of surgical procedures for 1995/96 is published simultaneously with this report.[7]

---

* see glossary, appendix B

Table S22

Classification of the operation - out-of-hours weekday operations

	Emergency	Urgent	Scheduled	Elective	Not answered	Total
Cardiothoracic	6	1	-	1	-	8
General/colorectal	58	64	3	-	1	126
Gynaecology	-	1	-	-	-	1
Neurosurgery	16	3	-	-	-	19
Ophthalmology	-	1	-	-	-	1
Oral/maxillofacial	-	-	-	-	-	0
Orthopaedic	2	15	2	1	-	20
Otorhinolaryngology	1	2	-	-	-	3
Plastic	1	-	1	-	-	2
Urology	3	3	1	1	-	8
Vascular	56	11	3	-	-	70
Total	**143**	**101**	**10**	**3**	**1**	**258**

There were 618 procedures done by surgeons below the grade of consultant; 260 (42%) of these were supervised by a more senior surgeon. For further discussion see the individual specialty sections (pages 99 to 137). There were 23 procedures done in the independent sector (four in hours and 19 out of hours). These were all done by consultants and if these patients are not included, then the figures are as follows:

Table S23 (qs 30, 31, 34 and 36)

Most senior operating surgeon - excluding independent sector (whole sample)

	Consultant	Associate specialist (supervised)		Clinical assistant (supervised)		Senior registrar (supervised)		Staff grade (supervised)		Registrar (supervised)		SHO (supervised)		Not answered
Cardiothoracic	68	-		-	-	6	(5)	-	-	4	(3)	-	-	-
General/colorectal	246	9	(4)	-	-	78	(26)	20	(6)	101	(39)	12	(5)	1
Gynaecology	46	-	-	1	(1)	4	(2)	1	(1)	8	(5)	1	(1)	-
Neurosurgery	21	-	-	-	-	14	(3)	1	(1)	22	(6)	-	-	-
Ophthalmology	7	-	-	-	-	1	(1)	1	-	1	(1)	1	(1)	-
Oral/maxillofacial	6	-	-	-	-	-	-	-	-	-	-	1	-	-
Orthopaedic	89	27	(11)	3	(2)	39	(15)	32	(12)	99	(41)	29	(16)	2
Otolaryngology	10	1	-	-	-	5	(2)	-	-	1	-	-	-	1
Plastic	5	-	-	-	-	4	(3)	-	-	1	-	1	(1)	-
Urology	61	1	-	-	-	3	(2)	-	-	13	(10)	-	-	-
Vascular	166	2	(2)	-	-	38	(13)	2	(1)	21	(10)	5	(2)	-
Total	**725**	**40**	**(17)**	**4**	**(3)**	**192**	**(72)**	**57**	**(21)**	**271**	**(115)**	**50**	**(26)**	**4**

There were 24 cases in which an SHO was the most senior operating surgeon and no supervision by a more senior surgeon was indicated on the surgical questionnaire. These figures consisted of 13 orthopaedic cases (only one of which was appropriate for an SHO), seven general surgical and colorectal cases of which only one (the drainage of perianal abscess) was thought to be suitable for an SHO, three vascular cases, one of which was certainly inappropriate, and one appropriate plastic surgery case (see the relevant surgical specialty sections).

Table S24 (qs 30, 31, 34 and 36)
Most senior operating surgeon - excluding independent sector (weekday - in hours)

	Consultant	Associate specialist (supervised)		Clinical assistant (supervised)		Senior registrar (supervised)		Staff grade (supervised)		Registrar (supervised)		SHO (supervised)		Total
Cardiothoracic	53	-	-	-	-	4	(4)	-	-	3	(3)	-	-	60
General/colorectal	134	-	-	-	-	26	(14)	9	(3)	29	(17)	5	(5)	203
Gynaecology	36	-	-	1	(1)	4	(2)	1	(1)	5	(4)	1	(1)	48
Neurosurgery	14	-	-	-	-	6	(2)	-	-	6	(4)	-	-	26
Ophthalmology	5	-	-	-	-	1	(1)	1	-	1	(1)	-	-	8
Oral/maxillofacial	4	-	-	-	-	-	-	-	-	-	-	-	-	4
Orthopaedic	61	21	(7)	1	(1)	20	(10)	17	(9)	55	(31)	13	(10)	188
Otorhinolaryngology	8	1	-	-	-	5	(2)	-	-	-	-	-	-	14
Plastic	4	-	-	-	-	2	(2)	-	-	-	-	1	(1)	7
Urology	47	-	-	-	-	2	(2)	-	-	11	(9)	-	-	60
Vascular	69	2	(2)	-	-	11	(5)	1	(1)	6	(4)	2	(1)	91
Total	435	24	(9)	2	(2)	81	(44)	29	(14)	116	(73)	22	(18)	709

Table S25 (qs 30, 31, 34 and 36)
Most senior operating surgeon - excluding the independent sector (weekday - out-of-hours)

	Consultant	Associate specialist (supervised)		Senior registrar (supervised)		Staff grade (supervised)		Registrar (supervised)		SHO (supervised)		Not answered	Total
Cardiothoracic	6	-	-	2	(1)	-	-	-	-	-	-	-	8
General/colorectal	51	3	(1)	23	(6)	6	(2)	38	(10)	4	(1)	-	125
Gynaecology	1	-	-	-	-	-	-	-	-	-	-	-	1
Neurosurgery	4	-	-	5	-	1	(1)	9	(1)	-	-	-	19
Ophthalmology	1	-	-	-	-	-	-	-	-	-	-	-	1
Oral/maxillofacial	-	-	-	-	-	-	-	-	-	-	-	-	-
Orthopaedic	4	2	(1)	1	-	3	-	6	-	3	(1)	1	20
Otorhinolaryngology	2	-	-	-	-	-	-	1	-	-	-	-	3
Plastic	1	-	-	1	-	-	-	-	-	-	-	-	2
Urology	6	-	-	1	-	-	-	1	(1)	-	-	-	8
Vascular	42	-	-	18	(5)	1	-	7	(3)	1	(1)	-	69
Total	118	5	(2)	51	(12)	11	(3)	62	(15)	8	(3)	1	256

Overall, registrars did 62/256 (24%) out-of-hours operations. Supervision was provided for 15 of these operations (24%). Can this lack of supervision provide adequate training?

Table S26 (qs 30, 31, 34 and 36)
Most senior operating surgeon - excluding the independent sector *(weekday - time not stated)*

	Consultant	Associate specialist (supervised)		Senior registrar (supervised)		Staff grade (supervised)		Registrar (supervised)		SHO (supervised)		Not answered	Tota
Cardiothoracic	2	-	-	-	-	-	-	-	-	-	-	-	
General/colorectal	10	-	-	5	(2)	-	-	3	(2)	1	(1)	1	2
Gynaecology	6	-	-	-	-	-	-	-	-	-	-	-	
Neurosurgery	1	-	-	1	(1)	-	-	-	-	-	-	-	
Ophthalmology	-	-	-	-	-	-	-	-	-	1	(1)	-	
Oral/maxillofacial	-	-	-	-	-	-	-	-	-	-	-	-	
Orthopaedic	11	2	(2)	4	(2)	4	(1)	7	(4)	5	(4)	1	3
Otorhinolaryngology	-	-	-	-	-	-	-	-	-	-	-	1	
Plastic	-	-	-	1	(1)	-	-	1	-	-	-	-	2
Urology	5	1	-	-	-	-	-	-	-	-	-	-	
Vascular	9	-	-	1	(1)	-	-	1	-	2	-	-	13
Total	**44**	**3**	**(2)**	**12**	**(7)**	**4**	**(1)**	**12**	**(6)**	**9**	**(6)**	**3**	**87**

Table S27 (qs 30, 31, 34 and 36)
Most senior operating surgeon - excluding the independent sector *(Saturday and Sunday)*

	Consultant	Associate specialist (supervised)		Clinical assistant (supervised)		Senior registrar (supervised)		Staff grade (supervised)		Registrar (supervised)		SHO (supervised)		Tot
Cardiothoracic	7	-	-	-	-	-	-	-	-	1	-	-	-	
General/colorectal	51	6	(3)	-	-	24	(4)	5	(1)	31	(10)	2	(1)	11
Gynaecology	3	-	-	-	-	-	-	-	-	3	(1)	-	-	
Neurosurgery	2	-	-	-	-	2	-	-	-	7	(1)	-	-	
Ophthalmology	1	-	-	-	-	-	-	-	-	-	-	-	-	
Oral/maxillofacial	2	-	-	-	-	-	-	-	-	-	-	1	-	
Orthopaedic	13	2	(1)	2	(1)	14	(3)	8	(2)	31	(6)	8	(4)	7
Otorhinolaryngology	-	-	-	-	-	-	-	-	-	-	-	-	-	
Plastic	-	-	-	-	-	-	-	-	-	-	-	-	-	
Urology	3	-	-	-	-	-	-	-	-	1	-	-	-	
Vascular	46	-	-	-	-	8	(2)	-	-	7	(3)	-	-	6
Total	**128**	**8**	**(4)**	**2**	**(1)**	**48**	**99)**	**13**	**(3)**	**81**	**(21)**	**11**	**(5)**	**29**

Consultants and senior registrars operated on 61% (178/291) of cases at weekends.

Table S28 (q1)
In which type of hospital did the final operation take place?

	A		B		C		D		E		F		G		Total
Cardiothoracic	9	*11%*	46	*54%*	23	*27%*	-	-	-	-	-	-	7	*8%*	**85**
General/colorectal	349	*74%*	114	*24%*	1	*<1%*	2	*<1%*	-	-	1	*<1%*	7	*1%*	**474**
Gynaecology	47	*75%*	14	*22%*	-	-	-	-	-	-	-	-	2	*3%*	**63**
Neurosurgery	8	*14%*	29	*50%*	21	*36%*	-	-	-	-	-	-	-	-	**58**
Ophthalmology	6	*55%*	3	*27%*	2	*18%*	-	-	-	-	-	-	-	-	**11**
Oral/maxillofacial	4	*57%*	3	*43%*	-	-	-	-	-	-	-	-	-	-	**7**
Orthopaedic	243	*76%*	67	*21%*	7	*2%*	-	-	2	*1%*	1	*<1%*	-	-	**320**
Otolaryngology	13	*69%*	4	*21%*	1	*5%*	-	-	-	-	-	-	1	*5%*	**19**
Plastic	7	*64%*	2	*18%*	2	*18%*	-	-	-	-	-	-	-	-	**11**
Urology	63	*79%*	13	*16%*	-	-	1	*1%*	1	*1%*	-	-	2	*3%*	**80**
Vascular	174	*73%*	58	*24%*	-	-	1	*<1%*	-	-	1	*<1%*	4	*2%*	**238**
Total	**923**	***68%***	**353**	***26%***	**57**	***4%***	**4**	***<1%***	**3**	***<1%***	**3**	***<1%***	**23**	***2%***	**1366**

A = District General   B = University/teaching   C = Surgical specialty

D = Other acute/partly acute   E = Community   F = Defence Medical

G = Independent

The operations done in the community hospitals were:

Bilateral total knee replacement	1
Open reduction/internal fixation left tibia and bone graft	1
Transurethral prostatectomy	1

Community hospitals have no resident medical staff. Can it be appropriate to do the surgery listed above in such an environment?

The operations done in the independent hospitals were:

Coronary artery bypass surgery	3
Mitral valve replacement and coronary artery bypass	1
Aortic valve replacement	1
Bronchoscopy, thoracoscopy and decortication via thoracotomy	1
Excision left submandibular gland	1
Oesophagogastrectomy	1
Attempted bouginage of malignant stricture occluding Roux loop	1
Open cholecystectomy and exploration of common bile duct	1
Laparotomy and small bowel resection	1
Re-exploration of abdomen, refashioning of ileo-ileal anastomosis	1
Laparotomy, separation of small bowel and lesions, drainage of paracolic abscess, oversewing of small hole in small bowel and left hemicolectomy with primary anastomosis	1
Laparotomy, resection of splenic flexure of colon and colostomy	1
Endoscopic assessment	1
Endometrial resection, laparotomy for intraperitoneal haemorrhage	1
Total abdominal hysterectomy and bilateral salpingo-oophorectomy	1
Right upper pole partial nephrectomy	1
TURP	1
Clamping of aorta and attempted resuscitation	1
Varicose vein surgery	1
Aortic iliac and femoral thrombectomy	1
Carotid endarterectomy	1

Submandibular gland excision and varicose vein surgery are not usually associated with death. In both cases there were additional factors and care was appropriate.

Table S29 (q2)
General availability of essential services

	Recovery area		Adult ICU		Adult HDU		Paediatric ICU/HDU		Total
Cardiothoracic	74	87%	81	95%	61	72%	38	45%	85
General/colorectal	473	>99%	451	95%	135	28%	137	29%	474
Gynaecology	62	98%	53	84%	29	46%	26	41%	63
Neurosurgery	56	97%	56	97%	40	69%	26	45%	58
Ophthalmology	11	100%	8	73%	5	45%	4	36%	11
Oral/maxillofacial	7	100%	7	100%	1	14%	3	43%	7
Orthopaedic	316	99%	292	91%	119	37%	98	31%	320
Otorhinolaryngology	19	100%	17	89%	10	53%	7	37%	19
Plastic	11	100%	9	82%	5	45%	6	55%	11
Urology	80	100%	74	93%	29	36%	15	19%	80
Vascular	237	>99%	237	>99%	77	32%	66	28%	238
Total	**1346**	99%	**1285**	94%	**511**	37%	**426**	31%	**1366**

Table S30 (qs 1 and 2)
Availability of essential services by type of hospital

	Recovery area		Adult ICU		Adult HDU		Paediatric ICU/HDU		Total
District General	919	>99%	877	95%	264	29%	227	25%	923
University/teaching	342	97%	338	96%	189	54%	172	49%	353
Surgical specialty	53	93%	47	82%	41	72%	21	37%	57
Other acute/partly acute	4	100%	2	50%	2	50%	1	25%	4
Community	3	100%	-		1	33%	-		3
Defence Medical	3	100%	3	100%	1	33%	-		3
Independent	22	100%	18	82%	13	59%	5	23%	23
Total	**1346**	99%	**1285**	94%	**511**	37%	**426**	31%	**1366**

The information concerning paediatric critical care services in tables 29 and 30 should be interpreted with caution as surgeons often replied with information relevant to an individual case rather than commenting on services generally available within a hospital.

Table S31 (q45)
If the patient's condition warranted an admission to an ICU/HDU, were you at any time unable to transfer the patient into an ICU/HDU within the hospital in which the surgery took place?

	Yes		No	Not applicable*	Not answered	Total
Cardiothoracic	1	1%	46	7	31	85
General/colorectal	18	4%	265	111	80	474
Gynaecology	4	6%	17	30	12	63
Neurosurgery	1	2%	49	6	2	58
Ophthalmology	-		3	6	2	11
Oral/maxillofacial	-		3	3	1	7
Orthopaedic	7	2%	111	122	80	320
Otorhinolaryngology	-		11	7	1	19
Plastic	-		5	4	2	11
Urology	4	5%	35	23	18	80
Vascular	10	4%	120	44	64	238
Total	**45**	*3%*	**665**	**363**	**293**	**1366**

* i.e. condition did not warrant admission to ICU/HDU

On 24 occasions there was no bed available in the intensive care unit. This mainly affected general, colorectal and vascular surgery. Fourteen of the patients who died had no access to the intensive care unit or HDU facilities as none existed in the hospital in which they had their surgery. These cases included surgery for perforated diverticular disease, strangulated femoral hernia, liver trauma, biliary surgery, abdominal trauma, aortic occlusion. Should surgeons perform this surgery in the absence of an ICU/HDU on site? Other reasons for non-admission to an ICU/HDU when it was required included: the closure of intensive care in three cases, the refusal of requested admission by the intensive care staff in two cases and two patients who died *en route* to an intensive care unit.

In seven of the deaths in children under 16 years of age the critical care services (i.e. ICU/HDU) were inadequate for children. These cases included surgery for perforated necrotizing enterocolitis, the repair of congenital diaphragmatic hernia, the resection of neuroblastoma, the repair of a ruptured liver, the exploration of an acute subdural haematoma and two cases of radical surgery for intrathoracic congenital anomalies. In all of these cases an ICU was available at the hospital, but it was often an adult ICU which doubled-up for treatment of children. All units undertaking major paediatric surgery should have dedicated paediatric intensive care and HDU services.

Table S32 (qs 20 and 41)
Admission to ICU immediately postoperatively, by ASA class

	ICU		HDU		Neither	Died in theatre	Not answered	Total
ASA 1	16	28%	2	4%	33	6	0	57
ASA 2	57	22%	16	6%	157	22	3	255
ASA 3	101	25%	13	3%	250	30	5	399
ASA 4	208	46%	25	6%	163	50	6	452
ASA 5	87	55%	5	3%	21	42	2	157
Not answered	9		3		27	4	3	46
Total	**478**	*35%*	**64**	*5%*	**651**	**154**	**19**	**1366**

Table S33 (qs 28 and 41)
Admission to ICU immediately postoperatively, by classification of operation*

	ICU		HDU		Neither	Died in theatre	Not answered	Total
Emergency	218	*54%*	16	*4%*	68	94	6	402
Urgent	170	*30%*	25	*4%*	339	29	8	571
Scheduled	58	*23%*	14	*6%*	154	18	4	248
Elective	32	*22%*	9	*6%*	89	13	1	144
Not answered	-		-		1	-	-	1
Total	**478**	*35%*	**64**	*5%*	**651**	**154**	**19**	**1366**

Table S34 (qs 16 and 26)
The most senior surgeon involved in decision-making prior to surgery:

	C		AS		CA		SR		SG		R		SHO		Total
Cardiothoracic	85	*100%*	-		-		-		-		-		-		85
General/colorectal	410	*86%*	4	*1%*	1	*<1%*	31	*7%*	10	*2%*	17	*4%*	1	*<1%*	474
Gynaecology	59	*94%*	-		-		3	*5%*	1	*2%*	-		-		63
Neurosurgery	57	*98%*	-		1	*2%*	-		-		-		-		58
Ophthalmology	11	*100%*	-		-		-		-		-		-		11
Oral/maxillofacial	7	*100%*	-		-		-		-		-		-		7
Orthopaedic	249	*78%*	11	*3%*	2	*1%*	20	*6%*	7	*2%*	29	*9%*	2	*1%*	320
Otorhinolaryngology	17	*89%*	1	*5%*	-		1	*5%*	-		-		-		19
Plastic	10	*91%*	-		-		-		-		1	*9%*	-		11
Urology	77	*96%*	-		-		2	*3%*	-		1	*1%*	-		80
Vascular	219	*92%*	2	*1%*	-		14	*6%*	-		3	*1%*	-		238
Total	**1201**	*88%*	**18**	*1%*	**4**	*<1%*	**71**	*5%*	**18**	*1%*	**51**	*4%*	**3**	*<1%*	**1366**

C = Consultant   AS = Associate specialist   CA = Clinical assistant
SR = Senior registrar   SG = Staff grade   R = Registrar
SHO = Senior house officer

◆ Overall there was a very high level of consultant involvement but there is considerable variation.

Orthopaedic surgery shows the lowest level of consultant involvement in decision-making.

---

* see glossary, appendix B

Table S35 (qs 16 and 26)
Consultant involvement

	Preoperatively						Intraoperatively						Any involvement	
	Consulted		Decision to operate		Either		Operating surgeon		Supervising		Either			
		%		%		%		%		%		%		%
Cardiothoracic	85	100	83	98	85	100	75	88	6	7	81	95	85	100
General/colorectal	397	84	385	81	410	86	253	53	49	10	302	64	417	88
Gynaecology	58	92	57	90	59	94	48	76	9	14	57	90	61	97
Neurosurgery	57	98	56	97	57	98	21	36	5	9	26	45	57	98
Ophthalmology	10	91	11	100	11	100	7	64	2	18	9	82	11	100
Oral/maxillofacial	7	100	7	100	7	100	6	86	-		6	86	7	100
Orthopaedic	238	74	229	72	249	78	89	28	60	19	149	47	260	81
Otorhinolaryngology	16	84	16	84	17	89	11	58	2	11	13	68	18	95
Plastic	9	82	9	82	10	91	5	45	3	27	8	73	10	91
Urology	76	95	76	95	77	96	63	79	9	11	72	90	78	98
Vascular	213	89	210	88	219	92	170	71	14	6	184	77	224	94
Total	**1166**	85	**1139**	69	**1201**	88	**748**	55	**159**	12	**907**	66	**1228**	90

◆ The overall involvement of consultants is commendable. Nineteen percent of orthopaedic cases (60 patients) and 12% of general/colorectal cases (57 patients) had no contact with consultants. This must be improved.

Table S36 (qs 16 and 26)
Classification of operation by most senior operating surgeon

	C		AS		CA		SR		SG		R		SHO		Not answered
		%		%		%		%		%		%		%	
Emergency	257	34	6	15	1	25	61	32	6	10	65	24	5	10	1
Urgent	223	30	20	50	1	25	91	47	42	74	157	58	36	72	1
Scheduled	162	22	12	30	1	25	25	13	5	9	35	13	7	14	1
Elective	106	14	2	5	1	25	15	8	4	7	13	5	2	4	1
Not answered	-		-		-		-		-		1	<1	-		-
Total	748	100	40	100	4	100	192	100	57	100	271	100	50	100	4

C = Consultant AS = Associate specialist CA = Clinical assistant
SR = Senior registrar SG = Staff grade R = Registrar
SHO = Senior house officer

Table S37 (q34)
Locum surgeons - most senior operating surgeon

	C	AS	SR	SG	(supervised)	R	(supervised)	SHO	(supervised)	All locums	
Cardiothoracic	3	-	1	-		-		-		4	5%
General/colorectal	17	-	3	-		12	(3)	-		32	7%
Gynaecology	2	-	1	-		1		-		4	6%
Neurosurgery	1	-	1	-		2		-		4	7%
Ophthalmology	-	-	-	-		-		-		-	-
Oral/maxillofacial	-	-	-	-		-		-		-	-
Orthopaedic	3	1	3	1	(1)	8	(3)	2	(-)	18	6%
Otorhinolaryngology	1	-	-	-		-		-		1	5%
Plastic	1	-	-	-		(-)		-		1	9%
Urology	4	-	1	-		1	(1)	-		6	8%
Vascular	9	-	2	-		-		-		11	5%
Total	**41**	**1**	**12**	**1**	**(1)**	**24**	**(7)**	**2**	**(-)**	**81**	**6%**

C = Consultant	AS = Associate specialist
SR = Senior registrar	SG = Staff grade
SHO = Senior house officer	

CA = Clinical assistant
R = Registrar

There were 19 cases where the most senior operating surgeon was an unsupervised locum trainee (either registrar or SHO). This is a small number of cases and the only inappropriate cases were in orthopaedic surgery where locum SHOs were operating solo on patients with fractured neck of femur.

It is apparent that, over the years since the original CEPOD report,[1] the provision of appropriately trained surgeons has improved. How do we eliminate the remaining areas of inappropriate behaviour?

Table S38 (q62)
Has this death been considered, (or will it be considered) at a local audit/quality control meeting?

	Yes		No	Not answered	Total
Cardiothoracic	73	86%	8	4	**85**
General/colorectal	430	91%	31	13	**474**
Gynaecology	34	54%	26	3	**63**
Neurosurgery	40	69%	14	4	**58**
Ophthalmology	4	36%	6	1	**11**
Oral/maxillofacial	5	71%	1	1	**7**
Orthopaedic	218	68%	89	13	**320**
Otorhinolaryngology	12	63%	6	1	**19**
Plastic	8	73%	3	0	**11**
Urology	69	86%	10	1	**80**
Vascular	215	90%	18	5	**238**
Total	**1108**	**81%**	**212**	**46**	**1366**

Table S39 (q63)
Did you have any problem in obtaining the notes (i.e. more than 1 week)?

	Yes		No	Not answered	Total
Cardiothoracic	6	7%	75	4	85
General/colorectal	54	11%	401	19	474
Gynaecology	9	14%	52	2	63
Neurosurgery	7	12%	47	4	58
Ophthalmology	3	27%	8	0	11
Oral/maxillofacial	1	14%	6	0	7
Orthopaedic	56	18%	251	13	320
Otorhinolaryngology	2	11%	17	0	19
Plastic	3	27%	8	0	11
Urology	13	16%	66	1	80
Vascular	31	13%	200	7	238
Total	**185**	*14%*	**1131**	**50**	**1366**

The problem of missing notes continues and has already been mentioned in the general data section (page 20).

Table S40 (q64)
Were all the notes available?

	Yes	No		Not answered	Total
Cardiothoracic	67	14	16%	4	85
General/colorectal	391	71	15%	12	474
Gynaecology	51	10	16%	2	63
Neurosurgery	41	12	21%	5	58
Ophthalmology	5	6	55%	-	11
Oral/maxillofacial	3	3	43%	1	7
Orthopaedic	240	67	21%	13	320
Otorhinolaryngology	17	2	11%	-	19
Plastic	10	1	9%	-	11
Urology	71	7	9%	2	80
Vascular	197	31	13%	10	238
Total	**1093**	**224**	*16%*	**49**	**1366**

If no, which part was inadequate/unavailable?

Postmortem report	93
Death certificate book	92
Anaesthetic notes	26
Postoperative notes	14
Operative notes	13
Preoperative notes	12
Nursing notes	11
Other notes	32
Not specified	4
Total (answers may be multiple)	**224**

Table S41 (q40)

Was the procedure performed SOLELY under local anaesthesia or sedation administered by the SURGEON?

	Yes		No	Not answered	Total
Cardiothoracic	-	-	76	9	85
General/colorectal	4	*1%*	434	36	474
Gynaecology	-	-	59	4	63
Neurosurgery	1	*2%*	55	2	58
Ophthalmology	5	*45%*	6	-	11
Oral/maxillofacial	1	*14%*	6	-	7
Orthopaedic	2	*1%*	312	6	320
Otorhinolaryngology	-	-	19	-	19
Plastic	2	*18%*	9	-	11
Urology	-	-	75	5	80
Vascular	7	*3%*	211	20	238
Total	**22**	*2%*	**1262**	**82**	**1366**

N.B. Tables S42 to S47 refer only to those cases for which both the anaesthetic and surgical questionnaires were returned to NCEPOD.

Throughout these tables, 'most senior anaesthetist' refers to the most senior anaesthetist present at the start of the anaesthetic; 'most senior surgeon' refers to the most senior operator, regardless of the presence in theatre of a more senior surgeon acting in a supervisory capacity.

Table S42

Most senior anaesthetist/ most senior surgeon by specialty *(All)*

	Consultant		Assoc. Spec.		Clin. Asst.		Senior registrar		Staff grade		Registrar		SHO		Other/ Not ans.		Total
	A	S	A	S	A	S	A	S	A	S	A	S	A	S	A	S	
Cardiothoracic	44	45	-	-	-	-	7	3	-	-	-	3	-	-	-	-	51
General/colorectal	164	191	9	6	8	-	50	50	12	16	56	74	49	12	2	1	350
Gynaecology	25	33	1	-	2	-	6	2	4	-	2	6	2	1	-	-	42
Neurosurgery	17	17	-	-	-	-	16	9	1	-	4	12	-	-	-	-	38
Ophthalmology	2	3	-	-	-	-	-	-	-	-	1	-	-	-	-	-	3
Oral/maxillofacial	3	4	-	-	-	-	-	-	-	-	1	-	-	-	-	-	4
Orthopaedic	89	67	9	19	5	3	11	24	12	26	37	63	62	24	1	-	226
Otolaryngology	10	9	1	1	-	-	1	3	-	-	1	-	1	-	-	1	14
Plastic	5	4	-	-	-	-	1	2	1	-	-	1	-	-	-	-	7
Urology	39	47	3	1	4	-	6	3	1	-	6	10	1	-	1	-	61
Vascular	111	134	2	2	-	-	29	26	7	1	18	11	10	5	2	-	179
Total	**509**	**554**	**25**	**29**	**19**	**3**	**127**	**122**	**38**	**43**	**126**	**180**	**125**	**42**	**6**	**2**	**975**

A = anaesthetist   S = surgeon

Of the above 975 cases, 551 (56%) operations were started between 08:00 and 18:00 hrs on a weekday, and 385 (39%) outside these times. NCEPOD does not know the time at which the remaining 39 procedures took place.

Table S43
Most senior anaesthetist/most senior surgeon by specialty *(Out of hours only)*

	Consultant		Assoc. Spec.		Clin. Asst.		Senior registrar		Staff grade		Registrar		SHO		Other/ Not ans.		Total
	A	S	A	S	A	S	A	S	A	S	A	S	A	S	A	S	
Cardiothoracic	6	6	-	-	-	-	2	1	-	-	-	1	-	-	-	-	8
General/colorectal	69	84	6	6	5	-	33	33	5	9	38	49	30	5	1	1	187
Gynaecology	1	1	-	-	-	-	-	-	-	-	-	1	1	-	-	-	2
Neurosurgery	5	5	-	-	-	-	9	4	-	-	3	8	-	-	-	-	17
Ophthalmology	-	1	-	-	-	-	-	-	-	-	1	-	-	-	-	-	1
Oral/maxillofacial	1	1	-	-	-	-	-	-	-	-	-	-	-	-	-	-	1
Orthopaedic	13	12	2	3	1	2	4	7	1	8	14	23	28	9	1	-	64
Otorhinolaryngology	1	1	-	-	-	-	-	-	-	-	-	-	-	-	-	-	1
Plastic	-	-	-	-	-	-	-	-	-	-	-	-	-	-	-	-	-
Urology	4	6	-	-	1	-	3	1	-	-	1	2	-	-	-	-	9
Vascular	53	69	1	-	-	-	17	16	2	1	13	7	8	2	1	-	95
Total	**153**	**186**	**9**	**9**	**7**	**2**	**68**	**62**	**8**	**18**	**70**	**91**	**67**	**16**	**3**	**1**	**385**

The high involvement of anaesthetic SHOs for out-of-hours procedures shows that anaesthesia is still too dependent upon junior trainees. (See also "Who operates when?"[7]).

Table S44
Most senior anaesthetist/most senior surgeon *(All)*

	Grade of anaesthetist								
	Consultant	Assoc. Spec.	Clin. Asst.	Senior registrar	Staff grade	Registrar	SHO	Other/ Not ans.	Total
Grade of surgeon									
Consultant	381	12	9	56	15	54	24	3	554
Associate specialist	16	1	-	1	-	2	9	-	29
Clinical assistant	-	-	-	-	-	1	2	-	3
Senior registrar	41	2	3	36	3	16	21	-	122
Staff grade	13	-	1	5	3	10	11	-	43
Registrar	46	5	3	28	15	39	41	3	180
SHO	11	5	3	1	2	4	16	-	42
Other	-	-	-	-	-	-	-	-	-
Not answered	1	-	-	-	-	-	1	-	2
Total	**509**	**25**	**19**	**127**	**38**	**126**	**125**	**6**	**975**

Table S45
Most senior anaesthetist/ most senior surgeon *(Out of hours only)*

Grade of surgeon	Consultant	Assoc. Spec.	Clin. Asst.	Grade of anaesthetist Senior registrar	Staff grade	Registrar	SHO	Other/ not ans.	Tot
Consultant	116	4	2	24	2	25	11	2	18
Associate specialist	3	1	-	1	-	1	3	-	
Clinical assistant	-	-	-	-	-	1	1	-	
Senior registrar	12	-	1	26	3	9	11	-	6
Staff grade	5	-	1	1	-	5	6	-	1
Registrar	13	3	1	15	3	29	26	1	9
SHO	4	1	2	1	-	-	8	-	1
Other	-	-	-	-	-	-	-	-	
Not answered	-	-	-	-	-	-	1	-	
Total	**153**	**9**	**7**	**68**	**8**	**70**	**67**	**3**	**38**

Table S46
Cases where both the most senior anaesthetist and the most senior surgeon were SHOs or registrars

	Weekday in hours	Weekday out of hours	Weekday time not stated	Saturday / Sunday	Total
General/colorectal	10	19	1	14	44
Gynaecology	-	-	-	1	1
Neurosurgery	-	1	-	-	1
Orthopaedic	23	5	2	19	49
Urology	-	1	-	-	1
Vascular	1	1	-	2	4
Total	**34**	**27**	**3**	**36**	**100**

Table S47
Cases where both the most senior anaesthetist and the most senior surgeon were SHOs or registrars, *and the most senior surgeon was unsupervised.*

	Weekday in hours	Weekday out of hours	Weekday time not stated	Saturday / Sunday	Total
General/colorectal	2	16	1	9	28
Gynaecology	-	-	-	1	1
Neurosurgery	-	1	-	-	1
Orthopaedic	11	4	2	12	29
Urology	-	-	-	-	-
Vascular	1	1	-	1	3
Total	**14**	**22**	**3**	**23**	**62**

These figures suggest that there is scope for improvement in the delivery of general/colorectal and orthopaedic surgery.

Cardiothoracic surgery

Table S48
List of procedures

Thoracic surgery

Pneumonectomy	4
Pleural decortication	4
Diagnostic thoracoscopy	3
Miscellaneous (one each of: bronchoscopy, pleurodesis, thoracotomy & open lung biopsy, pleuroperitoneal shunt, redo oesophagogastrectomy, rib resection & drainage of empyema, laparotomy for oesophageal perforation, thorascopic sympathectomy, thoracotomy & laparotomy).	9

Cardiac surgery

CABG	25
Aortic valve replacement	9
Repair of aortic arch/thoracic aorta	8
Mitral valve replacement	4
Closure of VSD	4
CABG & aortic valve replacement	4
CABG & mitral valve replacement	3
Redo mitral valve replacement	3
Re-exploration of thorax	3
Closure of ASD	2
Redo aortic valve replacement	2
Miscellaneous (one each of: repair right ventricle, Ross operation, correction of truncus arteriosus, tricuspid valve replacement, switch procedure, pulmonary artery banding, pulmonary valve repair, redo CABG, pulmonary embolectomy, pericardectomy, repair SVC, correction paraprosthetic leak).	12

◆ This specialty is consultant-based with 100% involvement in decision-making; 95% (81/85) operations were performed by senior surgeons i.e. consultants or senior registrars.

There were two unsupervised operations done by trainee surgeons. One was a CABG, done by an experienced senior registrar, and the other was a lung decortication done by a registrar. Both these procedures were suitable for the experience of the operator. In general the appropriateness of care, the occurrence of postoperative complications such as haemorrhage, and the proportion of deaths, bore no relationship to the grade of operator.

Despite the high 'hands-on' involvement of consultants, the return rate for questionnaires to the Enquiry was only 67% (87/130).

High risk cases

The patients who died were in high risk groups; emergency or urgent admissions and operations were common. There were 11 patients who were classified as ASA 5; they all underwent cardiovascular surgery. Their details are listed below.

Details of ASA 5 patients

Age (years)	Operation and death	Points
6	Intended shunt for congenital cardiac anomaly but died on table before shunt constructed.	Operation delayed for six days due to lack of ICU bed. Eventually became emergency procedure. Delay contributed to death.
24	Suture of lacerated right ventricle. Cardiac tamponade.	HIV +ve. Pericarditis. Aspiration of pericardium lacerated ventricle.
46	Crash CABG and aortic valve replacement following cardiac arrest in catheter lab. Died in theatre.	Very sick man with multiple pathologies. The decision to operate was difficult. Locum consultant.
50	Pulmonary embolectomy. Died in theatre.	Immobile patient as result of neurological disease.
57	Replacement of dissecting aneurysm of aortic arch. Died in theatre.	Patient with known hypertension and ischaemic heart disease.
62	Aortic valve replacement. Bleeding, stroke and cardiac failure.	Emergency procedure. Death expected.
64	Attempted repair of dissecting aneurysm of aortic arch. Died in theatre.	Originally misdiagnosed at referring hospital as myocardial infarction.
66	Replacement of aneurysmal aortic arch. Died in theatre.	High risk procedure.
73	Closure of post-infarct ventricular septal defect. Died in theatre.	High risk procedure.
77	Attempted redo aortic valve replacement. Died in theatre due to uncontrolled bleeding after sternotomy.	Referred to teaching hospital. Consultant surgeon of four years standing had no experience of this procedure. During the upper part of the sternotomy, the power saw cut into the previous ascending aortic replacement graft and the patient bled to death. This was a difficult case. Should the patient have been referred to another colleague or another hospital?
80	Redo mitral valve replacement. Died in theatre - left ventricular rupture.	Very high risk procedure.

There were also eight cases where the surgeon stated that the patient was expected to die. Four of these patients were ASA 5 and are included above. The remaining four cases (all of whom had cardiovascular surgery) were:

Age (years)	Operation and death	Points
32	Thoracotomy and laparotomy for suspected injuries following trauma. Death due to pulmonary valve incompetence and myocardial hypertrophy.	Patient had previous congenital cardiac disease (corrected as a child). Subsequent endocarditis led to pulmonary incompetence and sequelae. Known diabetes mellitus.
63	Emergency replacement of aortic valve and aneurysm of ascending aorta. Died on table.	Known peripheral vascular disease.
69	Emergency CABG after complication of angioplasty. Died on first operative day of cardiac failure.	Experienced senior registrar operating.
73	Redo mitral valve replacement, aortic valve replacement and CABG. Death on day 2 due to respiratory problems and heart failure.	High risk case recognised by surgeon. Appropriate care throughout.

Inappropriate operations

There were four operations where the decision to operate appears to have been unwise or where the procedure was unorthodox. Details of these cases are given below.

Age (years)	Sex	Diagnosis and procedure	Comment
59	M	Thoracoabdominal aortic aneurysm. Remodelling of aorta by deroofing aneurysm and patching with Dacron.	An unorthodox elective procedure for an extensive aneurysm. Died same day. Coroner's postmortem results not available to surgeon.
59	M	Recurrent carcinoma of oesophagus four years after initial oesophagogastrectomy. Resection of anastomotic recurrence and reanastomosis.	Died 48 hours after operation; cardiac dysrhythmia. No evidence of assessment for widespread disease. Was this an appropriate procedure?
61	M	Right thorascopic cervical sympathectomy for relief of anginal pain.	Severe angina on maximal therapy. Three previous CABGs - grafts patent. Died same day: acute cardiac failure.
72	F	Extensive carcinoma of oesophagus seen at endoscopy by thoracic surgical registrar. Attempted dilatation without further assessment caused a perforation of the oesophagus. Laparotomy and insertion of Celestin tube next day.	Death from peritonitis.

Delays

In 29 elective cases there were undue delays between the initial decision to operate and admission. The time ranged from three to 574 days (median 60 days); 25% of the patients waited more than 125 days. Apart from long waiting lists, delays were due to lack of ICU/HDU beds and lack of experienced staff. Once admitted, elective cases waited between 0 - 22 days for surgery (median 1.5 days); 75% of patients had surgery within three days of admission.

Availability of ICU/HDU

It is vital that a specialty which undertakes surgery in high risk patients has the ability to provide postoperative care for patients in the appropriate environment. For many this will be an ICU or at least an HDU. These units must be adequately staffed and available throughout the day and night. In this sample there were four instances where the surgeons stated that there was no adult ICU in the hospital undertaking cardiothoracic surgery and 12 occasions where the ICU was not open throughout the day and night i.e. for the full 24 hours. There should also be the correct provision of dedicated paediatric ICU beds when dictated by the surgical specialism of the unit. There were at least two instances where the lack of an ICU bed may have been related to the patient's death and a further case where care in the HDU would have been appropriate but did not happen.

A six-year-old child with congenital heart disease was kept waiting for a palliative shunt for four days because the ICU was "overwhelmed". He then suffered a cardiac arrest before surgery and failed to recover despite resuscitation and emergency surgery. The reporting surgeon and the authors considered that the subsequent delay contributed to the patient's death.

A 68-year-old man was transferred 300 miles whilst in cardiogenic shock. This was because there was no bed in the local cardiothoracic ICU. He had suffered a myocardial infarction five months previously which was treated with streptokinase. His condition became unstable after urgent angiography and he required an emergency quadruple coronary artery bypass graft. He died the following day due to cardiac failure despite inotropes and support with an intra-aortic balloon pump.

A 69-year-old man had an extended left pneumonectomy for a bronchial carcinoma. He was nursed on a general ward where he died 24 hours after surgery due to aspiration of vomit. He was then admitted to ICU and died. Patients having such major surgery need to be cared for in an HDU.

Thromboembolic prophylaxis

The use of prophylactic measures against thromboembolism is shown in the table below.

Table S49

Prophylaxis used?	Thoracic	Cardiac	Total
Yes	11	40	**51**
No	5	29	**34**

	Before/during operation			After operation		
	Total	Thoracic	Cardiac	**Total**	Thoracic	Cardiac
None	**38**	6	32	**32**	7	25
Heparin	**36**	6	30	**13**	6	7
Leg stockings	**15**	7	8	**11**	6	5
Calf compression	**5**	5	-	-	-	-
Warfarin	**2**	-	2	**2**	-	2
Heel support	**7**	-	7	-	-	-
Ripple mattress	**1**	1	-	**2**	1	1
Total cases (answers may be multiple)	**85**	**16**	**69**	**52**	**15**	**37**

There was one death from a pulmonary embolus.

A 45-year old woman was admitted with a unilateral pleural effusion. She had been treated for Hodgkin's lymphoma in the past. A thoracotomy was done to obtain biopsies and perform a decortication. Thromboembolic prophylaxis consisted of stockings and intra-operative calf compression. Two days after surgery she had a cardiac arrest and died. A postmortem examination revealed deep venous thromboses and a pulmonary embolus. There was a mucin-secreting adenocarcinoma in the right lung.

Would the use of heparin have influenced this course of events? In thoracic surgery consideration might be given to using pharmacological prophylaxis as an addition to a regimen for thromboembolic prophylaxis.

General/colorectal surgery

A total of 626 surgical questionnaires were sent out and 476 were returned, of which 474 were suitable for analysis. This is a return rate of 76%. One-hundred-and-fifty questionnaires were not returned:

No reason given	103
Notes lost	30
Surgeon left or retired	7
Surgeon declined to participate	1
Form returned blank	1
Miscellaneous	8
Total	**150**

The failure to retrieve the notes of 30 (30/626, 4.8%) patients who had died is disappointing and demonstrates a continuing problem on which NCEPOD has commented in previous reports (see also page 20). Even when surgeons did reply, they stated that there were 71 (15%) occasions when some part of the patient's record was missing. It appears that 105 surgeons who cared for patients undergoing general surgical and colorectal procedures were reluctant to participate in NCEPOD; since most of these surgeons failed to respond to reminders we do not know why they were reluctant to participate. This means that data concerning 105 (16.8%) patients who died were unavailable for review; the information presented by the Enquiry relies on the quantity and quality of the data gathered and we would urge surgeons to return all questionnaires fully and accurately completed.

Many of the patients were either very young (11 were less than 10 years old) or elderly (295/474, 62% being over the age of 70 years), and of high ASA class (385/474, 82% were ASA 3 or above). Variations between anaesthetists and surgeons in the use of the ASA classification were noted. Surgeons' retrospective classifications are probably less helpful than a contemporaneous assessment by an anaesthetist; this is an area where local agreement between specialties is required. Eighty-four percent (399/474) of patients were admitted as either emergency or urgent cases. In 322 cases (322/474, 68%) the surgeon felt that surgery carried a definite risk. There were equal numbers of men and women. More than 60% of patients had other major clinical problems yet only 17% of all patients were given the benefit of 'shared care' by the involvement of other specialties such as general medicine. Such involvement and joint decisions might have altered the outcome for some patients.

Table S50 (q15)
Was care undertaken on a formal shared basis with another specialty (excluding anaesthesia)?

Yes	85
No	383
Not answered	6
Total	**474**

The other specialties (may be multiple) were:

Other surgical specialty	25
General medicine	20
Gastroenterology	12
ICU intensivist	12
Care of the elderly	7
Neonatology	5
Haematology	4
Renal physician	4
Paediatrician	3
Cardiology	2
Chest physician	2
Accident & Emergency	1
Hepatology	1
Infectious diseases	1
Nephrology	1
Oncology	1
Palliative care	1

Hospitals continued to accept emergency cases, including trauma, despite the lack of adequate ICU backup. The table below shows the availability of critical care services for these patients who died.

Table S51
Availability of essential services

	Available in the hospital	Available 24hrs per day, 7 days per week
Recovery area	473	382
Adult ICU	451	406
Adult HDU	135	111
Paediatric ICU/HDU	137	121
Total cases	**474**	**474**

The resourcing of these essential services is clearly inadequate for the safe practice of major general and colorectal surgery. The magnitude of the problem is worrying because even hospitals which provide an ICU do not always staff them round the clock and at the weekends. It could be argued that hospitals that cannot provide adequate ICU/HDU facilities should not admit surgical cases (since unexpected problems may occur at any time) and a question must arise as to whether or not they are adequate establishments in which to conduct surgical training. There were some instances where the transfer of a patient, admitted as an emergency, to another hospital with an ICU bed was inevitable from the outset. One patient, the victim of a road accident, was transferred from the scene of the accident by helicopter to a hospital with no CT scanner and no ICU bed. Better liaison between the ambulance service and the receiving unit might have avoided this situation. Eighteen patients could not be admitted to an ICU (when indicated) in the hospital where the operation took place because of lack of resources.

Patients who are deemed to be high risk should not be taken to the operating theatre until there has been an appropriate appraisal of these risks and discussion between surgeons and anaesthetists. Where there is an inadequate provision of ICU and HDU facilities to deal with the presenting workload, it may be more appropriate to transfer the patient rather than deny him/her postoperative care in an ICU (see also page 91). There is no evidence in this specialty that surgeons and anaesthetists were using ICU inappropriately.

Table S52
List of procedures

These procedures may be multiple for any individual patient.

Oesophageal surgery

Open insertion of oesophageal tube	3
Feeding gastrostomy	2
Oesophageal transection for oesophageal varices	2
Oesophagectomy (all approaches for malignant disease)	2
Miscellaneous (one each of: injection of oesophageal varices, repair of oesophageal rupture, exploratory thoracotomy, insertion of percutaneous endoscopic gastrostomy)	4

It is noteworthy that three deaths occurred (two feeding gastrostomies and one PEG insertion) after the introduction of adjuvant feeding techniques. It seems unlikely that there were only three patients in need of nutritional support. Is there a failure to recognise malnutrition in surgical patients? NCEPOD does not, however, have details of the use of TPN.

Abdominal surgery

Laparotomy for acute mesenteric ischaemia (+/- small bowel resection)	52
"Open and shut" laparotomy for widespread malignancy	22
Small bowel resection (all causes)	29
Laparotomy for peritonitis (cause unknown)	15
Laparotomy and division of adhesions (+/- small bowel resection)	10
Enterocolic bypass	10
Partial gastrectomy	9
Laparotomy for postoperative intra-abdominal sepsis (+/- anastomotic dehiscence)	8
Laparotomy for haemorrhage/multiple trauma	8
Gastroenterostomy for gastric carcinoma	5
Mesenteric embolectomy	3
Total gastrectomy	3
Negative laparotomy	2
Gallstone ileus	2
Diagnostic laparoscopy	2
Miscellaneous (one each of: loop jejunostomy, gastroscopy, drainage of pelvic abscess)	3

Mesenteric infarction was a major cause of death and many laparotomies were diagnostic only. Many of the small bowel resections were associated with strangulated hernia surgery.

Surgery for complications of peptic ulcer

Bleeding gastric ulcer

Under-running of bleeding ulcer   7

Perforated gastric ulcer

Simple closure   6

Bleeding duodenal ulcer

Under-running of bleeding ulcer   9
Truncal vagotomy and pyloroplasty   5
Truncal vagotomy and gastroenterostomy   2
Endoscopic injection of bleeding ulcer   1
Gastroscopy only   1

Perforated duodenal ulcer

Oversewing and/or omental patch   21
Truncal vagotomy and pyloroplasty   2
Truncal vagotomy and gastroenterostomy   1

Miscellaneous

Duodenojejunostomy (massive perforated DU)   1
Oversewing perforated stomal ulcer   1
Laparotomy and gastrostomy for variceal bleeding   1

Hepatopancreatobiliary surgery

Cholecystectomy   23
(conversion of laparoscopic cholecystectomy 2, open cholecystectomy 21)
Splenectomy   9
Laparotomy for liver trauma   7
Laparotomy for pancreatitis   4
Pancreatic necrosectomy   4
Bypass surgery for malignant obstructive jaundice   3
Exploration of common bile duct   2
Miscellaneous (one each of: packing pancreatic bed, repair of spleen,   4
pancreaticoduodenectomy, mesocaval shunt)

Colorectal surgery

Surgery for malignancy

Right hemicolectomy	20
Anterior resection of rectum	7
Hartmann's procedure	6
Left hemicolectomy	5
Transverse colectomy	4
Transverse colostomy	4
Sigmoid colectomy	3
Abdominoperineal resection of rectum	2

Surgery for benign conditions

Hartmann's procedure for complicated diverticular disease	30
Ileostomy	21
Transverse colostomy	10
Subtotal colectomy	10
Sigmoid colectomy	9
Appendicectomy	9
Total colectomy	4
Refashioning of colostomy	3
Drainage of perianal sepsis	2
Miscellaneous	6

Hernia surgery (including coincidental procedures such as small bowel resection)

Strangulated inguinal hernia repair	13
Strangulated femoral hernia	9
Strangulated incisional hernia	7
Umbilical hernia repair	2
Miscellaneous (one each of: repair parastomal hernia, repair epigastric hernia, bilateral inguinal hernia repair, strangulated obturator hernia)	4

Miscellaneous procedures (often additional to other procedures)

Debridement for necrotising fasciitis	4
Biopsy of tumour mass	3
Repair of aortoduodenal fistula	3
Resuture of abdominal wound dehiscence	2
Nephrectomy	2
Miscellaneous (one each of: exploration of wound, incision and drainage of superficial abscess, repair of ruptured duodenojejunal flexure, above knee amputation, drainage of subphrenic abscess, feeding jejunostomy, mastectomy, axillary clearance, repair ruptured diaphragm)	9

The majority of these patients were appropriately managed and died as a result of the advanced disease and overwhelming comorbidity. When there was irresistible pressure from relatives to operate on seriously ill patients, the returns showed that the surgeons had discussed the realistic prognosis with both these relatives and the patients.

Patients may come to harm because their condition deteriorates whilst they are on a long waiting list. This certainly occurred in one case. When there is a long wait it is recommended that patients are re-assessed prior to surgery. There were 41 cases where referral to a surgeon was delayed either before or after admission to hospital. Thirteen patients were under the care of another specialty. This was particularly so for cases of gastrointestinal bleeding where physicians referred late and after transfusion of large volumes of blood. Gastrointestinal bleeding is a condition which should be managed by an integrated team of interested physicians and surgeons working to clearly defined protocols.[10]

There was still some inadequate preoperative assessment and preparation (sometimes compounded by misjudgements concerning fluid requirements) leading to operations being done on dehydrated patients; this was seen especially in those with a strangulated hernia.

There were other causes of delay in commencing surgical treatment in 21 patients. In seven cases there was no operating theatre space, three patients initially refused surgery, there was no ICU bed for one case and a shortage of nursing staff delayed another case. There were also nine miscellaneous causes of delay mainly due to queuing for an operating theatre space.

The surgical team

Table S53 (q14)
Specialty of consultant surgeon in charge at time of final operation before death

General surgery	452
Vascular surgery	2
Urology	5
Paediatric surgery	10
Transplantation surgery	2
Cardiothoracic surgery	1
Not answered	2
Total	**474**

◆ It is now exceptional to find a surgeon performing procedures in which he/she is not experienced.

Table S54 (qs 16 and 26)
The most senior surgeon involved in decision-making prior to surgery

		(locum)
Consultant	428	(25)
Associate specialist	17	-
Senior registrar	9	-
Clinical assistant	1	-
Staff grade	1	-
Registrar	17	(2)
Senior house officer	1	-
Total	**474**	

◆ Consultants were involved in the decision-making in 90% (428/474) of cases. The inclusion of senior registrars and associate specialists boosts this percentage to 96%.

Continuity of care was maintained by the practice of consultant surgeons handing over information about sick patients to colleagues prior to periods of annual leave.

Table S55 (q34)
Grade of most senior operating surgeon

		(locum)	With supervision?
Consultant	253	(17)	n/a
Associate specialist	9	-	4
Senior registrar	78	(3)	26
Staff grade	20	-	6
Registrar	101	(12)	39
Senior house officer	12	-	8
Not answered	1	-	-
Total	**474**		

◆ Senior surgeons operated on 340 (72%) of these ill patients. On only four occasions did an unsupervised basic surgical trainee operate on a patient who subsequently died. When compared with previous NCEPOD studies this is a great improvement.

Eighty-three percent (394) of the operations were emergency or urgent procedures indicating the acuteness and severity of these patients' illnesses.

Time of surgery

Fifty-one percent (244) of the operations after which patients died were done out of hours (see glossary, appendix B). The timing of these operations on patients who subsequently died contrasts markedly with the overall number of out-of-hours operations which is approximately 6% of all operations.[7] The higher number in this series reflects the seriousness of the patient's presenting condition and comorbidity. There will always be a need for some operations to be done out of hours because of the gravity of the patient's condition; however, the influence of the introduction of daytime emergency lists on the reduction of night-time operating in general is demonstrable.[7]

Postoperative complications

Table S56 (q46)
Postoperative complications

Not answered/none	36
Not applicable - death in theatre	21
Low cardiac output/other cardiac problems	295
Generalised sepsis	131
Respiratory distress	128
Renal failure	119
Haemorrhage/postoperative bleeding requiring transfusion	53
Stroke or other neurological problems	21
Other organ failure	16
Hepatic failure	16
DVT and/or pulmonary embolus	10
Anastomotic failure	8
Peripheral ischaemia	5
Nutritional problems	4
Problems with analgesia	3
Ureteric injury/fistula	2
Wound infection/dehiscence	2
Pressure sores	1
Other	28
Total cases *(answers may be multiple)*	**474**

This spectrum of complications is as might be expected for a group of ill patients who died after surgery. There was a low incidence of thromboembolism despite the very variable use of prophylaxis, see below.

Overall 93 patients (93/474, 19.6%) did not receive prophylaxis against thromboembolism. When prophylaxis was used, the method, timing and duration were variable (table S57).

Table S57 (q23)
Were any measures taken to prevent venous thromboembolism?

Yes	377	
No	93	
Not answered	4	

(May be multiple)	Before/during	After
None	112	204
Heparin	256	192
Leg stockings	205	145
Calf compression	90	11
Electrical stimulation of calves	7	3
Warfarin	3	-
Heel support	68	12
Ripple mattress	19	12
Other	2	3
Total	**474**	**453***

* (excludes death in theatre - 21 cases)

The question arises as to whether or not local protocols were being applied. It may be especially difficult for surgeons to apply local protocols to emergency cases when these are referred from other departments such as medicine where the dangers of thromboembolic disease following surgery may not always be appreciated.

Postmortem examinations and audit

Fifty-nine percent of these patients did not have a postmortem examination. Clinicians were inconsistent in their use of postmortem examinations. Pathologists often made value judgements (both positive and negative) about the standard of surgery which is outside their expertise.

Table S58 (qs 54 and 55)
Was a postmortem examination performed?

Coroner's PM	162
Hospital PM	31
No PM/not answered	281
Total	**474**

In the specialties of general surgery and colorectal surgery we cannot confirm that postmortem examinations gave any information of which surgeons were not already aware.

◆ The patients' deaths were discussed in local audit meetings in 91% (430/474) of cases. This is a commendable percentage of which general and colorectal surgeons should be proud. The audit process will be enhanced when patients' notes and the results of postmortem examinations are consistently available for discussions in audit.

Gynaecology

Table S59
List of procedures

Operations for benign gynaecological disease

Total abdominal hysterectomy (+/- bilateral salpingo-oophorectomy)	7
Vaginal hysterectomy (+/- anterior/posterior repair)	5
(one preceded by laparotomy and reduction of herniated bowel, one with BSO and diathermy to warts)	
Oophorectomy (unilateral or bilateral)	3
Procedures involving endoscopy (one hysteroscopy and one laparoscopy followed by laparotomy, adhesiolysis, oophorectomy)	2
Laparotomy for suspected intraperitoneal bleeding	2
Miscellaneous	3
Total (benign disease)	**22**

Operations for malignant gynaecological disease

Laparotomy (+/- biopsy)	11
Total abdominal hysterectomy (+/- bilateral salpingo-oophorectomy and including one subtotal hysterectomy)	9
Oophorectomy (+/- omentectomy)	9
Debulking (two colostomies in this group)	5
Procedures involving endoscopy (two laparoscopies and two hysteroscopies)	4
Simple vulvectomy	1
Miscellaneous	2
Total (malignant disease)	**41**

Total (all cases)	**63**

Commentary on gynaecology

- The return rate of questionnaires in gynaecology was 86% which is commendable.

- Gynaecology, a specialty with a large operative throughput, accounted for a relatively small number of sample cases (table S2 on page 76).

- Tables S23-S27 (pages 86 to 88) show that there was a high level of involvement of senior doctors (consultants, associate specialists and senior registrars) in the gynaecological operations shown. Only with weekend procedures (and there were only six in this study) did the percentage drop to 50%. However, consultants were involved in the preoperative decisions in over 90% of cases (see table S35, page 93). Only three of the six operations done at a weekend were performed by more junior doctors.

- Emergencies are often dealt with by staff below the consultant grade. Only 23% (15/63) of the procedures in this study were classified as 'urgent' or 'emergency' (table S12, page 81); 32% (20/63) of the deaths analysed were in patients admitted as emergencies (table S5, page 77). Twelve percent (7/63) of deaths analysed (table S21, page 85) followed operations done out of hours or at the weekends, which suggests that many emergencies find their way onto routine operating lists or dedicated daytime emergency lists.

- Of gynaecology patients, 56% (35/63) were graded by the gynaecologist as ASA 3, 4 or 5 (table S8, page 79), only 17% (11/63) had no co-existing problems (table S10, page 80) and in only 30% (19/63) was death not expected (table S11, page 81) confirming that it is the medically unfit and elderly women who are most at risk of death in gynaecological surgery.

- Delays in referral or admission (13%, 18/63 in table S18, page 84) or surgery (3%, 2/63 in table S19, page 84) and shortage of personnel (3% in table S20, page 85) played a minor part in the gynaecological deaths analysed.

- Only 54%, (34/63) of the deaths were apparently considered at a local audit meeting (table S38, page 94).

- Of the 63 deaths in gynaecology, 12 (19%) were due to pulmonary embolism and these are examined in more detail in the table below. All but four of these pulmonary emboli occurred in spite of appropriate precautions.

- In 43% (27/63) of the deaths there was some evidence of poor decision-making regarding the management particularly in cases where deaths were expected or likely.

Table S60
Deaths from pulmonary emboli

Age	Procedure and comments	Thromboprophylaxis
	Benign gynaecological disease	
45	Total abdominal hysterectomy, bilateral salpingo-oophorectomy for menorrhagia. Massive pulmonary embolus.	Heparin and stockings.
48	Fibroids. Total abdominal hysterectomy, bilateral salpingo-oophorectomy. Deep vein thrombosis and pulmonary embolus.	Heparin and stockings before and after operation.
55	Total abdominal hysterectomy and bilateral salpingo-oophorectomy for menorrhagia and fibroids.	Diabetes (90kg). No insulin. Heparin before and after operation.
72*	Laparotomy and right oophorectomy for benign cyst.	Three month delay had been advised because of decreased mobility. Previous myocardial infarction. Previous deep vein thrombosis and pulmonary embolus. Nearest ICU was three miles away. No heparin given preoperatively.
79	Vaginal hysterectomy and repair for procidentia.	No heparin given.
85	Vaginal hysterectomy and repair. Previous myocardial infarction.	No thromboprophylaxis.
	Malignant gynaecological disease	
51	Laparotomy and biopsies. Massive pulmonary embolus on second postoperative day.	Heparin prophylaxis.
61	Debulking of tumour. Pulmonary embolus was anaesthetist's diagnosis, massive stroke was the surgeon's diagnosis. No postmortem examination.	Heparin and stockings before and after operation.
63	Omentectomy and biopsies. Pulmonary embolus. Coroner's postmortem examination.	Heparin before operation.
64	Total abdominal hysterectomy and bilateral salpingo-oophorectomy for endometrial carcinoma with complete removal.	Overweight. Hypothyroid. Gout. On antihypertensives. No heparin.
71	Laparotomy, omental biopsies. Death on the first postoperative day due to presumed pulmonary embolus. No postmortem examination.	Heparin before operation.
81	Total abdominal hysterectomy and bilateral salpingo-oophorectomy for endometrial carcinoma. Large pulmonary embolus.	Heparin before and after operation.

There was a higher incidence of fatal pulmonary embolism in women operated on for benign disease (6/22, 27%) compared to 15% (6/41) in women who had operations for malignant diseases, an acknowledged high risk factor. The Royal College of Obstetricians and Gynaecologists has recently issued recommendations concerning thromboembolic prophylaxis in gynaecological surgery.[11]

Decision-making and 'inappropriate' surgery

This topic merits separate consideration as there were 22 cases, including one woman aged 72 who died from a pulmonary embolism, (see earlier * table S60) where decision-making or surgery appear retrospectively to have been inappropriate. These cases are tabulated below.

Table S61

Age	Operation and clinical details	Comments and points *(non-gynaecological malignancies in italics)*
	Benign gynaecological disease	
57	Oophorectomy for residual ovaries causing pain. Died 34 hours after surgery. Postmortem examination showed intraperitoneal haemorrhage although the vascular pedicles were intact. There was also evidence of sepsis and disseminated intravascular coagulopathy.	Past history of stroke and ischaemic heart disease. Possible inappropriate operation in a high risk patient.
78	Total abdominal hysterectomy, bilateral salpingo-oophorectomy and omentectomy for benign ovarian tumour. Difficulty with bleeding from mesentery. Death attributed to acute on chronic renal failure. No postmortem examination.	Chronic renal failure. *Chronic leukaemia.* Preoperative blood urea 10mmol/l and haemoglobin 9.8g/dl. Was surgery prudent?
	Malignant or presumed malignant gynaecological disease	
50	Ascites from liver metastases and liver failure. Open and close laparotomy.	What was the purpose of this operation?
60	Total abdominal hysterectomy and bilateral salpingo-oophorectomy for abnormal cytology after a cone biopsy. Deep pelvis and difficult anaesthesia. Postmortem examination showed acute left ventricular failure secondary to ischaemic heart disease and extensive coronary atheroma.	Diabetic. Previous myocardial infarction. Was repeat cone biopsy rather than pelvic clearance indicated?
64	Examination under anaesthesia, dilatation and curettage. Laparoscopy and mini-laparotomy for ascites and pleural effusion. No postmortem examination. Patient and husband wanted to know source of primary.	In hospital one month. Ascites and pleural effusion. Adenocarcinoma cells had been identified. Why operate?
65	Ovarian carcinomatosis. Omental biopsy and closure. Poor condition at operation.	Dyspnoea. Pleural effusions showed malignant cells. Why operate?

68	Extensive ovarian carcinoma. Some tumour on diaphragm. Total abdominal hysterectomy and bilateral salpingo-oophorectomy. Pelvic and aortic lymphadenectomy. Peritoneal biopsies. Resection ileum and caecum. 6 litre blood loss.	Obese, confused fluid-overloaded patient. Six unit intraoperative transfusion. Was such extensive surgery justified?
69	Total abdominal hysterectomy and bilateral salpingo-oophorectomy. History of postmenopausal bleeding for two months.	Ischaemic heart disease. Had third myocardial infarct some weeks before. Pipelle suggested CINIII. Smear suggested invasive disease. Operation done in the absence of a clear preoperative diagnosis.
70	Laparotomy and right salpingo-oophorectomy. Omental biopsy for abdominal mass and ascites.	*Carcinoma bronchus* previously treated by irradiation. Abdominal mass with ascites. CT guided ovarian biopsy had already shown ovarian carcinoma. Why operate?
73	Total abdominal and bilateral salpingo-oophorectomy for endometrial carcinoma. Died of cardiorespiratory failure.	Controlled congestive heart failure . Hypothyroidism. Ex-alcoholic. Depressed. Impaired renal function. Preoperative haemoglobin 9.7g/dl. Was preoperative assessment adequate?
75	Subtotal hysterectomy and bilateral salpingo-oophorectomy for endometrial carcinoma and umbilical hernia repair in a very obese woman. Died of heart failure. Operation done for bleeding despite irradiation.	Anaesthetist (who had previously anaesthetised for hysteroscopy, dilatation and curettage) said that she would not stand a hysterectomy.
77	Ligation of internal iliac vessels for postoperative haemorrhage after debulking operation for ovarian carcinoma with small bowel obstruction.	Patient had pleural effusion, congestive heart failure and atrial fibrillation and was on diuretic and Digoxin. Was surgery justifiable for someone in such poor condition?
78	Fixed retroperitoneal mass obstructing stomach found at operation. No pelvic disease. Died of renal failure.	Myocardial infarction 12 years previously. *Breast cancer diagnosis in 1990.* On Tamoxifen. Hypertensive. Became hypotensive with epidural bupivacaine.
80	Postmenopausal bleeding with an enlarged uterus. Hysteroscopy. Dilatation and curettage. Vulval biopsy. Died of presumed myocardial infarction on second postoperative day. No postmortem examination.	Past history of myocardial infarction and diverticulitis. Would a Pipelle aspiration have sufficed for diagnosis?
82	Advanced endometrial carcinoma. Examination under anaesthesia, hysteroscopy and dilatation and curettage. Cystoscopy. Postmortem examination showed extensive malignancy in pelvis.	Uraemic and dyspnoea at rest. Inappropriate surgery in a uraemic patient.
82	Excision of right ovarian carcinoma. Died of myocardial infarction. No postmortem examination.	Uraemic patient *with past history of transitional cell carcinoma of bladder.* The ICU and HDU were full.

83	Removal of ovarian tumour. Drainage of ascites. Regurgitated and inhaled in recovery room.	Mucinous ascites which had been tapped. Was this an appropriate operation?
83	Excision ovarian tumours. Died of acute myocardial infarction on the second postoperative day.	Confused patient in a geriatric unit. Known alcohol abuse. Doubly incontinent. Diagnosed as having ovarian malignancy one year previously. Was surgery appropriate?
83	Laparotomy and biopsy. Died of cardiac arrest on the first postoperative day. No postmortem examination.	Uraemic patient. SHO anaesthetist. Failed epidural. Was this an appropriate operation?
85	Ovarian carcinoma with omental metastases and other metastases involving stomach and spleen.	Presented with dyspnoea and pleural effusion. Effusion tapped. No cytology result before surgery.
88	Simple vulvectomy for Paget's disease of vulva. Died of congestive heart failure.	Congestive heart failure and ischaemic heart disease. Staff grade anaesthetist in DGH without HDU or ICU. Would local excision have been sufficient?

Eighteen of these 22 cases were managed in DGHs. Only two of the 19 cases of gynaecological malignancy or presumed malignancy were managed by gynaecological oncologists, but in the vast majority of cases other consultants (surgeons, urologists, oncologists, physicians) were involved in the decision-making and/or operating.

Ovarian cancer is the major cause of death from gynaecological malignancy largely because the majority of women present with advanced disease. Careful patient selection and preoperative assessment are important factors in the management of this cancer.

The developments in the subspecialty of gynaecological oncology and the Royal College of Obstetricians and Gynaecologists proposals for gynaecological cancer services[12] will hopefully encourage a more balanced approach to the management of the difficult cases. With the modern diagnostic services and resources available it has to be accepted that sometimes the most appropriate decision that can be made is **not to operate.** If surgery is undertaken, many women will require bowel surgery and should be prepared for this preoperatively. If the gynaecologists are uncertain about bowel surgery, they may wish to involve a general surgical colleague.

Insufficiently experienced surgeons

While the level of consultant cover was generally excellent, there were five instances when it appeared that insufficient experience of the operating surgeon may have played a role in the poor outcome.

Table S62

Age	Operation and death	Points
	Benign gynaecological disease	
39	Total abdominal hysterectomy for fibroids and prolonged periods. Estimated blood loss 1300ml. Two hour operation. Two previous caesarean sections and bladder mobilised with difficulty. Coroner's postmortem examination revealed aspiration pneumonitis. No haemorrhage or thrombosis at operation site.	Locum senior registrar doing a difficult hysterectomy.
63	Peritonitis. Laparotomy, right salpingo-oophorectomy and washout. Died of cardiac failure secondary to septicaemia on the second postoperative day.	Decision to operate taken and operation done on a Sunday by a registrar. Questionnaire very incomplete.
74	Hysteroscopy. Dilatation and curettage. Small bowel perforation. Died at home on the second postoperative day.	Registrar of one month experience operating. Unrecognised intraoperative complication. Sent home on the first postoperative day despite abdominal pain.
	Malignant gynaecological disease	
49	Carcinoma of endometrium. Died of overwhelming sepsis.	Senior registrar made over-ambitious attempts to remove an infected neoplastic uterus.
69	Stage II/III endometrial carcinoma. Laparotomy for massive intra-abdominal bleeding two days after total abdominal hysterectomy and bilateral salpingo-oophorectomy. Died on table of exsanguination.	Final operation done by a locum who had been an SHO for three years. An inexperienced surgeon dealing with a serious complication.

Comments

Despite the high input of consultant involvement in the decision-making the deaths following surgery for benign disease indicate that some cases might have either benefited from a greater medical input or a more definite policy for thromboembolism prophylaxis. In other instances there were examples of poor delegation of difficult operations and poor postoperative care particularly when there is persisting pain or infection.

Head and neck surgery

Commentary

◆ The three specialties involved in this section had an above average return rate for their surgical questionnaires. Consultants in otorhinolaryngology returned 90% (19/21) of questionnaires, oral/maxillofacial surgeons returned 88% (7/8) and ophthalmic surgeons returned 79% (11/14). This compares favourably with the overall surgical return rate of 76% (see page 19).

There were 11 deaths in this group which could not have been anticipated. One was due to myocardial infarction with no previous cardiac history and two patients experienced a ruptured abdominal aortic aneurysm soon after ophthalmic surgery.

Audit in all three specialties was low; 30% of cases were not considered at local audit meetings. There was also a low use of postmortem examinations and where Coroners' postmortem examinations were not indicated, hospital examinations were rarely requested. NCEPOD has made similar comments before.[6]

List of procedures

Otorhinolaryngology

Age	Sex	Operation and indication	Cause of death	Comment
3 days	M	Multiple congenital anomalies including tracheal stenosis. Tracheostomy and tracheal dilatation.	Respiratory failure.	Difficult patient with an impossible prognosis.
29	F	Tracheostomy.	Cardiorespiratory arrest.	Acute intermittent porphyria. Anoxic brain damage.
48	M	Diabetic with stridor due to retropharyngeal abscess (previously drained). Change of dressing.	Pulmonary embolus. DVT secondary to retropharyngeal abscess.	Thromboembolic prophylaxis given to patient throughout illness. No mention of diabetes mellitus in Coroner's postmortem examination report.
53	F	Breast carcinoma with metastases in nasopharynx causing epistaxis. Biopsy of nasopharynx and insertion of nasal packs.	Carcinomatosis and respiratory failure.	Epistaxis controlled and appropriate symptom control given.
54	F	Recurrent carcinoma of larynx. Total laryngectomy and thyroidectomy.	Cardiac failure.	Recurrence six years after irradiation. Known cardiac disease. Fluid overload in postoperative period.
62	F	Nasal polypi. Excision of nasal polyp proposed.	Acute cardiac failure.	Died at induction of anaesthesia. Probable suxamethonium anaphylaxis (see anaesthetic section).

Age	Sex	Operation and indication	Cause of death	Comment
63	M	Excision submandibular gland (benign).	Myocardial infarction in recovery area.	Preoperative ECG showed old inferior myocardial infarction.
67	F	Carcinoma of larynx. Direct laryngoscopy and biopsy. Tracheostomy.	Myocardial infarction.	Appropriate care.
67	M	Residual carcinoma of larynx after irradiation. Known ischaemic heart disease. Total laryngectomy.	Myocardial infarction.	Death 48 hours after surgery.
69	M	Recurrent carcinoma of larynx following irradiation. Chronic obstructive pulmonary disease. Total laryngectomy.	Myocardial infarction (confirmed at postmortem examination).	Death 24 hours after surgery.
70	M	Benign vocal cord nodules. Microlaryngoscopy, biopsy and laser excision.	Unknown.	Died at home three days after surgery.
72	M	Tracheostomy.	Gastrointestinal haemorrhage.	Massive GI bleeding from DU and hepatic encephalopathy. In ICU. Tracheostomy incidental.
73	M	Carcinoma of larynx. Right neck block dissection.	Myocardial infarction (confirmed at postmortem examination).	Third postoperative day. Unexpected carcinoma of kidney found at post mortem examination.
74	F	Emergency tracheostomy and laryngoscopy. Supraglottic oedema ? cause.	Septicaemia.	Death 48 hours after surgery. Postmortem examination showed laryngo-oesophago-epiglottitis.
75	M	Carcinoma of larynx. Percutaneous endoscopic gastrostomy.	Carcinomatosis.	Inevitable death.
77	M	Extensive carcinoma of larynx. Total laryngectomy.	Myocardial infarction.	Death 24 hours after surgery. No postmortem examination.
77	M	Right radical neck dissection. Carcinoma of larynx with cervical metastases two years after irradiation.	Myocardial infarction.	Death 48 hours after surgery.

Age	Sex	Operation and indication	Cause of death	Comment
78	M	Epistaxis. Known severe chronic obstructive pulmonary disease. Removal of nasal packing under general anaesthesia.	Respiratory failure.	Was the second procedure appropriate? It is usually possible to remove post nasal packs without anaesthesia.
81	F	Multinodular goitre and stridor. Urgent partial thyroidectomy.	Acute myocardial ischaemia.	Died on first postoperative day.

Eighteen of these nineteen operations were considered to be appropriate.

Oral/maxillofacial surgery

Age	Sex	Operation and indication	Cause of death	Comment
25	M	Road traffic accident with facial fractures. Haemorrhage from nasopharynx. Tracheostomy and ligation of external carotid artery.	Head injury. Subdural haemorrhage. Multiple fractures.	Died 24 hours after trauma. Full involvement of anaesthetists, neurosurgeons and orthopaedic surgeons.
28	M	Bleeding from recurrent mandibular sarcoma. Breakdown of previous reconstruction. Examination under anaesthetic and skin graft to back.	Torrential haemorrhage secondary to carotid artery "blow-out".	
64	M	Dental abscess. Severe ischaemic heart disease. Drainage of abscess and dental extraction under local anaesthesia.	Myocardial infarction.	Was in terminal stages of cardiac failure. Operation justified for pain relief. Full monitoring used and anaesthetist present. Died half an hour after procedure.
72	M	Recurrent post auricular squamous carcinoma. Resection of tumour and radical neck dissection. Myocutaneous flap reconstruction.	Cardiac failure.	Death three days postoperatively.
74	M	Facial trauma. Fixation of fractured maxilla and suturing of lacerations	Myocardial infarction (confirmed at postmortem examination).	No clear postoperative instructions were given concerning the management of this patient's airway or the removal of the wires.
74	M	Recurrent oral carcinoma. Resection of tumour and radical neck dissection. Tracheostomy.	Cardiac failure.	Death 48 hours postoperatively.
82	F	Bilateral bone grafts to temporomandibular joints. Recurrent dislocation of the jaw.	Cerebrovascular accident.	Death 24 hours postoperatively.

Care was appropriate in these cases.

Ophthalmology

Age	Sex	Operation and indication	Cause of death	Comment
70	M	Endophthalmitis following cataract extraction. Local antibiotic injections into anterior chamber.	Myocardial infarction (confirmed at postmortem examination).	
75	F	Glaucoma. Trabeculectomy.	Myocardial infarction.	Local anaesthetic. Died 24 hours after surgery.
77	M	Cataract. Severe emphysema. Cataract extraction.	Haemopneumothorax. Ruptured emphysematous bulla (confirmed at postmortem examination).	Operation under GA. Why was a local anaesthetic technique not used in view of lung disease?
79	F	Panophthalmitis. Enucleation.	Ruptured abdominal aortic aneurysm.	
80	M	Cataract, chronic obstructive pulmonary disease and senile dementia. Cataract extraction.	Status asthmaticus.	Local anaesthesia.
82	F	Cataract, ischaemic heart disease, diabetes mellitus. Cataract extraction.	Myocardial infarction.	General anaesthesia.
86	F	Cataract extraction and lens implant	Ruptured abdominal aortic aneurysm (confirmed at postmortem examination).	Initially a day case but converted to an in-patient in view of low blood pressure and anaemia. Ruptured aneurysm not diagnosed clinically.
88	M	Ectropion. Renal failure. Cardiac failure.	Acute cardiac failure.	Local anaesthesia. Died same day.
88	M	Cataract extraction and lens implant.	Haematemesis.	Died in another hospital 24 hours after cataract surgery.
89	F	Cataract extraction and lens implant. Diabetes mellitus, polymyalgia rheumatica and cardiac failure.	Acute cardiac failure.	General anaesthesia used.
92	M	Panophthalmitis. Enucleation.	Pulmonary embolus.	Presumed diagnosis - no postmortem examination.

The surgical procedures were all appropriate.

Neurosurgery

The return of questionnaires, though an improvement on the 1993/94 return, was still low (71%).

Table S63
List of procedures

Evacuation of acute subdural haematoma	15
Clipping of intracranial aneurysm	8
Evacuation of intracerebral haematoma	8
External ventricular drainage	8
Evacuation of traumatic extradural haematoma	4
Stereotactic biopsy of tumour	2
Evacuation of intracerebellar haematoma	2
Cervical spinal fusion	2
Suturing of scalp wounds	2
Miscellaneous (one each of: excision of cerebellar abscess, biopsy of brain stem tumour, lumbar laminectomy, spinal decompression, insertion of intracranial pressure monitor, debulking of meningioma, evacuation of chronic subdural haematoma)	7

There were a number of inappropriate operations carried out on moribund patients. Where these operations were for spontaneous or traumatic intracranial haemorrhage, especially in very elderly patients, this may not reflect upon the surgeon who carried out the operation but upon the difficulty in the assessment (for neurosurgeons) after the early intubation and ventilation of such patients in an emergency department as a life-saving procedure.

There was delay in diagnosis at non-specialist units due to lack of scanning facilities. Transfer of patients should take into account the availability of resources to diagnose and manage intracranial catastrophes.

The transfer of patients in certain circumstances gave cause for concern. It appeared that published standards for the transfer of head injuries were being flouted and patients were not transferred in a timely manner. [9, 13]

There were instances of burrholes being undertaken in non-specialist units and telephone advice being given without visual access to CT and MRI scans. It is to be emphasised that the practice of neurosurgery by giving advice on the telephone to non-specialists, without seeing images or the patient, is a retrograde step and is likely to lead to disaster. [14]

There were examples of operations carried out by inappropriate junior staff especially in elderly moribund patients.

An 80-year-old woman with a known breast carcinoma and previous strokes had a hydrocephalus drained with the insertion of a ventriculoperitoneal shunt at the same time as a mastectomy. She subsequently developed an acute on chronic subdural haematoma. A consultant decided that the haematoma should be drained but left the surgery to a locum SHO who operated unsupervised. The consultant neurosurgeon who completed and returned the surgical questionnaire stated that he had no idea as to the experience of this locum SHO.

Other examples of inappropriate procedures were:

Age	Sex	Operation & indication	Cause of death	Comment
73	F	Craniotomy and evacuation of intracerebral haematoma by unsupervised registrar.	Respiratory depression due to raised intracranial pressure.	Outcome expected to be poor. Surgery was probably not the appropriate treatment but the relatives wanted the surgical option pursued at all costs.
76	M	Craniotomy and evacuation of large acute subdural haematoma by unsupervised registrar.	Cardiorespiratory arrest.	Initially transferred as CT scanner not working and no ICU bed. The patient was moribund. Unsupervised registrar in post for five months.

Orthopaedic surgery

Table S64
List of procedures

	Total number	(Out-of-hours operations)[*]
Dynamic hip screw, or similar procedure for fractured neck of femur	126	(43)
Revision/removal/attention of dynamic hip screw	7	
Hemiarthroplasty for fractured neck of femur	95	(34)
Revision/removal/attention of hemiarthroplasty	1	
Total hip replacement for fractured neck of femur	1	(1)
Revision/removal/attention of total hip replacement	1	
Total hip replacement for arthritis	17	
Revision/removal/attention to above	9	(2)
Total knee replacement for arthritis	13	
Operations for fractured shaft of femur	16	(6)
Operations for fractured humerus/ulna/olecranon/dislocated shoulder	4	(2)
Operations for fractured acetabulum/dislocated hip	3	
Operations for f ractured tibia/fibula	2	(1)
Operations for fractured ankle	2	
Operations for fractured wrist	2	(2)
Operations for multiple fractures	7	(5)
Spinal operations	7	(2)
Arthroscopy	3	
Wound debridement	3	(1)
Above knee amputation	1	(1)
Below knee amputation	1	(1)
Total cases *(answers may be multiple)*	**320**	

Overall there were 231 operations done by grades of surgeon other than consultant. Of those 131 were unsupervised, see table S65.

Table S65
Unsupervised operations/total number of operations
(including 'not answered' and 'not known')

	Overall	Weekday in hours	Weekday time not stated	Weekday out of hours*	Saturday and Sunday
Senior house officer	10/29	3/13	1/5	2/3	4/8
Registrar	58/99	24/55	3/7	6/6	25/31
Staff grade	20/32	8/7	3/4	3/3	6/8
Senior registrar	24/39	10/20	2/4	1/1	11/14
Clinical assistant	1/3	0/1	-	-	1/2
Associate specialist	16/27	14/21	0/2	1/2	1/2
Other/not known	2/2	-	1/1	1/1	-
Subtotal (cases)	**131/231**	**59/127**	**10/23**	**14/16**	**48/65**
Consultant operations	89	61	11	4	13
Total	**320**	**188**	**34**	**20**	**78**

[*] see glossary, appendix B

From table S65 it can be seen that basic orthopaedic trainees i.e. SHOs, did 10 unsupervised operations of which six were done out of hours. Registrars did 58 unsupervised operations of which 31 were out of hours and at weekends. There is concern within the profession about basic orthopaedic trainees operating unsupervised, and an illustrative list of such cases is given below with comments. NCEPOD recommends the practice of trainees consulting seniors prior to operating.

Table S66
Examples of operations done by unsupervised SHOs in orthopaedic surgery

Age	Sex	Diagnosis and Procedure	Comment
83	F	Fractured neck of femur. Dementia and insulin-dependent diabetes. On steroids for polyarthritis. Unwell on admission with regurgitation of vomit. Dynamic hip screw and plate.	Both surgeon and anaesthetist were unsupervised SHOs. Died 24 hours postop. Aspiration of vomit.
85	M	Fractured neck of femur. Complex case - confused, anaemic, dehydrated, renal failure, atrial fibrillation. Hemiarthroplasty - technical problems. Postoperative coagulopathy and cardiac failure.	Consultant decision but SHO operation. Became ill over weekend and died three days postoperatively. Not considered for HDU.
87	F	Fractured neck of femur. Hemiarthroplasty.	Inappropriate delay due to lack of operating theatre (three days). Inappropriate surgeon.
89	F	Fractured neck of femur, hypothyroidism and dementia. Dynamic hip screw and plate.	Both surgeon and anaesthetist were unsupervised SHOs. Preoperatively ECG not seen by anaesthetist. Cardiac arrest on ward, transferred to ICU. Died within 24 hours after surgery.
90	F	Fractured neck of femur and dementia. Dynamic hip screw and plate.	Unsupervised surgeon and anaesthetist. Both SHOs.
93	F	Fractured neck of femur. Dynamic hip screw and plate.	Orthopaedic SHO made all decisions. Weekend operation by unsupervised locum SHO. Anaesthetist also SHO, and with no higher qualifications. Died second postoperative day - hyponatraemia and confusion. Sedated - respiratory failure.

Good surgical practice dictates that a consultant should be consulted regarding patient management and that the consultant should have established clinical guidelines and standardised management protocols for common conditions. It should be a consultant surgeon who decides that an operation is done. In order to provide an improved level of training, consultants should be available to supervise junior staff, especially when undertaking a major surgical procedure. In a specialty where the levels of supervision of SHOs and registrars were between 34% for SHOs and 59% for registrars (table S65), levels of supervision and consultant input cannot be viewed as good. In addition to the cases done by SHOs listed above, in the management of trauma there were too many cases where there was no consultant input.

There were delays for non-clinical reasons between admission and operation despite the establishment of trauma lists. This was particularly significant in the management of the fractures of the femoral neck. NCEPOD has discussed the matter previously[6] and is considered further in the "Who operates when?" report.[7]

Needless out-of-hours operating continues to occur (see table S64) and may be done by inappropriate staff with poor resources such as theatre availability and ancillary staff. This is especially recognised in the management of fractures of the femoral neck; resources must be available to undertake such procedures during the normal working day, and at weekends when required, with appropriate senior staff.

Plastic surgery

Commentary

There were 11 cases in this group and information about them is given on the following two pages.

◆ In all 11 cases the specialty of the surgeons caring for the patients was appropriate and in nine out of eleven cases the decision to operate was made at consultant level. In only two instances was the surgeon performing the procedure below the grade of senior registrar, and in four out of six instances in which consultants were not operating, consultants were immediately available.

◆ All of these patients had postmortem examinations.

Two patients (cases 7 and 8) died of massive pulmonary emboli and neither had thrombophrophylaxis during the final procedure.

In two circumstances, it was felt that the operation might with benefit have been avoided and, in one it was considered that a delay might have been beneficial, but it is possible that circumstances did not allow it.

Burns procedures	Age	Surgeon doing procedure	Specialty	Seniority of surgeon making decision to operate
1. Debridement of burns (60%). Insertion of subclavian line.	42	Senior registrar	Plastic	Senior registrar
2. Excision of burns (40%) and skin graft. Tracheostomy.	58	Consultant	Plastic	Consultant
3. Escharotomy to right upper limb.	66	Senior registrar	Plastic	Consultant
4. Excision of full thickness burns (10%) and split skin graft.	81	Senior registrar	General	Consultant
5. Debridement and grafting of burns (hand and arm).	85	SHO	Plastic	Consultant

Other procedures

	Age	Surgeon doing procedure	Specialty	Seniority of surgeon making decision to operate
6. Facial bipartition. Revision of cleft lip.	4	Consultant and team	Cranio-facial	Consultant
7. Debridement of necrotic transverse rectus abdominis myocutaneous flap site (breast carcinoma two years previously).	56	Consultant	Plastic	Consultant
8. Right superficial parotidectomy for large tumour.	64	Consultant	Plastic	Consultant
9. Resection of intraoral malignancy. Radical lymphadenectomy. Reconstruction with free tissue transfer and microsurgical anastomoses (nine hour procedure).	72	Consultant and team	Plastic	Consultant
10. Debridement of necrotic olecranon with a radial forearm flap (five hour procedure).	76	Senior registrar	Plastic	Consultant
11. Debridement and grafting of tibial lacerations.	81	Registrar	Plastic	Registrar

Co-existing problems	Postoperative complications	Comments
Inhalational burns. Renal failure. Sepsis.	Sepsis. Cardiac and renal failure.	Patient transferred four days after burns from another hospital (because of ward closure) for the final operation, which was one in a series.
	Septicaemia and renal failure	
Respiratory disease. Cardiovascular complications. Alcoholism.	Respiratory hepatic and renal failure.	Could the escharotomy have been done in the ward without general anaesthesia?
Alcoholism.	Airway problem. Possible inhalation of vomit. Died of respiratory failure 7 hours postoperatively.	No anaesthetic questionnaire completed.
Atherosclerosis.	Cerebrovascular accident.	
Congenital neurological anomalies.	Raised intracranial pressure.	Child was seriously underweight. Would delay to older age have been beneficial? Might elective postoperative ventilation have reduced the risk of raised intracranial pressure?
	Massive pulmonary embolism.	DVT prophylaxis (given for original TRAM flap) was not reintroduced for debridement.
	Massive pulmonary embolism.	No anaesthetic questionnaire available. No thromboprophylaxis.
Contralateral neck dissections some years previously.	Haemorrhage. Hyperpyrexia. Chest infection. Pulmonary oedema and pleural effusions.	
Confused debilitated patient.	Bronchopneumonia.	
Chronic bronchitis.	Respiratory failure.	Would conservative treatment have been more appropriate and should the decision to operate have been taken above registrar level?

Urology

Table S67
List of procedures

Transurethral resection of prostate (one followed by laparotomy for capsular perforation)	31
Cystoscopy (flexible or rigid, +/- bladder biopsy or washout, bladder neck incision)	9
Nephrectomy (three radical, one of them with hysterectomy, ovarian cystectomy and omentectomy)	9
Transurethral resection of bladder tumour	7
Ureteric operations (one with right hemicolectomy)	6
Operations to control haemorrhage (five open, one evacuation of bladder haematoma)	6
Laparotomy (various procedures)	5
Partial cystectomy (combined with sigmoid colectomy and hysterectomy)	1
Radical orchidectomy	1
Transvesical prostatectomy	1
Miscellaneous	4
Total	**80**

Commentary

There were 80 deaths reported in this specialty. Sixty-five of these patients were aged over 70 years and the majority were men.

There was a high level of appropriateness within the delivery of care in this specialty but there were four (5%) operations where the procedure was done by a surgeon with no special interest in urology. These were as follows:

Table S68
Procedures done by surgeons with no special interest in urology

Procedure	Age	Specialty of surgeon	Cause of death
Repeat TURP.	71	General	Pulmonary embolism.
Laparotomy for pelvic abscess after repeat TURP.	72	General and gastroenterology	Sepsis and ischaemic heart disease.
TURP and bladder biopsy.	74	Vascular	Myocardial infarct on the first postoperative day.
TURP.	83	General and gastroenterology	Postoperative haemorrhage.

In only one case (the last of the above cases) might a surgeon with urological training have produced a better outcome.

Thirty-one (39%) of the deaths in this study followed transurethral resection of the prostate (TURP). Preoperatively surgeons had assessed the risk of death in 28 (90%) of these patients as small. Further analysis of the group of patients who died after TURP showed that they were older than other urological patients in this sample, but in other respects these patients could not be distinguished from patients having other urological procedures.

The main cause of death after TURP was coronary artery disease or pulmonary oedema. The incidence of death in which coronary artery disease and pulmonary oedema feature is noteworthy in a group of patients in whom the risk of perioperative death was considered small or non-existent in 90% of cases. This reflects the fact that TURP is associated with considerable haemodynamic disturbances due to:

a) high volumes of irrigating fluids (and their possible absorption)
b) the use of regional blocks
c) the failure to diagnose and adequately replace blood loss
d) cold irrigating fluids
e) inappropriate secretion of antidiuretic hormone

While it is not possible to draw conclusions about these matters from the information provided in the questionnaires, the monitoring of fluid balance and postoperative haematocrit, haemoglobin and electrolyte levels after TURP or indeed any endoscopic procedures are matters which should be the subject of further research.

Alternatives to TURP (such as the use of indwelling catheters and stents) need more emphasis in the very old and the very frail.

Vascular surgery

Table S69
List of procedures

Aneurysm surgery (ruptured)	134
Aneurysm surgery (non-ruptured)	8
Lower limb revascularisation including embolectomy	44
Amputations (all levels)	28
Laparotomy for mesenteric occlusion	4
Carotid surgery	3
Fasciotomy	3
Laparotomy	3
Reconstruction for occlusive aortic disease (including revisional surgery)	3
Laparotomy for vascular trauma	2
Laparotomy for haemorrhage	2
Varicose veins surgery	1
Lumbar sympathectomy	1
Second look laparotomy	1
Evacuation of haematoma	1
Total cases	**238**

Commentary

Eighty-one percent of the surgical questionnaires were returned to NCEPOD.

The patients for vascular surgery were in higher age groups, the peak in the eighth decade, and were of high ASA grading. They therefore represent a high risk group with high incidence of concomitant cardiac and respiratory disease alongside the vascular problems.

The majority of the admissions were as emergencies; in 8.8% (21/238) the referral or admission was delayed. This was mainly due to a failure to recognise the clinical condition (19 cases), the lack of a bed in one case and the lack of an available vascular specialist in another. After admission there were 17 cases where there was a delay between admission and surgery; this was due to factors other than clinical.

There were eight patients with a ruptured abdominal aortic aneurysm in whom there was a delay between admission and surgery. On three occasions the diagnosis was missed by non-vascular specialties; three patients were admitted to hospitals with no available ICU beds and died during transfer to another hospital and two patients died whilst efforts were made to find an appropriate surgeon. Amongst patients with other vascular problems, delays were caused by patients' reluctance to undergo surgery (3), delayed referral (2), lack of available radiological services (1), lack of operating time (1), absence of an ICU bed (1) and the non-availability of an appropriate vascular surgeon (1).

In ten cases the patient should have been admitted to an ICU/HDU but the surgeon was unable to make this transfer either pre- or postoperatively. In nine instances this was due to the lack of a bed and in one case the patient died in the recovery ward before admission to ICU. It is in the patient's best interests to be transferred to a centre where there is vascular competence and appropriate support services. Where the patient's condition allows, this move should take place before surgery. On one occasion, the outcome was doubtful after emergency aneurysm surgery, but an ICU bed was requested for the patient. No such bed was available locally and it was necessary to contact seven hospitals before an ICU bed was successfully identified for this patient. Despite transfer the patient subsequently died.

On another occasion an unsuspected ruptured iliac artery aneurysm was found at laparotomy. There was no ICU bed at the local hospital so, after surgery, it was necessary to transfer the patient to a neighbouring hospital where there was a vacant ICU bed.

Specialist vascular surgeons treated 10% of the patients, but if general surgeons who stated an interest in vascular surgery are included then two-thirds of these patients who died were treated by appropriate surgeons. This does, however, leave approximately a third of patients who were treated by surgeons with no vascular interest (see table S70, page 137). NCEPOD does not have data to comment on whether or not the outcome for this group of patients treated by surgeons who are not in any way specialised in vascular surgery are worse than those for patients treated by surgeons with a special interest.

The surgeons dealing with the cases listed in table S70 (page 137) sometimes found themselves in situations where their skills were inadequate. There were instances where an inappropriate surgeon had difficulty in gaining control of the aorta above a leaking abdominal aortic aneurysm; there were also injuries to the left renal vein in the process of gaining control. An experienced vascular surgeon might not have had such problems.

Other examples of lack of expertise included the use of an inappropriate graft (both type and size) for aortic reconstruction, inability to achieve adequate haemostasis after an emergency aortic graft and faulty techniques when dealing with, for example, an aortocaval fistula and a fasciotomy.

Senior surgeons i.e. consultants, senior registrars and associate specialists were involved in the decision-making in all but three cases and 26 patients had surgery done by trainee surgeons. Seven of these 26 operations were supervised by senior staff. Amongst the 19 unsupervised operations were three cases done by basic surgical trainees i.e. SHOs; these comprised two amputations and one laparotomy for undiagnosed ruptured abdominal aortic aneurysm. It may be inappropriate for some basic trainees to perform amputations unsupervised although there is no evidence that inexperience produces defective stumps.[15] The remaining cases done by unsupervised registrars were:

Transfemoral embolectomy	5
Above knee amputation	4
Below knee amputation	4
Through knee amputation	1
Femoro-femoral crossover graft and femoropopliteal bypass	1
Laparotomy for acute abdomen (undiagnosed ruptured abdominal aortic aneurysm)	1

It is unlikely that the outcome for any of these patients would have changed had supervision been present, but there is no doubt that some operations would have been quicker, and the training component of these surgical procedures would have been enhanced, had consultant surgeons been present. Consultant surgeons should be present in theatre if the surgery is beyond the competence of the trainee or the operation is not going well.

Three cases were reported where there was a shortage of personnel; this was due to shortage of skilled assistance on one occasion, a consultant anaesthetist on another and in the third case the shortage was not specified.

One-hundred-and-sixty-eight of these patients who died had emergency surgery and a further 38 had urgent procedures (see glossary, appendix B). These figures reinforce the gravity of the surgical presentation and the increased likelihood of an unfavourable outcome after surgery. Approximately 60% of these procedures were done out of hours and yet the overall involvement of consultants in the operating theatre was approximately 80% (170/238). These figures demonstrate a very heavy out-of-hours commitment for consultants dealing with elderly patients with vascular problems.

There were four deaths after vascular surgery in which angioplasty had been involved at an earlier stage. Two patients died from massive retroperitoneal haemorrhage from a damaged external iliac artery despite salvage surgery. (In one of these cases the surgeon was unaware that an interventional procedure was taking place). The other two patients, both with diabetes mellitus and other pathologies, developed medical complications following failed angioplasty and subsequent thrombectomy.

Interventional radiologists are often asked to treat patients who are unfit for reconstructive arterial surgery when the alternative may be loss of a limb. It is vital that radiologists and surgeons liaise and carefully plan treatment and surgical cover in the event of a complication.

Conclusions

Vascular surgery is a high risk specialty with a high consultant input which is frequently out of hours. Emergency cover for vascular surgery should be provided by consultants with a declared interest in vascular surgery. Improved outcomes will probably follow earlier referral, specialisation and the development of shared care of patients between specialists. These advances will need to be coupled with the greater availability of emergency theatres and associated critical care services.

Table S70
Cases done by surgeons with interests other than vascular, and with no regular vascular practice

Procedure	Weekday - in hours	Weekday - out of hours*	Weekday - no stated time	Weekend	Total
Repair of ruptured abdominal aortic aneurysm	10	12	4	10	36
Open and close laparotomy for ruptured abdominal aortic aneurysm	7	5	-	5	17
Unilateral femoral embolectomy	3	3	-	3	9
Bilateral femoral embolectomy	2	-	-	1	3
Above knee amputation	2	2	-	1	5
Laparotomy for bleeding after repair abdominal aortic aneurysm	1	-	-	-	1
Exploration of thrombosed aortic graft	1	1	-	-	2
Repair bilateral false aneurysms	1	-	-	-	1
Repair of artery (trauma)	-	1	-	-	1
Fasciotomy	-	1	-	-	1
Mesenteric embolectomy	-	1	-	-	1
Laparotomy for trauma	-	1	-	-	1
Right hemicolectomy and repair of limb of aortobifemoral graft	-	1	-	-	1
Amputation of toes	-	-	1	-	1
Total	**27**	**28**	**5**	**21**	**80**

---

* see glossary, appendix B

Positive points indicated by the symbol ◆ in the surgical sections

For the total sample:

there was a very high level of consultant involvement in preoperative decision-making and in the subsequent surgery.

For individual specialties:

in cardiothoracic surgery consultants were involved in the decision-making for all patients.

in general and colorectal surgery it was exceptional to find a surgeon performing procedures with which he/she was unfamiliar or inexperienced.

within the specialties of general, colorectal and plastic surgery senior surgeons were involved in the majority of decision-making and operating.

audit was widely practised in general surgery.

there was an appropriately high level of postmortem examinations in plastic surgery.

there was a high return rate for questionnaires from specialties involved in head and neck surgery (otorhinolaryngology, oral/maxillofacial and ophthalmology).

Pathology

Pathology

Advisors

NCEPOD wishes to thank the consultant pathologists who acted as advisors to the Enquiry and prepared the section on pathology:

Professor J Bradfield		(South & West)
Dr B Conroy		(South Thames)
Dr N Cooper		(Northern & Yorkshire)
Dr S S Cross	*Chairman*	(Trent)
Dr P Millard		(Anglia & Oxford)

Review process and sample

The members of the advisory group of consultant pathologists represented academic, district general and forensic pathology practice. The group met on four occasions and reviewed 470 postmortem examination reports of which 421 were those performed at the request of H M Coroner (henceforth referred to as Coroners') and 49 were consent hospital examinations. Data from the surgical questionnaires indicated that in 714 cases in the overall NCEPOD review postmortem examination examinations had been made, so only 66% (470/714) of postmortem examination reports had been submitted for review. This is a similar percentage to reviews in previous years and it is disappointing that more postmortem examination reports are not being made available to the Enquiry. Data relating to pathology from the 1366 surgical questionnaires were also reviewed.

KEY POINTS

- Referral of perioperative deaths to the Coroner may be close to full reporting of cases for this sample of early postoperative deaths.

- A higher rate of requesting hospital consent postmortem examinations would have beneficial effects for medical audit and education.

- The cranial cavity should be examined in all Coroners' postmortem examinations and all hospital postmortem examinations where permission for this has been given.

- A clinicopathological correlation should be included in all postmortem examinations.

- Eighty-eight percent of postmortem examination reports were graded as satisfactory or better by the group.

- The efficiency of transmission of postmortem examination reports to the clinical team, although nearly 80%, must be improved, and liaison with the Coroner's office is essential here.

Deaths reportable to the Coroner and postmortem examination requests

Table P1 (q54)
Was the death reported to the Coroner?

Yes	1116	*82%*
No	203	*15%*
Not answered	32	*2%*
Not known/not recorded	15	*1%*
Total	**1366**	

In previous NCEPOD reports[4, 5] the failure to identify deaths reportable to the Coroner has been a theme. In this sample 82% of deaths were reported to the Coroner and this is much higher than figures in previous reports: 56% in 91/92 and 56% in 92/93. This may be due to greater recognition by surgical teams of the circumstances in which cases should be reported to the Coroner[16-18] but it may also be a bias introduced by the different sample criteria for cases in different years' enquiries, as all the cases for 1994/95 were of patients who died within three calendar days of surgery. Not all deaths occurring after surgery will have to be reported to the Coroner but the majority will fall into one of the many categories of referral and 82% is more likely to represent adequate reporting than figures below 60%.

Table P2 (q54a)
If yes, was a Coroner's postmortem examination ordered and performed?

Yes	633	*57%*
No	457	*41%*
Not answered	12	*1%*
Not known/not recorded	14	*1%*
Total	**1116**	

Table P3 (q55)
If a Coroner's postmortem examination was not performed, was a hospital postmortem examination undertaken?

Yes	81	*11%*
No	524	*71%*
Not answered	110	*15%*
Not known/not recorded	18	*2%*
Total	**733**	

Table P4 (q55)
If no, why not?

Cause of death/diagnosis known	270	*52%*
Relative-related	120	*23%*
Coroner felt not necessary	12	*2%*
Not requested (not further specified)	18	*3%*
Other	12	*2%*
Not stated	87	*17%*
Not known/not recorded	19	*4%*
Total *(answers may be multiple)*	**524**	

The low rate of hospital consent postmortem examinations in patients who died in hospital after operative procedures remains worrying. There have been numerous studies which show the fallibility of clinical diagnoses made without the confirmation of postmortem examination.[19-21] In most of these studies the rate of major discrepancies between antemortem diagnoses and postmortem examination findings is about 30%[19] and the joint recommendation from the Royal Colleges of Surgeons, Physicians and Pathologists, titled "The Autopsy and Audit",[22] has emphasised the importance of increasing the number of postmortem examination requests. The 12 cases where a hospital consent postmortem examination was not performed because it was stated that the Coroner felt it was not necessary could be an artefact of questionnaire design since once a case has not been accepted by the Coroner it reverts back to the discretion of the clinicians as to whether to request a postmortem examination.

Table P5 (q60)
Who performed the postmortem examination?

Specialist pathologist	115	*16%*
Consultant pathologist	478	*67%*
Junior pathologist	36	*5%*
Not answered	56	*8%*
Not known/not recorded	29	*4%*
Total	**714**	

The main pathology specialties recorded were forensic, neuropathology and paediatric pathology. No specialties outside histopathology (e.g. microbiology, clinical chemistry or general practice) were recorded.

Review of postmortem examination reports

The "Guidelines for Postmortem Reports" was published by the Royal College of Pathologists in August 1993[23] and distributed to all Members and Associates of the Royal College of Pathologists so all pathologists performing the postmortem examinations in this review should have been aware of these guidelines. The guidelines state that a postmortem examination report should normally include the following components:

- Demographic details
- History
- External examination
- Internal examination
- Histology report
- Summary of findings
- Commentary/conclusions
- Cause of death in OPCS format

The advisory group of pathologists used these guidelines as the exemplar for postmortem examination reports (see Appendix E) and only reports which fulfilled all the recommendations were graded as excellent; e.g. any reports that did not include a histology report could not be graded as excellent.

Table P6
Is the report typewritten?

Yes	470	*100%*
Total	**470**	

It is gratifying that all reports in this year's enquiry were typewritten, the first year that this has occurred.

Table P7
Is a clinical history provided?

Yes	385	*82%*
No	85	*18%*
Total	**470**	

If yes, the clinical history is:

Unacceptably brief, obscure, uninformative	2	*<1%*
Poor	15	*4%*
Satisfactory	143	*37%*
Good	155	*40%*
Fully detailed, clear, informative	70	*18%*
Total	**385**	

A clear concise clinical history stating the facts necessary to the understanding of the postmortem examination results should be present in all reports. Such a history was absent in 18% (85/470) of cases which is disappointing and this percentage was similar in Coroners' and consent hospital postmortem examinations so it was not due to constraints placed upon the format of Coroners' reports. It was recognised that in the current litigious climate the clinical history given by the pathologist should only include incontrovertible facts about the case with no opinions on the care of the patient and no opinions on diagnosis derived from previously uninterpreted data in the clinical notes. This constraint may well lead to shorter clinical histories but it is still possible to convey the facts of the case. When the history was given, the vast majority were at least satisfactory; 58% were graded good or excellent.

Table P8
The description of external appearances is:

Unacceptably brief, inadequately detailed	16	*3%*
Poor	40	*9%*
Satisfactory	150	*32%*
Good	212	*45%*
Fully detailed, clear, informative	52	*11%*
Total	**470**	

Table P9
Were scars and incisions measured?

Yes	284	*60%*
No	159	*34%*
Not applicable	27	*6%*
Total	**470**	

Table P10
The gross description of the internal organs is:

Unacceptably brief, inadequately detailed	12	*3%*
Poor	39	*8%*
Satisfactory	142	*30%*
Good	214	*46%*
Fully detailed, clear, informative	63	*13%*
Total	**470**	

Table P11
Number of organs weighed (paired organs count as 1):

None	51	*11%*
1	23	*5%*
2	25	*5%*
3	19	*4%*
4	9	*2%*
5	34	*7%*
6	295	*63%*
7	8	*2%*
8	1	*<1%*
9	1	*<1%*
more than 9	1	*<1%*
Total	**470**	

The modal number of organs weighed remained six which usually represented weights of the brain, heart, lungs, liver, kidneys and spleen. The weight of individual organs can be important in some cases, e.g. assessment of cardiac ventricular hypertrophy or pulmonary oedema, but in some cases with pathology such as ruptured aortic aneurysm, organ weights would contribute little or no additional information.

Table P12
Were the skull and brain examined?

Yes	434	*92%*
No	36	*8%*
Total	**470**	

Consent for hospital postmortem examinations may contain restrictions on the extent of the examination which may exclude examination of the cranial cavity but in Coroners' postmortem examinations the cranial cavity should always be examined: this did not occur in 7% of cases in this review. The cranial cavity may contain the pathology which caused death and may be unrelated to any surgical procedures. In this review such pathology included an unknown astrocytoma which caused death after a routine hysterectomy.

Table P13
Is the operation site described?

Yes	432	*92%*
No	35	*7%*
Not applicable	3	*1%*
Total	**470**	

A postmortem examination on a perioperative death should always include a description of the operation site and it was disappointing that this was absent in 7% of reports.

Table P14
Is the gross examination appropriate to the clinical problem?

Yes	461	*98%*
No	9	*2%*
Total	**470**	

Table P15
Samples were taken for:

Histology	109	*23%*
Microbiology	2	*<1%*
Toxicology	5	*1%*
Other	3	*1%*
None of these investigations	352	*75%*
Total (*answers may be multiple*)	**470**	

Table P16
A thorough postmortem examination in this case would have called for:

Histology	439	*93%*
Microbiology	5	*1%*
Toxicology	7	*1%*
Other	2	*<1%*
None of these investigations	25	*5%*
Total (*answers may be multiple*)	**470**	

Table P17
Is a histological report included with the postmortem examination report?

Yes	72	*15%*
No	398	*85%*
Total	**470**	

When present, the histological report is:

Unacceptably brief, inadequately detailed	1	*1%*
Poor	0	*0%*
Satisfactory	27	*38%*
Good	27	*38%*
Fully detailed, clear, informative	17	*24%*
Total	**72**	

When absent, does the lack of histology detract significantly from the value of this report?

Yes	258	*65%*
No	140	*35%*
Total	**398**	

In Coroners' cases there still appeared to be uncertainty about the cases for which it is permissible to retain tissue for histology and even in hospital consent postmortem examinations histology is not performed in all cases. The figures given in table P17 may be lower than the actual number of cases in which histology was performed since the histology report may have been issued separately from the main postmortem examination report and may not have reached NCEPOD. In many cases histology is useful to confirm macroscopic findings, e.g. to type tumours discovered at postmortem examination, or to detect pathologies not apparent at macroscopic examination which may have contributed to the cause of death, e.g. bronchopneumonia.[24] There may be some cases, ruptured atheromatous abdominal aortic aneurysm is an example, where histology is unlikely to make any contribution to knowledge about the cause of death and retention of tissues from a Coroner's postmortem examination might be difficult to justify. This is reflected in the advisory group's assessment that in 35% of cases, the absence of histology did not detract significantly from the overall value of the postmortem examination report. In this the advisory group's views differ from the Royal College of Pathologists guidelines[23] which suggest that samples for histology should be taken in all cases.

Table P18
Is a summary of lesions present?

Yes	99	21%
No	371	79%
Total	**470**	

When present, does this correspond accurately to the text report?

Yes	97	98%
No	2	2%
Total	**99**	

Table P19
Is an OPCS cause of death present?

Yes	449	96%
No	21	4%
Total	**470**	

When present, does it correspond accurately to the text report?

Yes	412	92%
No	37	8%
Total	**449**	

Does it follow OPCS formatting rules?

Yes	402	90%
No	47	10%
Total	**449**	

Table P20
Is a clinico-pathological correlation present?

Yes	253	54%
No	217	46%
Total	**470**	

If yes, the clinico-pathological correlation is:

Unacceptably brief, obscure, uninformative	8	3%
Poor	12	5%
Satisfactory	102	40%
Good	98	39%
Fully detailed, clear, informative	33	13%
Total	**253**	

The "Guidelines for Postmortem Reports"[23] suggest that information found at postmortem examination can be summarised in the three forms examined in these tables and that each has a distinct function. The summary of lesions will give all pathological lesions present at postmortem examination whether or not they are relevant to the cause of death. The clinicopathological correlation will be a summary relating the postmortem examination findings with the clinical history/diagnoses and the cause of death. The OPCS format cause of death is given for the purposes of death certification and educational purposes in hospital consent postmortem examinations (where a certificate of the cause of death will have been completed before the postmortem examination is carried out).[25-27] This review shows that a formal summary of lesions is rarely included in reports. This may reflect the preponderance of Coroners' postmortem examinations where pathologists may not wish to include summary information which is not relevant to the cause of death. An OPCS format cause of death was given in the majority of cases but was absent in 22% of hospital consent postmortem examinations. The group felt that it should be given in all hospital consent postmortem examinations with a qualifying statement such as "the cause of death could be formulated as:" to indicate that the medical certificate of the cause of death will have already been completed. A clinico-pathological correlation was present in only 54% of reports and the group found this very disappointing. This is the section of the report which clinicians are most likely to read since it should distil the postmortem examination findings into an easily understood form. Some causes of death, such as ruptured atheromatous abdominal aortic aneurysm, are self-explanatory and would require a very brief clinico-pathological summary, but any case where an operation has been performed and death is not immediately due to the pathology for which the operation was undertaken will require a more detailed clinico-pathological correlation. The group acknowledged that pathologists should confine themselves to matters of fact and pathological interpretation with no judgemental statements on surgical technique or clinical care.

Table P21
Overall score for the postmortem examination

Unacceptable, laying the pathologist open to serious professional criticism	8	2%
Poor	48	10%
Satisfactory	204	43%
Good	193	41%
Excellent, meeting all standards set by the RCPath guidelines	17	4%
Total	**470**	

Eighty-eight percent of postmortem examination reports were graded as satisfactory or better which is encouraging. The percentage of reports graded as excellent remains similar to previous years' reviews despite the rigorous application of the Royal College of Pathologists' Guidelines as assessment criteria.

Table P22

When the history, ante-mortem clinical diagnosis and cause of death are compared with the postmortem examination findings, this postmortem examination demonstrates:

A discrepancy in the cause of death or in a major clinical diagnosis, which if known, might have affected treatment, outcome or prognosis.	7	*1%*
A discrepancy in the cause of death or in a major diagnosis, which if known, would probably not have affected treatment, outcome or prognosis.	28	*6%*
A minor discrepancy.	0	*0%*
Confirmation of essential clinical findings.	339	*72%*
An interesting incidental finding.	26	*6%*
A failure to explain some important aspect of the clinical problem as a result of a satisfactory postmortem examination	9	*2%*
A failure to explain some important aspect of the clinical problem as a result of an unsatisfactory postmortem examination.	9	*2%*
The cause of death, which was not known before postmortem examination.	129	*27%*
Total *(answers may be multiple)*	**470**	

The figures in this table have a different distribution to previous years' reviews because the new category of "established the cause of death which was not known before postmortem examination" was added. The group felt this addition were necessary since there was a substantial proportion of cases where the clinicians did not make a clinical diagnosis before the patient died and so apparent discrepancies could not be assessed. A major category for referral of cases to the Coroner is that the cause of death is unknown by the doctors caring for the patient and this is reflected in the 27% of cases which fell into the new category. "Confirmation of essential clinical findings" remains the most frequent category but this is not surprising since many cases were of a catastrophic pathology (such as ruptured aortic aneurysm) which was diagnosed immediately on presentation but from which the patient died during or soon after operative intervention. The figure for failure to explain some important aspect of the clinical problem as a result of an unsatisfactory postmortem examination is low (2%) but effort should be continued to reduce this to zero.

Transmission of the postmortem examination findings

Table P23 (q56)

Was the surgical team informed of the date and time of the postmortem examination?

Yes	260	*36%*
No	373	*52%*
Not answered	42	*6%*
Not known/not recorded	39	*5%*
Total	**714**	

Table P23 suggests that in only 36% of cases were the clinicians informed of the date and time of postmortem examination. This figure may be artificially low since the clinician completing the surgical questionnaire for NCEPOD may not be the same clinician who was informed about the postmortem examination and this information would probably not have been recorded in the patient's notes. It is obviously desirable that the clinical team should always be told when the postmortem examination is being performed, but it is clearly important that clinicians who wish to attend a postmortem examination ordered by the Coroner do inform the Coroner's office of this, so that appropriate arrangements can be made. This is particularly important when the Coroner's postmortem examination is taking place at a site away from the hospital, for example in a public mortuary. In this situation, without prior information, the Coroner's officers and pathologist may be unaware of the clinician's desire to attend.

Table P24 (q56a)
If yes, which member of the surgical team attended the postmortem examination?

None	124	48%
House officer	18	7%
Senior house officer	45	17%
Registrar	31	12%
Staff grade	2	1%
Senior registrar	11	4%
Associate specialist	4	2%
Consultant	42	16%
Other	4	2%
Not known/not recorded	10	4%
Total (answers may be multiple)	**260**	

Table P25 (q56b)
If the surgical team were informed of the date and time of the postmortem examination but did not attend, why not?

Unavailable/other commitments	86	69%
Nothing to be gained/diagnosis known	18	15%
Other	21	17%
Not known/not recorded/not answered	8	6%
Total (answers may be multiple)	**124**	

It is desirable that a member of the clinical team should attend the postmortem examination to allow discussion between the pathologist and clinician about the case with demonstration of the findings. With job plans which include more fixed commitments this is likely to be less possible in the future and pathologists should consider methods of recording their findings as visual images for display at regular clinicopathological conferences.

Table P26 (q57)
Did the surgical team receive a copy of the postmortem report?

Yes	557	78%
No	84	12%
Not answered	65	9%
Not known/not recorded	8	1%
Total	**714**	

It is obviously desirable that the surgical team should always receive a copy of the postmortem examination report. In a few areas there still seems to be a difficulty with release of reports on Coroners' postmortem examinations to clinicians and this, combined with the known inaccuracy of internal mail systems, may account for the deficit from 100% in this table. In the cases where a Coroner's postmortem report was not received by the surgical team, however, it is not known whether this had been requested initially. Liaison with the Coroner's office is important here, particularly if the postmortem examination is conducted away from the hospital, to ensure that the Coroner's office is aware that a particular clinician has requested a copy of the postmortem report.

Table P27 (qs 57a and 48)
How long after the patient's death was the first information received giving the postmortem examination results?

7 days or fewer	186	*26%*
8 to 30 days	90	*13%*
31 days to 60 days	34	*5%*
More than 60 days	49	*7%*
Not answered*	355	*50%*
Total	**714**	

* May indicate that no written information was received

The information in this table conflicts with the information in table P24 in that in 52% of cases some member of the clinical team did attend the postmortem examination and so would have received information (albeit verbal) within seven days of the patient's death.

Table P28 (question 59)
Was the pathological information given useful i.e. did it contribute additional information to the understanding of the case?

Yes	394	*55%*
No	228	*32%*
Not answered	50	*7%*
Not known/not recorded	42	*6%*
Total	**714**	

If no, why not?

Cause of death/diagnosis already known	140	*61%*
Did not fully explain/confirm the cause of death	20	*9%*
Other	13	*6%*
Not stated	55	*24%*
Total	**228**	

The question in table P28 asks whether the postmortem examination report contributed additional information to the understanding of the case and the phrasing of the question suggests that cases which confirmed essential clinical findings would be given a negative reply. The figure of 55% of cases in which the postmortem examination report did contribute additional information to the understanding of the case illustrates the value of the postmortem examination in audit and education and this percentage was the same for Coroners' and hospital postmortem examinations.[28, 29]

References

References

1   Buck N, Devlin H B, Lunn J N. *The Report of a Confidential Enquiry into Perioperative Deaths.* Nuffield Provincial Hospitals Trust and The King Edwards' Hospital Fund for London. London, 1987.

2   Campling E A, Devlin H B, Lunn J N. *The Report of the National Confidential Enquiry into Perioperative Deaths 1989.* London, 1990.

3   Campling E A, Devlin H B, Hoile R W, Lunn J N. *The Report of the National Confidential Enquiry into Perioperative Deaths 1990.* London, 1992.

4   Campling E A, Devlin H B, Hoile R W, Lunn J N. *The Report of the National Confidential Enquiry into Perioperative Deaths 1991/1992.* London, 1993.

5   Campling E A, Devlin H B, Hoile R W, Lunn J N. *The Report of the National Confidential Enquiry into Perioperative Deaths 1992/1993.* London, 1995.

6   *The Report of the National Confidential Enquiry into Perioperative Deaths 1993/1994.* NCEPOD. London, 1996.

7   Campling E A, Devlin H B, Hoile R W, Ingram G S, Lunn J N. *Who Operates when?.* NCEPOD. London, 1997

8   NAHAT briefing No. 74. Birmingham, 1994.

9   *Recommendations for the Transfer of Patients with Acute Head Injuries to Neurosurgical Units.* The Neuroanaesthesia Society of Great Britain and Ireland and the Association of Anaesthetists of Great Britain and Ireland. London 1996.

10 Lennard-Jones J E (Chairman of the Working Group). *Guidelines for good practice in and audit of the management of upper gastrointestinal haemorrhage.* Journal of the Royal College of Physicians of London. Vol 26 No 3, July 1992.

11 *Report of the RCOG Working Party on Prophylaxis Against Thromboembolism in Gynaecology and Obstetrics.* March 1995.

12 *A Policy Framework for Commissioning Cancer Services.* A Joint Working Group Response by The Royal College of Obstetricians and Gynaecologists and The British Gynaecological Cancer Society. January 1997.

13 Munro H M, Laycock J R D. *Inter-hospital transfer: Standards for ventilated neurosurgical emergencies.* British Journal of Intensive Care 1993; 3: 210-214.

14 The Society of British Neurological Surgeons. *Safe Neurosurgery.* 1993.

15 Cosgrove C M, Ashley S, Thornberry D J, Wilkins D C. *The incidence of defective amputation stumps is not influenced by the surgeon's experience.* Br. J. Surg. Vol 84, Suppl. 1, May 1997.

16 Start R D, Delargy-Aziz Y, Dorries C P, et al. *Clinicians and the coronial system: ability of clinicians to recognise reportable deaths.* BMJ 1993;306:1038-1041.

17 Leadbeatter S, Knight B. *Reporting deaths to Coroners: all the legal aspects of dying need re-examining.* BMJ 1993;306:1018

18 Start R D, Usherwood T P, Carter N, et al. *General practitioners' knowledge of when to refer deaths to a coroner.* Br J Gen Pract 1995;45:191-193.

19 Underwood J C E: Autopsies and Clinical Audit; in Cotton D W K, Cross S S (eds). *The Hospital Autopsy.* Oxford, Butterworth-Heinemann, 1993, pp 163-172.

20 Hoel D G, Ron E, Carter R, et al. *Influence of death certificate errors on cancer mortality trends.* J Natl Cancer Inst 1993;85:1063-1068.

21 Robinson I A, Marley N J E. *Factors predicting cases with unexpected clinical findings at necropsy.* J Clin Pathol 1996;49:909-912.

22 *The Autopsy and Audit.* Report of the Joint Working Party of the Royal College of Pathologists, the Royal College of Physicians of London and The Royal College of Surgeons of England. London 1991.

23 The Royal College of Pathologists. *Guidelines for Postmortem Reports.* London, The Royal College of Pathologists, 1993.

24 Reid W A. *Cost effectiveness of routine postmortem histology.* J Clin Pathol 1987;40:459-461.

25 Leadbeatter S. *Semantics of death certification.* J R Coll Physicians London 1986;292:129-132.

26 Slater D N. *Certifying the cause of death: an audit of wording inaccuracies.* J Clin Pathol 1993;46:232-234.

27 James D S, Bull A D. *Information on death certificates: cause for concern?.* Clin Pathol 1996;49:213-216.

28 Chen K. *The coroner's necropsy - an epidemiological treasure trove.* J Clin Pathol 1996;49:698-699.

29 O'Sullivan JP. *The coroner's necropsy in sudden death: an under-used source of epidemiological information.* J Clin Pathol 1996;49:737-740.

Appendices

Appendix A - Abbreviations

BP	Blood pressure
CCF	Coronary cardiac failure
CCU	Coronary care unit
CFAM	Cerebral function analysing monitor
CT	Computerised tomography
CVP	Central venous pressure
D&C	Dilatation and curettage
DGH	District General Hospital
DU	Duodenal ulcer
DVT	Deep vein thrombosis
ECG	Electrocardiogram
GA	General anaesthetic
HDU	Higher dependency unit
ICU	Intensive care unit
IHD	Ischaemic heart disease
IDDM	Insulin dependent diabetes mellitus
IPPV	Intermittent positive pressure ventilation
iv/im	intravenously, intramuscularly
LMA	Laryngeal mask
LVF	Left ventricular failure
MI	Myocardial infarction
MRI	Magnetic resonance imaging
MUA	Manipulation under anaesthesia
OPCS	Office of Population Censuses and Surveys (now the Office for National Statistics)
PE	Pulmonary embolism
sc	subcutaneous
SHO	Senior house officer
TPN	Total parenteral nutrition
TURP	Transurethral resection of prostate

Appendix B - Glossary

ADMISSION

Elective - at a time agreed between the patient and the surgical service.

Urgent - within 48 hours of referral/consultation.

Emergency - immediately following referral/consultation, when admission is unpredictable and at short notice because of clinical need.

AMERICAN SOCIETY OF ANESTHESIOLOGISTS (ASA) CLASSIFICATION OF PHYSICAL STATUS

ASA 1 a normal healthy patient.

ASA 2 a patient with mild systemic disease.

ASA 3 a patient with severe systemic disease that limits activity but is not incapacitating.

ASA 4 a patient with incapacitating systemic disease that is a constant threat to life.

ASA 5 a moribund patient who is not expected to survive for 24 hours with or without an operation.

(NCEPOD) CLASSIFICATION OF OPERATIONS

Emergency

Immediate life-saving operation, resuscitation simultaneous with surgical treatment (e.g. trauma, ruptured aortic aneurysm). Operation usually within one hour.

Urgent

Operation as soon as possible after resuscitation (e.g. irreducible hernia, intussuception, oesophageal atresia, intestinal obstruction, major fractures). Operation within 24 hours.

Scheduled

An early operation but not immediately life-saving (e.g. malignancy). Operation usually within three weeks.

Elective

Operation at a time to suit both patient and surgeon (e.g. cholecystectomy, joint replacement).

OUT OF HOURS

NCEPOD's definition of out-of-hours operating includes all operations started between 18.01 and 07.59 on a weekday, as well as operations performed at any time on a Saturday or Sunday.

RECOVERY AND SPECIAL CARE AREAS

(Definitions used by the Association of Anaesthetists of Great Britain and Ireland)

High dependency unit

A high dependency unit (HDU) is an area for patients who require more intensive observation, treatment and nursing care than can be provided on a general ward. It would not normally accept patients requiring mechanical ventilation, but could manage those receiving invasive monitoring.

Intensive care unit

An intensive care unit (ICU) is an area to which patients are admitted for treatment of actual or impending organ failure, especially when mechanical ventilation is necessary.

Recovery area

A recovery area is an area to which patients are admitted from an operating theatre, and where they remain until consciousness has been regained, respiration and circulation are stable and postoperative analgesia is established.

NATIONAL CONFIDENTIAL ENQUIRY INTO PERIOPERATIVE DEATHS

35-43 Lincoln's Inn Fields, London, WC2A 3PN

ANAESTHETIC QUESTIONNAIRE (DEATHS) 1994/95

QUESTIONNAIRE No.   A ☐☐☐☐

DO NOT PHOTOCOPY ANY PART OF THIS QUESTIONNAIRE

QUESTIONNAIRE COMPLETION

The information you supply is important. It must be accurate if valid conclusions are to be drawn.

Neither the questions nor the choices for answers are intended to suggest standards of practice.

Please **enclose** a copy of the ANAESTHETIC record and of the fluid balance chart(s). Any identification will be removed in the NCEPOD office.

Many of the questions can be answered by "Yes" or "No".
Please insert the relevant **number** in the appropriate box eg

☐ 1 for Yes

☐ 2 for No

Where multiple choices are given, please insert the relevant letter(s) of your answer in the box(es), and leave the remaining boxes blank.

Eg question 12a

☐ C

☐ D

indicates that advice was sought from both a Senior Registrar and a Consultant.

Where more details are requested, please write in BLOCK CAPITALS.

Consultants or junior staff may write to the NCEPOD office under separate cover, quoting th questionnaire number.

All original copies of correspondence will be confidential (**but do not retain copies of your correspondence**).

The whole questionnaire will be shredded when data collection is complete.

In case of difficulty, please contact the NCEPOD office on:

071-831-6430

HAVE YOU ENCLOSED COPIES OF THE ANAESTHETIC RECORD AND FLUID BALANCE CHARTS?

PROXY ANAESTHETISTS

1 If you were not involved in any way with this anaesthetic and have filled out this questionnaire on behalf of someone else, please indicate your position.

A Chairman of Division
B College Tutor
C Duty Consultant
D Other Consultant
E Other (please specify)

☐ 1

HOSPITAL

2 In what type of hospital did the anaesthetic take place?

A District General Hospital or equivalent
B University/Teaching Hospital
C Surgical Specialty Hospital
D Other Acute/Partly Acute Hospital
E Community Hospital
F Defence Medical Services Hospital
G Independent Hospital
H Other (please specify)

☐ 2

THE ANAESTHETIST(S)

3 Grade(s) of all anaesthetist(s) who were present at the start of this anaesthetic.
Enter the appropriate letter for each person present.

A Senior House Officer
B Registrar
C Senior Registrar
D Consultant
E Staff Grade
F Associate Specialist
G Clinical Assistant
H General Practitioner
I Hospital Practitioner
J Other (please specify)

☐☐☐☐☐☐☐☐☐☐ A B C D E F G H I J   3

We want to know about the experience of the **most senior anaesthetist** in the operating room at the **start** of this procedure.

Questions 4 to 11 inclusive refer to **this** anaesthetist

4 Year of primary medical qualification

☐☐ 4

Please state country: _____   4a

5 Year of first full-time anaesthetic training post ☐☐☐ 5

Which higher diploma in **anaesthesia** is held?

☐ A none

☐ B Fellowship (Royal College, College or Faculty)

Year of award

☐ C DA (or Part 1 FRCA) ☐☐☐☐ 5a

☐ D Part 2 FRCA ☐☐☐☐

☐ E Other (please specify) ☐☐☐☐

6 Was this anaesthetist employed in a locum capacity? ☐ 6

Yes = 1   No = 2

7 Is this locum post part of a recognised training programme? ☐ 7

Yes = 1   No = 2

8 How long had this locum anaesthetist been in **this** post at the time of this operation? ☐ 8

☐ year(s) ☐ month(s) ☐ week(s) ☐ day(s)

9 Is this locum post an exchange one with another country? ☐ 9

Yes = 1   No = 2

10 Is this locum anaesthetist accredited by the Royal College of Anaesthetists? ☐ 10

Yes = 1   No = 2

11 If the most senior anaesthetist present was **not** in a training grade, please enter the appropriate letters in the boxes provided if he/she has regular weekly (ie more than 50 operations per year) NHS commitments in anaesthesia for the following:

☐☐☐☐ 11

A cardiac surgery   A

B children under 3 years old   B

C neurosurgery   C

D none of the above   D

12 Did the anaesthetist (of whatever grade) **seek advice** at any time from another anaesthetist (not mentioned in question 3)? ☐ 12

Yes = 1   No = 2

If **yes**, grade(s) of anaesthetist(s) from whom advice sought:

A Senior House Officer   A

B Registrar   B

C Senior Registrar   C

D Consultant   D ☐☐☐☐☐☐☐☐☐☐ 12a

E Staff Grade   E

F Associate Specialist   F

G Clinical Assistant   G

H General Practitioner   H

I Hospital Practitioner   I

J Other (please specify)   J

13 Did any colleague(s) (not mentioned in question 3) **come to help** at any time? ☐ 13

Yes = 1   No = 2

If **yes**, grade(s) of anaesthetist(s) **who came to help**:

A Senior House Officer   A

B Registrar   B

C Senior Registrar   C

D Consultant   D ☐☐☐☐☐☐☐☐☐☐ 13a

E Staff Grade   E

F Associate Specialist   F

G Clinical Assistant   G

H General Practitioner   H

I Hospital Practitioner   I

J Other (please specify)   J

14   Date of patient's birth:

						14
D	D	M	M	Y	Y	

15   Age of patient at time of operation:

———— Y ———— M   15

16   Date of admission to hospital in which final operation took
place eg 05 04 93 (5 April 1993):

						16
D	D	M	M	Y	Y	

17   Time of admission:

				17
				(use 24 hour clock)

18   Date of final operation:

						18
D	D	M	M	Y	Y	

19   Date of death:

						19
D	D	M	M	Y	Y	

20   Was the patient transferred **from** another hospital?

Yes = 1   No = 2   ☐ 20

21   If **yes**, had the patient's condition apparently deteriorated during transfer?

Yes = 1   No = 2   Not known = 3   ☐ 21

If **yes**, please explain:

_____

_____

_____

22   Primary pre-operative diagnosis:

_____

_____

23   What operation was planned?

_____

_____

24   What operation was performed, if different?

_____

_____

25   If this operation was the most recent in a sequence, please list the previous procedures.

Procedure: Date

_____

_____

_____

Please enclose a copy of all anaesthetic records

26   Classification of operation (last before death). See definitions below.

A   Emergency
B   Urgent
C   Scheduled
D   Elective   ☐ 26

DEFINITIONS

A   **Emergency**
Immediate life-saving operation, resuscitation simultaneous with surgical treatment (eg trauma, ruptured aortic aneurysm). Operation usually within one hour.

B   **Urgent**
Operation as soon as possible after resuscitation (eg irreducible hernia, intussusception, oesophageal atresia, intestinal obstruction, major fractures). Operation within 24 hours.

C   **Scheduled**
An early operation, but not immediately life-saving (eg malignancy). Operation usually within 3 weeks.

D   **Elective**
Operation at a time to suit both patient and surgeon (eg cholecystectomy, joint replacement).

27 Was a record of the patient's weight available?

Yes = 1   No = 2   ☐ 27

If **yes**, what was this weight?

If **no**, the estimated weight was _____ kg

28 Was a record of the patient's height available?

Yes = 1   No = 2   ☐ 28

If **yes**, what was this height? _____ cm

If **no**, estimated height was _____ cm

29 Was an anaesthetist **consulted** by the surgeon (as distinct from informed) before the operation?

Yes = 1   No = 2   ☐ 29

30 Where did the anaesthetist assess the patient before the operation?

A   Ward
B   Outpatient Department
C   Theatre Suite
D   Accident and Emergency Department
E   ICU/HDU
F   Other (please specify) _____

☐☐☐☐☐☐ A B C D E F   30

G   Patient not assessed ☐ G

30a Was **this** anaesthetist present **at the start of the operation?**

Yes = 1   No = 2   ☐ 30a

---

31 Which of the following investigations, relevant to the anaesthetist, were done before the anaesthetic? (Including tests carried out in the referral hospital and available before the operation.)

PLEASE WRITE RESULTS IN THE SPACE NEXT TO THE TEST NAME

Indicate which test(s) by insertion of the appropriate letter in each box.

☐ A ☐ B ☐ C ☐ D ☐ E ☐ F ☐ G ☐ H ☐ I ☐ J ☐ K 31 ☐ L ☐ M ☐ N ☐ O ☐ P ☐ Q ☐ R ☐ S ☐ T ☐ U ☐ V ☐ W ☐ X ☐ Y

A   None

B   Haemoglobin _____ $gm.litre^{-1}$

C   Packed cell volume (haematocrit) _____

D   White cell count _____ $x10^9.litre^{-1}$

E   Sickle cell test (eg Sickledex) _____

F   Blood group +/- cross match _____

G   Coagulation screen _____

H   Plasma electrolytes   Na _____ $m\,mol.litre^{-1}$

I   K _____ $m\,mol.litre^{-1}$

J   Cl _____ $m\,mol.litre^{-1}$

K HCO_3 _____ $m\,mol.litre^{-1}$

L   Blood urea _____ $m\,mol.litre^{-1}$

M   Creatinine _____ $micro\,mol.litre^{-1}$

N   Serum albumin _____ $g.litre^{-1}$

O   Bilirubin (total) _____ $micro\,mol.litre^{-1}$

P   Glucose _____ $m\,mol.litre^{-1}$

Q   Amylase _____

R   Urinalysis (ward or lab) _____

S   Blood gas analysis _____

T   Chest x-ray _____

U   Electrocardiography _____

V   Respiratory function tests _____

W   Special cardiac investigation (eg cardiac catheterization) _____

X   Special neurological investigation (eg imaging) _____

Y   Others relevant to anaesthesia (please specify) _____

_____

AMERICAN SOCIETY OF ANESTHESIOLOGY CLASSIFICATION OF PHYSICAL STATUS

CLASS 1
The patient has no organic, physiological, biochemical, or psychiatric disturbance. The pathological process for which the operation is to be performed is localized and does not entail a systemic disturbance.

Examples: a fit patient with inguinal hernia;
fibroid uterus in an otherwise healthy woman.

CLASS 2
Mild to moderate systemic disturbance caused either by the condition to be treated surgically or by other pathophysiological processes.

Examples: non-, or only slightly limiting organic heart disease
mild diabetes
essential hypertension
anaemia.

Some might choose to list the extremes of age here, either the neonate or the octogenarian, even though no discernible systemic disease is present. Extreme obesity and chronic bronchitis may be included in this category.

CLASS 3
Severe systemic disturbance or disease from whatever cause, even though it may not be possible to define the degree of disability with finality.

Examples: severely limiting organic heart disease
severe diabetes with vascular complications
moderate to severe degrees of pulmonary insufficiency
angina pectoris or healed myocardial infarction.

CLASS 4
Severe systemic disorders that are already life threatening, not always correctable by operation.

Examples: patients with organic heart disease showing marked signs of cardiac insufficiency
persistent angina or active myocarditis
advanced degree of pulmonary, hepatic, renal or endocrine insufficiency.

CLASS 5
The moribund patient who has little chance of survival but is submitted to operation in desperation.

Examples: the burst abdominal aneurysm with profound shock
major cerebral trauma with rapidly increasing intracranial pressure
massive pulmonary embolus.

Most of these patients require operation as a resuscitative measure with little if any anaesthesia.

35   Please enter the patient's preoperative ASA status (Note we do not use the E subclassification)

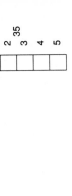

	1
2	35
3	
4	
5	

---

32   Coexisting medical diagnoses (please enter the appropriate letter in a box, **and specify the disorder in the space next to the category**).

A   none
B   respiratory
C   cardiac
D   neurological ⁣ 32
E   endocrine
F   alimentary
G   renal
H   hepatic
I   musculoskeletal
J   vascular
K   haematological
L   genetic abnormality
M   obesity
N   sepsis (specify site)
O   other (please specify)

33   What drug or other therapy was the patient receiving regularly at the time of operation (but excluding premedication or drugs for anaesthesia)?

Please specify drugs in the space below.

34   Was there any history of a drug reaction?

Yes = 1   No = 2   34

If **yes**, specify drug and reaction:

Were premedicant drugs prescribed?

Yes = 1   No = 2   ☐ 40

If **yes**, please enter the appropriate letter in each box, and specify drugs and dose in the space next to each category.

A   Atropine _____

B   Chloral hydrate _____

C   Diazepam (eg Valium) _____

D   Droperidol _____

E   Fentanyl _____

F   Glycopyrronium (Robinul) _____

G   Hyoscine (Scopolamine) _____

H   Lorazepam (eg Ativan) _____

I   Ketamine _____   40a

J   Metoclopramide _____

K   Midazolam (Hypnovel) _____

L   Morphine _____

M   Papaveretum (Omnopon) _____

N   Pethidine _____

O   Prochlorperazine (eg Stemetil) _____

P   Temazepam _____

Q   Promethazine (eg Phenergan) _____

R   Trimeprazine (Vallergan) _____

S   Non-steroidal analgesics _____

T   Other (please specify) _____

☐☐☐☐☐☐☐☐☐☐☐☐☐☐☐☐☐☐☐☐ (A–T)

PREPARATION OF PATIENT BEFORE OPERATION

36   When was the last fluid given by mouth?   ☐ 36

A   more than 6 hours before operation

B   between 4-6 hours before operation

C   less than 4 hours before operation

D   not known/not recorded

Please specify nature and volume if known.

37   Indicate measures taken to reduce gastric acidity and volume, as prophylaxis against acid aspiration.

A   none

B   antacids

C H_2 antagonists

D   metoclopramide

E   proton pump inhibitor (eg omeprazole)

F   nasogastric/stomach tube

G   other (please specify)

☐☐☐☐☐☐☐ (A–G)   37

38   Did the patient receive intravenous fluid therapy in the 12 hours before induction?

Yes = 1   No = 2   ☐ 38

If **yes**, please send copies of the fluid balance charts.

39   Were measures taken to improve or protect the cardiorespiratory system **before** induction of anaesthesia?

Yes = 1   No = 2   ☐ 39

If **yes**, please indicate which measure(s) by entering a letter for each.

A   antibiotic therapy

B   bronchodilators (specify nature and dose)

C   diuretics

D   inotropes or vasoactive drugs (specify nature and dose)   39a

E   cardiac resuscitation eg external cardiac compression

F   chest physiotherapy

G   air way management eg oral airway, tracheostomy, controlled ventilation

H   steroids

I   pleural aspiration

J   oxygen therapy (as distinct from preoxygenation)

K   other (please specify)

41 Was **non-invasive** monitoring established just **before** the induction of anaesthesia?

Yes = 1   No = 2   ☐ 41

If **yes**, please indicate

A	ECG							
B	BP							
C	pulse oximetry							
D	capnography							41a
E	inspired oxygen							
F	temperature							
G	other (please specify)							

☐☐☐☐☐☐☐

If **yes** to question 41 what was the blood pressure immediately before induction?

_____ / _____ mmHg

42 Was **invasive** monitoring established **before** induction of anaesthesia eg CVP, arterial line?

Yes = 1   No = 2   ☐ 42

If **yes**, please indicate;

A	CVP
B	arterial line
C	pulmonary arterial line
D	blood gas analysis
E	other (please specify)

☐☐☐☐☐ (A B 42a C D E)

43 Were any measures taken (before, during or after operation) to prevent venous thrombosis?

Yes = 1   No = 2   ☐ 43

If **yes**, please enter letter for each measure taken;

		Before or during	After
A	aspirin	☐	☐
B	heparin	☐	☐
C	dextran infusion	☐	☐
D	leg stockings	☐	☐
E	calf compression	☐	☐ (43a)
F	electrical stimulation of calves	☐	☐
G	warfarin	☐	☐
H	heel supports	☐	☐
I	ripple mattress	☐	☐
J	plaquenil	☐	☐
K	other (please specify)	☐	☐

44 Time of start of anaesthetic:
(enter "X" in boxes if times not recorded)

☐☐☐☐ 44
(use 24 hour clock)

45 Time of start of surgery:

☐☐☐☐ 45
(use 24 hour clock)

46 Time of transfer out of operating room:
(ie to recovery, ICU etc)

☐☐☐☐ 46
(use 24 hour clock)

If you are not able to provide the **times**, please indicate total duration of operation
(ie time of start of anaesthetic to time of transfer):

_____ hours   _____ mins

47 What was the grade of the most senior **surgeon** in the operating room?

☐ 47

A	House Officer
B	Senior House Officer
C	Registrar
D	Senior Registrar
E	Associate Specialist
F	Clinical Assistant
G	Staff Grade
H	Consultant
I	Other (please specify)

48 Was there a trained anaesthetist's assistant (ie ODA, SODA, anaesthetic nurse) present for this case?

Yes = 1   No = 2   ☐ 48

If **no**, please explain

_____

_____

FLUIDS DURING OPERATION

49 Is there an anaesthetic record for this operation in the notes?

Yes = 1   No=2

☐ 49

If **yes**, please send a complete copy of it with this questionnaire to the NCEPOD office. (We will delete/remove identification marks).

If **no**, please give as full an account as possible of the anaesthetic below. Please include details of anaesthetic agents, drugs, routes of administration, breathing systems, and tube size.

50 What was the assessed blood loss during operation?

☐☐☐☐☐ 50 ml

51 Did the patient receive intravenous fluids **DURING** the operation?

Yes = 1   No = 2

☐ 51

If **yes**, please indicate which;

	Fluid (indicate type by inserting appropriate letter)	Total volume during operation (mls)

51a **Crystalloid**

A Dextrose 5%
B Dextrose 4% saline 0.18%
C Dextrose 10%
D Saline 0.9%
E Hartmann's (compound sodium lactate)
F Other (please specify)

☐☐☐☐ ☐☐☐☐☐ 51a

51b **Colloid (and others)**

A Modified gelatin (Gelofusine, Haemaccel)
B Human albumin solution
C Starch (HES)
D Dextran
E Mannitol (Please specify concentration)
F Other (please specify)

☐☐☐☐ ☐☐☐☐☐ 51b

51c **Blood**

A Whole blood
B Platelets
C Fresh frozen plasma
D Other component (please specify)

☐☐☐ ☐☐☐☐ 51c

52   Were monitoring devices used during the management of this anaesthetic?

Yes = 1   No = 2   ☐ 52

If **yes**, please indicate **which** monitors were used.

Please enter appropriate letter(s) in boxes:

	Anaesthetic Room	Operating Room
A ECG		
B pulse oximeter		52a
C indirect BP		
D pulse meter		
E oesophageal or precordial (chest wall) stethoscope		
F fresh gas O_2 analyser		
G inspired gas O_2 analyser		
H inspired anaesthetic vapour analyser		
I expired CO_2 analyser		
J airway pressure gauge		
K ventilation volume		
L ventilation disconnect device		
M peripheral nerve stimulator		
N temperature (state site) _____		
O urine output		
P CVP		
Q direct arterial BP (invasive)		
R pulmonary arterial pressure		
S intracranial pressure		
T EEG/CFAM/evoked responses		
U other (please specify)		
V anaesthetic room not used		

53   Did anything hinder full monitoring?

Yes = 1   No = 2   ☐ 53

If **yes**, please specify: (eg bilateral arm surgery, radiotherapy, skin pigmentation, inaccessibility, non-availability of monitors).

_____

POSITION OF PATIENT

54   What was the position of the patient during surgery?   ☐ 54

A   supine
B   lateral
C   prone
D   sitting
E   knee-elbow
F   lithotomy (inc. Lloyd-Davies)
G   jack knife
H   head down
I   head up
J   on special orthopaedic table (please specify) _____
K   other (please specify)

_____

TYPE OF ANAESTHESIA

55   What type of anaesthetic was used?   ☐ 55

A   general alone (56-59)
B   local infiltration alone
C   regional alone (60-61, and 63)
D   general and regional (56-61)
E   general and local infiltration (56-59)
F   sedation alone (62-63)
G   sedation and local infiltration (62-63)
H   sedation and regional (60-63)

Please now answer the questions indicated in brackets, and then continue from question 64.

GENERAL ANAESTHESIA

56 Did you take precautions **at induction** to minimise pulmonary aspiration?

Yes = 1   No = 2   ☐ 56

If **yes**, please indicate which;

A cricoid pressure
B postural changes – head up
C postural changes – head down
D postural changes – lateral
E preoxygenation without inflation of the lungs
F aspiration of nasogastric tube
G trachea already intubated on arrival in theatre
H other (please specify)

☐☐☐☐☐☐☐☐ 56a
A B C D E F G H

57 How was the airway established during anaesthesia?

A face mask (with or without oral airway)
B laryngeal mask
C orotracheal intubation
D nasotracheal intubation
E endobronchial
F tracheostomy
G patient already intubated prior to arrival in theatre suite
H other (please specify)

☐☐☐☐☐☐☐☐ 57
A B C D E F G H

58 If the trachea was intubated, how was the position of the tube confirmed?

A tube seen passing through cords
B chest movement with inflation
C auscultation
D expired CO_2 monitoring
E oesophageal detector device
F other (please specify)

☐☐☐☐☐☐ 58
A B C D E F

59 Were there any problems with airway maintenance or ventilation?

Yes = 1   No = 2   ☐ 59

If **yes**, please specify

REGIONAL ANAESTHESIA

60 If the anaesthetic included a regional technique, which method was used?

A epidural – caudal
B   lumbar
C   thoracic
D interpleural
E intravenous regional
F cranial or peripheral nerve blocks (please specify)
G plexus block (eg brachial, 3-in-1 block)
H subarachnoid (spinal)
I surface (eg for bronchoscopy)

☐☐☐☐☐☐☐☐☐ 60
A B C D E F G H I

61 Which agent was used? Please specify drug(s) and dosage(s);

A local
B narcotic
C other (please specify)

☐☐☐ 61
A B C

SEDATION (as opposed to General Anaesthesia)

62 Which sedative drugs were given for this procedure (excluding premedication)?

A inhalant
B narcotic analgesic
C benzodiazepine
D sub-anaesthetic doses of IV anaesthetic drugs
E other (please specify)

☐☐☐☐☐ 62
A B C D E

63 Was oxygen given?

Yes = 1   No = 2   ☐ 63

If **yes**, for what reason?

A routine
B otherwise indicated (please specify indications)

☐☐ 63a
A B

RECOVERY FROM ANAESTHESIA

Definitions

(as used by the Association of Anaesthetists of Great Britain and Ireland)

A **recovery area** is an area to which patients are admitted from an operating room, **where they remain until** consciousness is regained and ventilation and circulation are stable.

A **high dependency unit** (HDU or area A) is an area for patients who require more intensive observation and/or nursing care than would normally be expected on a general ward. Patients who require mechanical ventilation or invasive monitoring would not be admitted to this area.

An **intensive care unit** (ICU) is an area to which patients are admitted for treatment of actual or impending organ failure who may require technological support (including mechanical ventilation of the lungs and/or invasive monitoring).

64 Which special care areas (see definitions above) **exist** in the hospital in which the operation took place?

A   recovery area or room equipped and staffed for this purpose
B   high dependency unit   64
C   intensive care unit
D   other (please specify)
E   none of the above

65 Where did this patient go on leaving theatre?   ☐ 65

A   recovery area or room equipped and staffed for this purpose
B   high dependency unit
C   intensive care unit
D   specialised ICU
E   ward
F   another hospital
G   other (please specify)
H   died in theatre

If the patient died in theatre please move to question 73

66 Was that an optimal location for this patient?   ☐ 66

Yes = 1   No = 2

If **no**, please explain.

67 Would this destination for patients represent your normal practice after this procedure?   ☐ 67

Yes = 1   No = 2

If **no**, please explain.

Were you unable at any time to transfer the patient into an ICU, HDU, etc?   ☐ 68

Yes = 1   No = 2

If **yes**, why?

A   closed at night
B   closed at weekend
C   understaffing
D   lack of beds   68a
E   no ICU or HDU in hospital
F   other (please specify)

RECOVERY AREA/ROOM

If the patient did not enter a recovery room, please move to question 72.

Were monitoring devices used, or investigations carried out during the management of this patient in the recovery room?   ☐ 69

Yes = 1   No = 2

If **yes**, please indicate which monitors were used.

Enter the letter(s) in each appropriate box;

A   ECG
B   pulse oximeter
C   indirect BP
D   pulse meter
E   oesophageal or precordial (chest wall) stethoscope
F   inspired gas O_2 analyser
G   expired CO_2 analyser
H   airway pressure gauge   69a
I   ventilation volume
J   ventilator disconnect device
K   peripheral nerve stimulator
L   temperature (state site)
M   urine output
N   CVP
O   direct arterial BP (invasive)
P   blood gas analysis
Q   pulmonary arterial pressure
R   intracranial pressure
S   cardiac output
T   other (please specify)

CRITICAL EVENTS DURING ANAESTHESIA OR RECOVERY

70   Time of transfer from recovery area:

☐☐☐☐ 70

(use 24 hour clock)

(enter "X" in boxes if not recorded)

71   Where did this patient go next (ie after the recovery room)?

☐ 71

A   ward
B   high dependency unit
C   intensive care unit
D   specialised ICU
E   home
F   another hospital
G   died in recovery area
H   other (please specify)

72   Was controlled ventilation used postoperatively?

☐ 72

Yes = 1   No = 2

If yes, why?

☐☐☐☐☐☐☐☐

A   routine management
B   respiratory inadequacy
C   cardiac inadequacy
D   control of intracranial pressure or other neurosurgical indications   72a
E   part of the management of pain
F   poor general condition of patient
G   to allow recovery of body temperature
H   other reasons (please specify)

73   Did any of the following events, which required specific treatment, occur during anaesthesia or immediate recovery (ie the first few hours after the end of the operation)?

☐ 73

Yes = 1   No = 2

If yes, please specify nature by insertion of the appropriate letter(s) in a box.

☐☐☐☐☐☐☐☐   ☐☐☐☐   ☐☐☐☐☐☐☐☐   ☐☐☐☐

A   air embolus
B   airway obstruction
C   anaphylaxis
D   arrhythmia
E   bradycardia (to or less than 50% of resting)
F   bronchospasm
G   cardiac arrest (unintended)
H   convulsions
I   disconnection of breathing system   73a
J   hyperpyrexia (greater than 40°C or very rapid increase in temperature)
K   hypertension (increase of more than 50% resting systolic)
L   hypotension (decrease of more than 50% resting systolic)
M   hypoxaemia (please state oxygen saturation)
N   misplaced tracheal tube
O   pneumothorax
P   pulmonary aspiration
Q   pulmonary oedema
R   respiratory arrest (unintended)
S   tachycardia (increase of 50% or more)
T   unintentional delayed recovery of consciousness
U   ventilatory inadequacy
V   excessive spread of regional anaesthesia (eg total spinal, overextensive epidural)
W   wrong dose or overdose of drug
X   other (please specify)

Please specify location of patient, treatment and outcome.

_____

_____

_____

_____

74 Was there any mechanical failure of equipment during anaesthesia or recovery?

Yes = 1   No = 2   ☐ 74

If **yes**, please specify:

A   equipment for IPPV
B   suction equipment
C   syringe drivers
D   infusion pump
E   instrumental monitor (please specify)
F   other (please specify)

☐☐☐☐☐☐ 74a

If the patient died in the theatre please move to question 79

75 What were the complications or events after this operation?

Please enter a letter for each, and specify in the space below each category:

A   ventilatory problems (eg pneumonia, pulmonary oedema)   ☐

B   cardiac problems (eg acute LVF, intractable arrhythmias, post-cardiac arrest)   ☐

C   hepatic failure   ☐

D   septicaemia   ☐ 75

E   renal failure   ☐

F   central nervous system failure (eg failure to recover consciousness)   ☐

G   progress of surgical condition   ☐

H   electrolyte imbalance   ☐

I   haematological disorder/coagulopathy   ☐

J   other (please specify)   ☐

Please give an account of any adverse events during this period.

_____

_____

Were drugs given in the first 48 hours after operation for pain?

Yes = 1   No = 2   ☐ 76

If **yes**, which drug type?

A   opiate / opioid
B   local analgesic
C   non-steroidal analgesic
D   general (inhaled) anaesthetic
E   other (please specify)

☐☐☐☐☐ 76a

Which method / route?

A   intra-muscular injection
B   oral
C   rectal
D   continuous intravenous infusion
E   PCA (patient-controlled analgesia)
F   continuous epidural
G   PCEA (patient-controlled epidural analgesia)
H   inhaled
I   other (please specify)

☐☐☐☐☐☐☐☐☐ 76b

77 Did complications occur as a result of these analgesic methods?

Yes = 1   No = 2   ☐ 77

If **yes**, please specify

78 Were other sedative/hypnotic or other drugs given?

Yes = 1   No = 2   ☐ 78

If **yes**, which?

A   propofol
B   midazolam
C   other benzodiazepine
D   other (please specify)

☐☐☐☐ 78a

DEATH

79 Date of death:

D	D	M	M	Y	Y

79

Time of death:

79a

(use 24 hour clock)

80 Place of death:

A   theatre

B   recovery area

C   intensive care unit

D   high dependency unit

E   ward

F   home

G   another hospital

H   other (please specify)

80

81 Cause of death:

_____

_____

82 Do you have morbidity/mortality review meetings in your department?

Yes = 1   No = 2

82

If **yes**, will this case be, or has it been discussed at your departmental meeting?

Yes = 1   No = 2

82a

83 Has a consultant anaesthetist seen and agreed this form?

A   yes

B   no

C   not applicable (completed by consultant)

83

A B C

PLEASE CONTINUE ON TO NEXT PAGE

Please use this sheet to provide extra information to help the advisory group of anaesthetists to understand aspects of this case which may not be apparent from your answers to the questions. Please write clearly.

REMINDER

Have you enclosed copies of the
anaesthetic record and fluid balance charts?

THANK YOU FOR TAKING THE TIME TO COMPLETE THIS
QUESTIONNAIRE

YOU MUST NOT KEEP A COPY OF THIS QUESTIONNAIRE

Please return it in the reply-paid envelope provided to:

NCEPOD
35-43 Lincoln's Inn Fields
LONDON
WC2A 3PN

If you wish to inform the NCEPOD office of any other details of this case,
please do so on a separate sheet, but include the number of the questionnaire.

CONSULTANT ANAESTHETISTS ONLY

We would like to publish the names of all

consultants who have returned completed questionnaires.

Please help us by providing your initials and surname.

This page will be removed from the questionnaire on receipt.

Initials _____ Surname _____

SURGICAL QUESTIONNAIRE (DEATHS) 1994/95

QUESTIONNAIRE No. | S | | | | |

DO NOT PHOTOCOPY ANY PART OF THIS QUESTIONNAIRE

QUESTIONNAIRE COMPLETION

This questionnaire should be completed with reference to the **last** operation before the death of the patient specified by the NCEPOD office. If you feel that this was not the **main** operation in the period before the patient's death, you may give additional information.

The **whole** questionnaire will be shredded when data collection is complete. The information will be filed anonymously.

Neither the questions nor the choices for answers are intended to suggest standards of practice.

Please enclose a copy of all the relevant surgical operation notes, the postmortem reports and the postmortem request form if available. Any identification will be removed in the NCEPOD office.

Many of the questions can be answered by "yes" or "no". **Please insert a tick (✓) in the appropriate box.**

Where multiple choices are given, please insert the tick(s) in the appropriate box(es).

Where more details are requested for an answer, please write in **BLOCK CAPITALS.**

In case of difficulty, please contact the NCEPOD office on:

071-831-6430

HAVE YOU ENCLOSED COPIES OF THE
OPERATION AND POSTMORTEM NOTES?

---

relevant. **(Please write clearly for the benefit of the specialist group who will be reviewing the questionnaire.)**

If you wish to inform the NCEPOD office of any further details of this case, please do so on a separate sheet, quoting the questionnaire number.

1 In which type of hospital did the final operation take place?

- a District General (or equivalent)
- b University/Teaching
- c Surgical Specialty
- d Other Acute/Partly Acute
- e Community
- f Defence Medical Services
- g Independent
- h Other (please specify)

☐☐☐☐☐☐☐☐ a b c d e[1] f g h

SPECIAL CARE AREAS

Definitions

(As used by the Association of Anaesthetists of Great Britain and Ireland)

A recovery area is an area to which patients are admitted from an operating room, where they remain until consciousness is regained and ventilation and circulation are stable.

A high dependency unit (HDU) is an area for patients who require more intensive observation and/or nursing care than would normally be expected on a general ward. Patients who require mechanical ventilation or other organ support would not be admitted to this area.

An intensive care unit (ICU) is an area to which patients are admitted for treatment of actual or impending organ failure who may require technological support (including mechanical ventilation of the lungs and/or invasive monitoring).

2 Are the following areas available in the hospital in which the final operation took place? (see definitions above):

a Theatre recovery area

Yes ☐
No ☐ 2a

If **yes**, is this available and staffed 24 hours per day, 7 days per week?

Yes ☐
No ☐

If **no**, please specify times when available

---

b Adult ICU

Yes ☐
No ☐ 2b

If **yes**, is this available and staffed 24 hours per day, 7 days per week?

Yes ☐
No ☐

If **no**, please specify times when available

---

c Adult HDU

Yes ☐
No ☐ 2c

If **yes**, is this available and staffed 24 hours per day, 7 days per week?

Yes ☐
No ☐

If **no**, please specify times when available

---

d Paediatric ICU/HDU

Yes ☐
No ☐ 2d

If **yes**, is this available and staffed 24 hours per day, 7 days per week?

Yes ☐
No ☐

If **no**, please specify times when available

PATIENT DETAILS

3 Date of birth

☐☐ ☐☐ ☐☐ 3
D D M M Y Y

4 Date of final operation

☐☐ ☐☐ ☐☐ 4
D D M M Y Y

5 Sex

Male ☐ a
Female ☐ b 5

6 What diagnosis was recorded in the notes at the time of admission?

_____

_____

_____

7 Date of admission:

☐☐ ☐☐ ☐☐ **7**
D D M M Y Y

8 Admission category:

a Elective - at a time agreed between patient and surgical service ☐ a **8**

b Urgent - within 48 hours of referral / consultation ☐ b

c Emergency - immediately following referral / consultation ☐ c

If **elective**, date placed on waiting list or entered into admission diary:

☐☐ ☐☐ ☐☐ **8a**
D D M M Y Y

9 What was the pathway for this admission?

a Transfer as an inpatient from another acute hospital ☐ a **9**

b Referral from a General Medical or General Dental Practitioner ☐ b

c Admission following a previous outpatient consultation (please state date of referral) ☐ c

☐☐ ☐☐ ☐☐
D D M M Y Y

d Admission via A&E department ☐ d

e Other (please state) ☐ e

10 Type of referring hospital:

a District General
b University/Teaching
c Surgical Specialty
d Other Acute/Partly Acute
e Community
f Defence Medical Services
g Independent
h Other (please specify)

☐☐☐☐☐☐☐☐ **10**
a b c d e f g h

Why was the patient transferred?

_____

Did the patient's condition deteriorate during transfer?

Yes ☐ **10a**
No ☐

If **yes**, please specify

_____
_____
_____

PREOPERATIVE CARE

11 To what type of area was the patient **first** admitted?

a Surgical ward (including surgical specialties)
b Gynaecological/Obstetric ward
c Medical ward
d Mixed medical/surgical ward
e Geriatric ward
f Admission ward
g A&E holding area (or other emergency admission ward)
h Day unit
i Direct to theatre
j ICU
k Coronary care unit (CCU)
m HDU
n Other (please specify)

☐☐☐☐☐☐☐☐☐☐☐☐☐ **11**
a b c d e f g h i j k m n

_____

12 Was the patient originally admitted to the hospital (in which the final surgery took place) under the care of the surgeon whose team undertook the final operation?

Yes ☐
No ☐ 12

If **no**, what **was** the source of referral to the Consultant Surgeon?

a A medical specialty (please specify) ☐ a
_____

b Another surgical specialty (please specify) ☐ b
_____ 12a

c Same surgical specialty (please state reason for referral) ☐ c
_____

d Other (please specify) ☐ d
_____

Date and time of transfer to surgical team undertaking final operation.

Date ☐☐ ☐☐ ☐☐   Time ☐☐☐☐ 12b
     D D M M Y Y   (use 24 hour clock)

Date of first consultation following referral:

☐☐ ☐☐ ☐☐ 12c
D D M M Y Y

13 Was there any delay in either the referral or the admission of this patient?

Yes ☐
No ☐ 13

If **yes**, please specify.
_____
_____
_____

14 Specialty of Consultant Surgeon in charge <u>at time of final operation</u> before death.

a General
b General with special interest in Paediatric Surgery
c General with special interest in Urology
d General with special interest in Vascular Surgery
e General with special interest in Gastroenterology
f General with special interest in Endocrinology
g General with special interest in (please specify) _____
h Vascular
i Urology
j Transplantation
k Accident and Emergency
l Cardiac/Thoracic/Cardiothoracic
m Gynaecology
n Neurosurgery
o Ophthalmology
p Oral/Maxillofacial
q Orthopaedic
r Otolaryngology
s Paediatric
t Plastic
u Other(please specify)

a ☐ b ☐ c ☐ d ☐ e ☐ f ☐ g ☐ h ☐ i ☐ j ☐ k ☐ l ☐ m ☐ n ☐ o ☐ p ☐ q ☐ r ☐ s ☐ t ☐ u ☐   14

15 Was care undertaken on a formal shared basis with another specialty (excluding anaesthesia)?

Yes ☐
No ☐ 15

If **yes**, please specify.
_____

16 What was the grade of the most senior surgeon **consulted** before the operation?

Please tick both columns if a locum.

Locum?

a	House Officer	
b	Senior House Officer	
c	Registrar	
d	Senior Registrar	
e	Consultant	
f	Staff Grade	
g	Clinical Assistant	
h	Associate Specialist	
i	Other (please specify)	16

_____

17 Please state the working diagnosis by the most senior member of the surgical team;
(PLEASE USE BLOCK CAPITALS)

_____

_____

_____

18 What operation was proposed by the most senior member of the surgical team?
(PLEASE USE BLOCK CAPITALS)

_____

_____

_____

19 What was the immediate indication for the proposed operation?
(PLEASE USE BLOCK CAPITALS)

_____

_____

_____

20 ASA class:

| 1 |
| 2 | 20 |
| 3 |
| 4 |
| 5 |

American Society Of Anesthesiology (A.S.A.) Classifications Of Physical Status

Class 1
This patient has no organic, psychological or psychotic disturbance. The pathological process for which operation is to be performed is localised and does not entail a systemic disturbance.

Class 2
Mild to moderate systemic disturbance or distress caused by either the condition to be treated surgically or by other pathophysiological processes.

Class 3
Severe systemic disturbance or disease from whatever cause, even though it may not be possible to define the degree of disability with finality.

Class 4
Severe systemic disorders that are already life-threatening, not always correctable by operation.

Class 5
The moribund patient who has little chance of survival but is submitted to operation in desperation.

21 Were there any coexisting problems **(other than the main diagnosis)** at the time of final surgery?

Yes
No   21

If **yes**, please put a tick in each appropriate box and specify the disorder in the space provided

a	Malignancy	a
b	Respiratory	b
c	Cardiac	c
d	Renal	d
e	Haematological	e
f	Gastrointestinal	f
g	Vascular	g 21a
h	Sepsis	h
i	Neurological	i
j	Endocrine (including diabetes mellitus)	j
k	Musculoskeletal	k
m	Psychiatric	m
n	Alcohol-related problems	n
o	Drug addiction	o
p	Genetic abnormality	p
q	Other (please specify)	q

PREOPERATIVE PREPARATION

22 What precautions or therapeutic manoeuvres were undertaken preoperatively (excluding anaesthetic room management) to improve the patient's preoperative condition?

Enter a tick in each appropriate box.

a	None
b	Cardiac support drugs or antidysrhythmic agents
c	Gastric aspiration
d	Intravenous fluids
e	Correction of hypovolaemia
f	Urinary catheterisation
g	Blood transfusion
h	Diuretics
i	Anticoagulants
j	Vitamin K
k	Antibiotics (pre- or intraoperative)
m	Bowel preparation (specify method used)
n	Chest physiotherapy
o	Oxygen therapy
p	Airway protection (eg in unconscious patients)
q	Tracheal intubation
r	Mechanical ventilation
s	Nutritional support
t	Others (please specify)

22

23 Were any measures taken (before, during or after operation) to prevent venous thromboembolism?

Yes ☐ No ☐ 23

If **yes**, specify method(s):

Before/during   After

a	Heparin
b	Leg stockings
c	Calf compression
d	Electrical stimulation of calves
e	Warfarin
f	Dextran infusion
g	Heel support
h	Ripple mattress
i	Other (please specify)

23a

---

24 Did the patient's medication (excluding premedication) in any way contribute to the fatal outcome in this case?

Yes ☐ No ☐ 24

If **yes**, please explain:

_____

_____

25 Previous operations. If the final operation was the most recent in a <u>sequence</u> please list the other procedures. (PLEASE USE BLOCK CAPITALS) Please send **all** relevant operation notes.

Operation	Date	Specialty and grade of operating surgeon
a		
b		
c		
d		

26 Which grade of surgeon made the **final decision to operate**?

Please tick both columns if a locum.

         Locum?

a	House Officer
b	Senior House Officer
c	Registrar
d	Staff Grade
e	Senior Registrar
f	Clinical Assistant
g	Associate Specialist
h	Consultant
i	Other (please specify)

26

Date of decision to operate:

D D M M Y Y

26a

D D M M Y Y

	M	T	W	Th	F	Sa	Sun	30a

Please circle day:

Was this on a

a   Public Holiday?   a
b   Extra-statutory holiday (NHS)?   b   30b
c   Neither?   c

31   Time of start of operation:
(not including anaesthetic time)

31

(use 24 hour clock)

32   Duration of operation (not including anaesthetic time):

_____ hrs _____ mins

Cardiac cases only:

33   Ischaemic time: _____ hrs _____ mins

Which grades of surgeon were present in the operating room during the procedure?

Please tick both columns if a locum.

		Locum?
a	House Officer	
b	Senior House Officer	
c	Registrar	
d	Staff Grade	33
e	Senior Registrar	
f	Clinical Assistant	
g	Associate Specialist	
h	Consultant	
i	Other (please specify)	

34   What was the grade of the **most senior operating surgeon** (as distinct from surgeons present in an assisting or supervisory capacity)?

Please tick both columns if a locum.

		Locum?
a	House Officer	
b	Senior House Officer	
c	Registrar	
d	Staff Grade	34
e	Senior Registrar	
f	Clinical Assistant	
g	Associate Specialist	
h	Consultant	
i	Other (please specify)	

_____

a   Not expected
b   Small but significant risk   27
c   Definite risk
d   Expected

27a

If death was **expected**, specify the anticipated benefit of the operation.

_____
_____

OPERATION

28   Classify the **final** operation (see definitions below and choose the category most appropriate to the case).

a   Emergency
b   Urgent   28
c   Scheduled
d   Elective

Definitions

a   **Emergency**
Immediate life-saving operation, resuscitation simultaneous with surgical treatment (eg trauma, ruptured aortic aneurysm). Operation usually **within one hour.**

b   **Urgent**
Operation as soon as possible after resuscitation (eg irreducible hernia, intussusception, oesophageal atresia, intestinal obstruction, major fractures). Operation usually **within 24 hours.**

c   **Scheduled**
An early operation but not immediately life-saving (eg malignancy). Operation usually **within 3 weeks.**

d   **Elective**
Operation at a time to suit both patient and surgeon (eg cholecystectomy, joint replacement).

29   Were there any delays (between admission and surgery) due to factors other than clinical?

Yes | | 29
No | |

If **yes**, please specify:

_____
_____

35 How long had this surgeon spent in **this** grade in **this** specialty?

_____ yrs _____ mths

35a How many similar procedures had **THIS** surgeon performed **in the previous 12 months?**
(If not known, please enter an estimate)

_____ procedures

36 If the most senior operator was not a consultant, was a more senior surgeon **immediately available, ie. in the operating room/suite?**

Yes ☐ 36
No ☐

If **yes**, please specify grade and location.

Grade _____

Location _____

37 Final operation undertaken:
(PLEASE USE BLOCK CAPITALS)

_____
_____
_____

N.B. PLEASE ENCLOSE A COPY OF THE OPERATION NOTES.

37a If the operation undertaken was different to that proposed, please explain.

_____
_____
_____
_____

38 Please state the diagnosis established at operation:
(PLEASE USE BLOCK CAPITALS)

_____
_____
_____
_____

39 Were there any unanticipated intra-operative problems?

Yes ☐ 39
No ☐

If **yes**, please specify.

_____
_____

40 Was the procedure performed **SOLELY** under local anaesthetic or sedation **administered by the SURGEON?**

Yes ☐ 40
No ☐

If **yes**, which of the following were recorded during or immediately after the procedure?

☐ a ☐ b ☐ c ☐ d ☐ e ☐ f 40a

a   Blood pressure

b   Pulse

c   ECG

d   Pulse oximetry

e   Other (please specify) _____

f   None

POSTOPERATIVE CARE

41 Was the patient admitted to an ICU or HDU immediately after leaving the theatre suite (see definitions above question 2)?

☐ a ☐ b ☐ c 41

a   Intensive Care Unit

b   High Dependency Unit

c   Neither of the above

41a If **neither**, was the patient admitted to an ICU/HDU after an initial period on a routine postoperative ward?

☐ a ☐ b ☐ c 41a

a   Intensive Care Unit

b   High Dependency Unit

c   Neither of the above

If either **a** or **b**, after how many days postoperatively?

_____ days

If the patient was admitted to an ICU or HDU please answer questions 42 to 45.

If the patient was not admitted to an ICU or HDU, please continue from question 45.

42 What were the indications for the admission to ICU/HDU (this can be a multiple entry)?

- a Routine for this surgical procedure
- b Specialist nursing
- c Presence of experienced intensivists
- d General monitoring
- e Metabolic monitoring
- f Ventilation
- g Surgical complications
- h Anaesthetic complications
- i Co-incident medical diseases
- j Inadequate nursing on general wards
- k Transfer from hospital without facilities
- m Other (please specify)

[boxes: a b c d 42 e f g h i j k m]

43 Discharge from ICU/HDU was due to:

- a Death
- b Elective transfer to ward
- c Pressure on beds
- d Other (please specify)

[boxes: a b 43 c d]

44 Was the patient subsequently readmitted to an ICU/HDU?

Yes [   ]
No [   ] 44

If **yes**, please give details.

_____

_____

45 If the patient's condition warranted an admission to an ICU/HDU, were you at any time unable to transfer the patient into an ICU/HDU within the hospital in which the surgery took place?

Yes [   ] a 45
No [   ] b
Condition did not warrant admission to ICU/HDU [   ] c

If **yes**, why?

_____

_____

46 Please specify the postoperative complications:

- a Haemorrhage/postoperative bleeding requiring transfusion
- b Upper respiratory obstruction
- c Respiratory distress
- d Generalised sepsis
- e Wound infection/dehiscence
- f Anastomotic failure
- g Cardiac arrest
- h Low cardiac output/other cardiac problems
- i Hepatic failure
- j Renal failure
- k Endocrine system failure
- l Stroke or other neurological problems
- m Persistent coma
- n Other organ failure (please specify)
- o Problems with analgesia
- p DVT and/or pulmonary embolus
- q Fat embolus
- r Orthopaedic prosthetic complication
- s Pressure sores
- t Peripheral ischaemia
- u Urinary tract infection
- v Urinary retention/catheter blockage
- w Ureteric injury/fistula
- x Nutritional problems
- y Other(please specify)

[boxes: a b c d 46 e f g h i j k l m n o p q r s t u v w x y]

47 Was there a shortage of personnel in this case?

Yes [   ]
No [   ] 47

If **yes**, which?

- a Consultant surgeons
- b Trainee surgeons
- c Consultant anaesthetists
- d Trainee anaesthetists
- e Skilled assistants
- f Nurses
- g ODAs
- h Porters
- i Other (please specify)

[boxes: a b c d 47a e f g h i]

DEATH

48   Date of death:

48   [ ][ ][ ][ ][ ][ ]
D D M M Y Y

49   Time of death:

49   [ ][ ][ ][ ]
(use 24 hour clock)

50   Place of death:

a   Theatre
b   Recovery room
c   Ward
d   ICU/HDU
e   CCU
f   Home
g   Another acute hospital
h   Other (please specify)

50   a [ ] b [ ] c [ ] d [ ] e [ ] f [ ] g [ ] h [ ]

51   Was cardiopulmonary resuscitation attempted?

Yes [ ] 51
No [ ]

If **no**, was this a decision made preoperatively?

Yes [ ] 51a
No [ ]

52   What was the immediate **clinical** cause of death (this need not be a duplication of the death certificate)?
(PLEASE USE BLOCK CAPITALS)

_____

_____

_____

CAUSE OF DEATH (this is a facsimile of the death certificate: please complete it accordingly, using BLOCK CAPITALS).

53   I (a)   Disease or condition directly leading to death

_____

_____

     (b)   Other disease or condition, if any, leading to I(a)

_____

_____

     (c)   Other disease or condition, if any, leading to I(b)

_____

_____

     II   Other significant conditions CONTRIBUTING TO THE DEATH but not related to the disease or condition causing it

_____

_____

54   Was the death reported to the Coroner?

Yes [ ] 54
No [ ]

If **yes**, was a Coroner's postmortem ordered and performed?

Yes [ ] 54a
No [ ]

55   If a Coroner's postmortem **was** performed, please answer questions 56 to 61.

If a Coroner's post mortem **was not** performed, was a hospital postmortem undertaken?

Yes [ ] 55
No [ ]

If **no**, why not?

_____

N.B. If a post mortem was not performed, please move to question 62.

56 Was the surgical team informed of the date and time of postmortem?

Yes ☐
No ☐ 56

56a If **yes**, which member of the surgical team attended the postmortem?

- a None
- b House Officer
- c Senior House Officer
- d Registrar
- e Staff Grade
- f Senior Registrar
- g Associate Specialist
- h Consultant
- i Other (please specify) _____

56a ☐☐☐☐☐☐☐☐☐

56b If a surgeon **did not** attend the postmortem, why not?

_____
_____

57 Did the surgical team receive a copy of the postmortem report?

Yes ☐ a
No ☐ b
Informal report or verbal message ☐ c 57

57a If **yes**, when was this received?

☐☐ ☐☐ ☐☐
D D M M Y Y 57a

58 Please list the relevant findings of the postmortem. **(PLEASE USE BLOCK CAPITALS)**

_____
_____
_____
_____
_____
_____

PLEASE SEND A COPY OF ALL POSTMORTEM REPORTS AND POSTMORTEM REQUEST FORM IF AVAILABLE

59 Was the pathological information given useful, ie did it contribute additional information to the understanding of the case?

Yes ☐ a
No ☐ b 59
None received ☐ c

If **no**, why not?

_____
_____

60 Who performed the postmortem?

- a Specialist pathologist
- b Consultant pathologist
- c Junior pathologist
- d Not known

☐☐☐☐ 60

61 Are you aware of any subspeciality of the pathologist involved?

Yes ☐
No ☐ 61

If **yes**, please specify.

_____
_____

AUDIT

62   Has this death been considered, (or will it be considered) at a local audit/quality control meeting?

Yes ☐
No ☐ 62

63   Did you have any problems in obtaining the patient's notes (ie more than 1 week)?

Yes ☐
No ☐ 63

If **yes**, how long did they take to reach you? _____

64   Were all the notes available?

Yes ☐
No ☐ 64

If **no**, which part was inadequate/unavailable?

a   Preoperative notes
b   Operative notes
c   Postoperative notes
d   Death certificate book
e   Nursing notes
f   Anaesthetic notes
g   Postmortem report
h   Other notes (please specify) _____

☐☐☐☐☐☐☐☐ a b c d e f g h

64a

65   Has the consultant surgeon seen and agreed this form?

Yes ☐
No ☐ 65

66   Date questionnaire completed

☐☐ ☐☐ ☐☐
D D M M Y Y
66

THANK YOU FOR TAKING THE TIME TO COMPLETE THIS QUESTIONNAIRE

<u>YOU MUST NOT KEEP A COPY OF THIS QUESTIONNAIRE</u>

Please return it in the reply-paid envelope provided to:

NCEPOD
35-43 Lincoln's Inn Fields
LONDON
WC2A 3PN

THIS QUESTIONNAIRE IS THE PROPERTY OF NCEPOD

Appendix E - Pathology proforma

GENERAL FEATURES OF THE AUTOPSY REPORT

The report is typewritten   ☐ Yes   ☐ No

A clinical history is provided   ☐ Yes   ☐ No
When present the clinical history is   ☐ 1 Unacceptably brief, obscure, uninformative
                                                             ☐ 2 Poor
                                                             ☐ 3 Satisfactory
                                                             ☐ 4 Good
                                                             ☐ 5 Fully detailed, clear, informative

A summary of lesions is present   ☐ Yes   ☐ No
When present this corresponds accurately to the text report ☐ Yes   ☐ No

An OPCS cause of death is present   ☐ Yes   ☐ No
When present this corresponds accurately to the text report ☐ Yes   ☐ No
When present this follows OPCS formatting rules   ☐ Yes   ☐ No

A clinico-pathological correlation is present   ☐ Yes   ☐ No
When present the clinico-pathological correlation is   ☐ 1 Unacceptably brief, obscure, uninformative
                                                             ☐ 2 Poor
                                                             ☐ 3 Satisfactory
                                                             ☐ 4 Good
                                                             ☐ 5 Fully detailed, clear, informative

SPECIFIC FEATURES OF THE AUTOPSY REPORT

The description of external appearances is   ☐ 1 Unacceptably brief, inadequately detailed
                                                             ☐ 2 Poor
                                                             ☐ 3 Satisfactory
                                                             ☐ 4 Good
                                                             ☐ 5 Fully detailed, clear, informative

Scars and incisions are measured   ☐ Yes   ☐ No   ☐ N/A

The gross description of internal organs is   ☐ 1 Unacceptably brief, inadequately detailed
                                                             ☐ 2 Poor
                                                             ☐ 3 Satisfactory
                                                             ☐ 4 Good
                                                             ☐ 5 Fully detailed, clear, informative

Organs weighed (paired organs score 1)   ☐ 0 ☐ 1 ☐ 2 ☐ 3 ☐ 4 ☐ 5 ☐ 6 ☐ 7 ☐ 8 ☐ 9 ☐ >9

The skull and brain have been examined   ☐ Yes   ☐ No
The operation site is described   ☐ Yes   ☐ No
The gross examination is appropriate to the clinical problem ☐ Yes   ☐ No

Samples have been taken for: ☐ 1 Histology
                                                             ☐ 2 Microbiology
                                                             ☐ 3 Toxicology
                                                             ☐ 4 Other
                                                             ☐ 5 None of these

In my judgement samples should have been taken for: ☐ 1 Histology

☐ 2 Microbiology

☐ 3 Toxicology

☐ 4 Other

☐ 5 None of these

A histology report is included with the PM report   ☐ Yes   ☐ No

When present the histological report is: ☐ 1 Unacceptably brief, inadequately detailed

    ☐ 2 Poor

    ☐ 3 Satisfactory

    ☐ 4 Good

    ☐ 5 Fully detailed, clear, informative

When absent does the lack of histology detract significantly   ☐ Yes   ☐ No
from the value of this report?

My overall score for this autopsy is: ☐ 1 Unacceptable, laying the pathologist open
    to serious professional criticism

    ☐ 2 Poor

    ☐ 3 Satisfactory

    ☐ 4 Good

    ☐ 5 Excellent, meeting all standards set by
    RCPath booklet

CLINICAL RELEVANCE

When the history, antemortem clinical diagnosis and cause of death are compared with the postmortem findings, this autopsy demonstrates (more than one answer will often apply):

☐ 1   A discrepancy in the cause of death or in a major diagnosis, which if known, might have affected treatment, outcome or prognosis

☐ 2   A discrepancy in the cause of death or in a major diagnosis, which if known, would probably not have affected treatment, outcome or prognosis

☐ 3   A minor discrepancy

☐ 4   Confirmation of essential clinical findings

☐ 5   An interesting incidental finding

☐ 6   A failure to explain some important aspect of the clinical problem, as a result of a satisfactory autopsy

☐ 7   A failure to explain some important aspect of the clinical problem, as a result of an unsatisfactory autopsy

ANY FEATURES WHICH MIGHT BE QUOTED IN THE NCEPOD REPORT:

Appendix F - Participants

Consultant anaesthetists

These consultant anaesthetists returned at least one questionnaire relating to period 1 April 1994 to 31 March 1995. We are not able to name all of the Consultants who have done so as their names are not known to us.

Abbott P.
Abdel-Salam M.G.
Abercrombie C.A.
Ackers J.W.L.
Adams C.N.
Ahearn R.S.
Ahmed M.
Aitken H.A.
Aitkenhead A.R.
Al Hajij W.W.
Al Quisi N.K.S.
Alagesan K.
Albin M.Z.
Alexander J.P.
Allan D.J.
Allen S.C.
Allt-Graham J.
Amoroso P.
Anderson I.
Anderson J.D.
Andrew D.S.
Andrew L.
Antrobus J.H.L.
Aquilina R.
Archer P.L.
Arrigoni P.B.
Ashby M.
Ashton W.
Aspbury J.N.
Ather T.
Austin T.R.
Baguley I.
Bailey P.W.
Bailie R.
Bajorek P.
Baker G.M.
Baker J.R.
Baldock G.J.
Ballance J.
Ballance P.G.
Balmer H.G.R.
Bamber P.A.

Bardgett D.M.M.
Barker G.L.
Barker P.
Barman D.N.
Barnett M.B.
Barry P.
Barton F.
Baskett P.J.F.
Batchelor A.M.
Batchelor G.N.
Bavister P.H.
Baxter P.J.C.
Baxter R.C.H.
Bayoumi M.
Beasley J.M.
Beaugie A.V.
Beeby C.P.
Beers H.T.B.
Beese E.
Bell C.F.
Bellis D.
Bembridge M.
Bennett J.A.
Bennett P.J.
Berridge J.C.
Bexton M.
Bhar D.
Bill K.M.
Billingham I.S.
Bird K.J.
Bird T.M.
Biswas M.
Black A.
Blackburn A.
Blumgart C.
Blundell M.D.
Bone M.E.
Boobyer M.D.
Bourne J.A.
Bowen D.J.
Bowley C.J.
Boylan M.K.G.

Boyle A.S.
Bradfield H.G.C.
Braithwaite P.
Bramwell R.G.B.
Braude N.
Bray M.
Brayshaw S.A.
Breckenridge J.L.
Brim V.B.
Brock P.J.
Brooker J.
Brooks A.M.
Brown G.C.S.
Brown L.A.
Brown P.M.
Browne G.A.
Brownlie G.
Buckley C.J.
Buckley P.M.
Buist R.
Bulmer J.N.
Burchett K.R.
Burlingham A.N.
Burn M.C.
Burnley S.
Burridge P.M.
Buxton B.J.
Cadle D.R.
Calder I.
Cameron B.
Campbell D.N.
Carmichael J.C.G.
Carnie J.C.
Carter A.J.
Carter M.I.
Cartwright P.D.
Casey W.F.
Cash T.I.
Cashman J.N.
Cave W.P.
Chakrabarti P.
Chalmers E.P.D.

Chamberlain M.E.
Charters P.
Charway C.L.
Chhaya U.H.
Child D.A.
Choksi M.A.
Choudhry A.
Christian A.S.
Christmas D.
Church J.J.
Clark G.
Clark J.M.
Clarke H.L.
Clarke K.
Clarke T.N.S.
Clyburn P.
Cobley M.
Cockroft S.
Codman V.A.
Cody M.
Coe A.J.
Coghill J.C.
Cohen M.
Cole J.R.
Collier I.F.
Colville L.J.
Colvin M.P.
Coniam S.W.
Conn A.G.
Conroy P.T.
Conway M.
Conyers A.B.
Cook P.R.
Cooper A.E.
Cooper A.M.C.
Cooper C.M.
Cooper J.B.
Cooper R.
Corser G.C.
Cory C.E.
Cotter J.
Cousins D.J.

Craddock K.H.
Craddock S.C.
Cranston A.J.
Creagh-Barry P.
Crew A.D.
Crooke J.W.
Crosse M.M.
Cruickshank R.H.
Cunliffe M.
Curran J.P.
Dako J.A.
Dalton J.R.
Daly P.E.
Dann W.L.
Daum R.E.O.
Davies C.
Davies D.W.L.
Davies G.K.
Davies J.R.
Davies K.H.
Davies K.J.
Davies M.
Davies M.H.
Davies R.
Davies S.
Davis M.
Day C.D.
Daykin A.
Dean S.G.
Denny N.M.
Derbyshire D.R.
Derrington M.C.
Desborough R.C.
Desgrand D.
Desmond M.J.
Devlin C.
Dewar A.K.
Diamond A.W.
Dickenson J.E.
Dickson D.
Dixon A.M.
Dixon J.
Dobson M.B.
Dobson P.M.S.
Dodd P.
Dowdall J.W.
Dowling R.M.
Downer J.
Dowson S.
Du Boulay P.M.
Dumont S.
Duncan N.H.
Duncan P.W.
Dunn S.R.
Dunne J.

Dunnet J.
Dunnill R.P.H.
Duthie A.M.
Eadsforth P.
Eames G.M.
Earlam C.
Eastley R.J.
Eatock C.R.
Edbrooke D.L.
Edmondson W.C.
Elliott P.
Elliott R.H.
Elsworth C.
Eltoft M.E.
Emmott R.S.
Eppel B.
Erskine W.A.R.
Evans D.H.C.
Evans J.A.
Ewah B.N.
Ewart I.A.
Ewart M.C.
Fahy L.T.
Fairbrass M.J.
Falconer R.
Farling P.A.
Farquharson S.
Fenner S.
Ferguson A.
Ferguson B.J.M.
Field G.
Fischer H.B.J.
Flynn M.J.
Forster S.
Foster J.M.
Foster S.
Foxell R.M.
Francis G.A.
Francis I.
Frater R.A.S.
Frazer R.S.
Freeman R.
Freeman R.M.
Frimpong S.
Frossard J.
Fry D.I.
Fryer J.M.
Furness G.
Furniss P.
Fuzzey G.J.J.
Gabrielczyk M.
Galea P.J.
Galizia E.J.
Gamble J.A.S.
Gargesh K.

Garrett C.P.O.
Geadah M.
Gerrish S.P.
Ghandour F.M.
Ghosh N.
Gibson J.S.
Gill N.
Gill S.S.
Gillbe C.
Gillespie I.A.
Goldberg P.
Goodwin A.P.L.
Goold J.E.
Gooneratne D.S.
Gordon H.L.
Goroszeniuk T.
Gothard J.W.W.
Gough J.D.
Gough M.B.
Govenden V.
Graham I.F.M.
Graham R.F.
Gray H.S.J.
Grayling G.G.
Gregory M.
Gregory M.A.
Grewal M.S.
Griffiths D.P.G.
Griffiths F.J.
Grummitt R.
Haden R.M.
Hall P.J.
Hall R.M.
Hall-Davies G.
Hamer M.S.F.
Hamilton J.N.
Haque A.K.M.
Hargreaves J.
Hargreaves M.
Harley D.H.
Harley N.F.
Harper J.
Harris D.
Harris T.J.B.
Harrison C.A.
Harrison K.M.
Hartopp I.K.
Harvey D.C.
Harvey P.B.
Haslett W.H.K.
Hawkins S.
Hawkins T.J.
Hawley K.
Healy M.
Heath M.L.

Hebblethwaite R.
Hebden M.W.
Hegarty J.E.
Hegde R.T.
Heidelmeyer C.F.
Heining M.P.D.
Henderson P.A.L.
Henderson R.
Herrema I.H.
Hicks I.
Hicks J.B.
Higgs B.D.
Hill H.
Hills M.M.
Hipkin A.M.
Hirsch N.P.
Hitchings G.M.
Hoad D.J.
Hodgson R.M.H.
Hollis N.
Holmes J.W.L.
Holmes W.
Hood G.
Hooper M.B.
Hopkins P.M.
Horton J.N.
Housam G.D.
Hovell B.C.
Howard R.F.
Howell E.
Howell P.J.
Howell R.S.C.
Huddy N.C.
Hudecek I.P.
Hudson R.B.S.
Huggins N.J.
Hughes A.
Hughes K.
Hull C.J.
Hunter S.J.
Hurley J.E.
Hurwitz D.S.
Hussain A.
Hutchings P.J.G.
Hutchinson H.T.
Hutchinson J.
Imrie M.M.
Iyer D.
James M.L.
James R.H.
Jash K.
Jayaratne B.
Jeevananthan V.
Jefferies G.
Jeffs N.G.

Jellicoe J.A.	Lamb A.S.T.	Mackay L.J.	Morgan C.J.
Jenkins B.J.	Lamberty J.	MacKenzie J.	Morgan G.A.R.
Jephcott G.	Lamplugh G.	Mackersie A.	Morgan M.
Jessop E.	Lane J.R.	McKinlay R.G.C.	Morgan-Hughes J.O.
Jeyaratnam P.	Lanham P.R.W.	McKinney M.	Morrison A.
Johnston C.G.	Lanigan C.	McKnight C.K.	Moss E.
Johnston J.R.	Latimer R.D.	McLaren I.M.	Moss P.
Johnston K.	Laurence A.S.	McLellan I.	Moxon M.A.
Johnston P.	Leach A.B.	Macleod K.G.A.	Moyle J.T.B.
Johnstone R.D.	Lee K.G.	McLoughlin K.H.	Mulvein J.T.
Jones D.F.	Lenz R.J.	Macmillan R.R.	Mundy J.V.B.
Jones D.F.	Lesser P.J.A.	McNeill H.G.	Murphy P.
Jones D.O.	Lewis D.G.	McPherson J.J.	Murray J.F.
Jones H.E.	Lewis M.A.H.	McVey F.	Myerson K.R.
Jones H.M.	Lindsay W.A.	Madden A.P.	Nalliah R.
Jones I.W.	Ling S.	Magee P.T.	Nandi K.
Jones M.J.T.	Linsley A.	Maginness J.M.F.	Navaratnarajah M.N.
Jones R.E.	Linter S.P.K.	Mahoney A.	Newbegin H.
Jones R.M.	Lintin S.	Maile C.J.D.	Newby D.M.
Jones S.E.F.	Loach A.B.	Male C.G.	Newman V.J.
Kassi A.G.	Loader B.W.	Mallaiah S.	Newton D.E.F.
Kay P.M.	Locker I.	Manser J.	Newton M.
Keep P.J.	Lockwood G.	Marczak A.	Nightingale J.
Kelly D.R.	Loh L.	Marjot R.	Nightingale P.
Kelly E.P.	Longbottom R.T.	Marsh A.M.	Notcutt W.G.
Kelly J.M.	Lothian M.	Marsh R.H.K.	Nott M.R.
Kenny N.T.	Loughran P.G.	Marshall A.G.	Nunn G.F.
Kent A.P.	Loveland R.	Marshall F.P.F.	O'Donovan N.P.
Keogh B.F.	Lowe S.S.	Marshall M.A.	O'Keeffe N.
Kerr L.I.	Loyden C.F.	Martin A.	Okell R.W.
Kershaw E.J.	Ludgrove T.	Martin A.J.	Olivelle A.
Kestin I.G.	Lumb A.B.	Mason C.J.	Oosthuysen S.A.
Khan I.A.	Lumley J.	Massey N.J.A.	Ordman A.
Khawaja A.A.	Lung C.P.	Mather S.P.	Orr D.A.
Kidd J.	Lutton M.	Mathias I.M.J.	Orton J.K.
Kilpatrick S.M.	Luxton M.C.	Matthews N.C.	Packham R.N.
Kimberley A.	Lynch M.	Matthews P.J.	Paddle J.S.
King N.W.	Lytle J.	Matthews R.F.J.	Padfield A.
Kinnell J.D.	McAra A.	Mawson P.J.	Padfield N.L.
Kipling R.M.	Macartney I.D.	Meadows D.P.	Padmanabhan H.
Kirby I.J.	McAteer E.M.	Mercer N.P.	Page R.J.E.
Kneeshaw J.	McAteer M.P.	Michael W.	Pais W.A.
Knight P.F.	McCallum I.J.	Michel R.	Palmer R.
Kokri M.S.	McCallum M.I.D.	Milaszkiewicz R.M.	Pappin J.C.
Kotting S.	McCarthy G.	Millar J.	Park R.
Kraayenbrink M.A.	McCaughey W.	Miller R.I.	Park W.G.
Krapez J.R.	McCollum J.S.C.	Miller-Jones C.M.H.	Parker J.R.
Krishnan A.	McComish P.B.	Milligan K.R.	Parsloe M.
Kulasinghe N.	McFadzean W.A.	Milne L.A.	Patel D.K.
Kumar V.	MacFarlane D.W.	Mirakhur R.K.	Pateman J.A.
Kurer F.	McGeachie J.F.	Mitchell M.D.	Pathirana D.U.S.
Lack J.A.	McGhee T.D.	Monk C.	Paul S.
Laffey D.A.	McGowan W.A.W.	Moore M.R.	Peebles-Brown A.E.
Lake A.P.J.	McHutchon A.	Moore N.A.	Pegg M.S.
Lalitha K.	Mackay I.R.	Moore P.	Pennefather S.H.

Appendix F - Participants (anaesthetists)

Perkins D.H.
Perriss B.W.
Peterson A.C.
Petros A.
Phillips D.C.
Phillips G.
Phillips P.D.
Pick M.
Piggott S.E.
Pinchin R.M.E.
Platt M.W.
Plummer R.B.
Pocklington A.G.
Ponte J.C.
Poobalasingam N.
Poole D.
Porterfield A.J.
Potter C.J.F.
Powell D.R.
Powell H.
Powell J.N.
Power K.J.
Power S.J.
Pradhan V.S.
Price K.A.
Pridie A.K.
Prince G.D.
Proctor E.A.
Prosser J.A.
Pryn S.J.
Purcell G.
Pyne A.
Radford P.
Rafferty M.P.
Raithatha H.H.
Raitt D.G.
Rajasekaran T.
Ralph S.
Ralston C.
Ramachandran A.
Rampton A.J.
Ramsay T.M.
Randall N.P.C.
Rao I.N.
Rao M.V.S.
Raper J.M.
Ratcliffe R.M.H.
Ravalia A.
Ravenscroft P.J.
Rawlinson W.A.L.
Read M.
Rebstein S.E.
Redman D.R.O.
Redman L.R.
Redpath A.

Reilly C.S.
Rhodes S.P.
Rice C.P.
Richards D.C.
Richards M.J.
Richmond D.J.H.
Richmond M.N.
Riddell G.S.
Rimell P.J.
Ritchie P.
Ritchie P.A.
Robbie D.S.
Roberts M.G.
Roberts W.O.
Robertson J.A.
Robertson S.
Robinson D.A.
Robinson D.J.C.
Robinson F.P.
Robinson K.N.
Rodgers R.C.
Rogers C.
Rogers P.
Roscoe B.
Rose A.
Rose N.
Ross S.
Rouse J.M.
Royle P.
Royston N.
Rucklidge M.A.
Ruff S.J.
Russell G.
Ryan D.A.
Saddler J.M.
Sagar D.A.
Sahal B.B.
St John-Jones L.
Sale J.P.
Saleh A.
Salib Y.M.
Samak R.V.
Samuel I.O.
Sanders D.
Sanghera S.
Saunders D.A.
Scallan M.J.H.
Schmulian C.
Scott A.C.
Scott P.V.
Scott R.B.
Scott-Knight V.
Seagger R.A.
Searle A.E.
Seethalakshmi K.

Sekar M.
Sellers W.F.S.
Sellwood W.G.
Sen A.
Sengupta P.
Seymour A.H.
Shanks A.B.
Shannon C.J.
Sharawi R.
Sharpe T.D.E.
Shewan D.M.
Short S.
Shribman A.J.
Sides C.A.
Silk J.M.
Silver J.
Simpson J.
Simpson M.E.
Singh K.H.P.
Singh R.K.
Siriwardhana S.A.
Sivaloganathan G.
Skelly A.
Skinner A.C.
Smith B.A.C.
Smith B.L.
Smith H.S.
Smith I.D.
Smith J.B.
Smith M.
Smith M.B.
Smith P.
Smith P.A.
Sneyd J.R.
Somanathan S.
Somerville I.D.
Songhurst L.Z.
Soni N.C.
Speedy H.M.S.
Spencer E.
Spencer H.A.
Spilsbury R.A.
Spreadbury P.L.
Sprigge J.S.
Srivastava S.
Stacey R.
Stanley J.C.
Stanton J.M.
Starkey C.
Steven C.M.
Stielow E.
Stock J.G.L.
Stokes M.
Stray C.M.
Street M.

Stride P.C.
Strong J.E.
Stubbing J.F.
Sullivan P.M.
Summerfield R.J.
Sumner E.
Sutherland I.C.
Sutton D.N.
Sweeney B.P.
Swindells S.
Tackley R.M.
Taggart P.C.M.
Tannett P.G.
Tatham P.F.
Tattersall M.P.
Taylor M.
Taylor M.B.
Teturswamy G.
Thomas A.N.
Thomas D.G.
Thomas D.I.
Thompson E.M.
Thompson J.F.W.
Thomson J.
Thorn J.L.
Thornberry A.
Thornley B.
Thorpe M.H.
Thorpe P.M.
Tobias M.A.
Tomlinson J.H.
Tordoff S.
Trask M.D.
Turley A.
Turner G.
Turtle M.J.
Tweedie D.G.
Tweedie I.
Twentyman C.
Twohig M.M.
Ulyett I.
Valijan A.
van Mourik G.
Van Ryssen M.E.P.
Vanner R.G.
Veitch G.
Vella L.M.
Veness A.M.
Verghese C.
Verma R.
Vohra A.
Wade M.J.
Wadon A.J.
Waite K.
Walker J.A.

Appendix F - Participants (anaesthetists)

Walker M.A.
Walmsley A.J.
Walsh E.
Walters F.
Ward M.E.
Ward R.M.
Warner J.A.
Waterland J.
Watkins T.G.
Watson D.A.
Watson D.M.
Watson N.A.
Webb T.B.
Welchew E.A.
Weller R.
Wells J.K.G.
Wemyss-Gorman P.B.
West D.
Whelan E.
Whitaker D.K.
Whitburn R.
White J.B.
Will R.
Willatts D.G.
Williams A.B.
Williams E.M.
Williams L.J.
Wilson C.M.
Wilton H.J.
Wise C.C.
Withington P.S.
Wolfe M.J.
Wood C.H.
Woodall N.M.
Woodsford P.V.
Wort M.
Wray G.
Wright M.M.
Wright P.
Xifaras G.P.
Yates D.W.
Yates J.E.J.
Young D.
Young P.N.
Zaki M.A.
Zilkha T.R.

Appendix G - Participants

Consultant surgeons and gynaecologists

These consultant surgeons and gynaecologists returned at least one questionnaire relating to the period 1 April 1994 to 31 March 1995

Ackroyd C.E.
Ackroyd J.S.
Adam R.F.
Adamson A.
Affifi R.
Afshar F.
Al-Asadi A.D.
Al-Fallouji M.
Al-Mukhtar A.M.
Alderman P.M.
Aldoori M.I.
Aldridge M.C.
Aldridge M.J.
Alexander D.J.
Ali A.L.
Ali M.A.A.
Allan A.
Allan D.
Allen N.
Allen P.R.
Allen T.R.
Allum W.H.
Anderson R.J.L.
Andrew D.R.
Andrews B.G.
Andrews N.
Angus P.D.
Antrobus J.N.
Appleton G.
Appleyard I.
Arafa M.
Armitage N.C.
Armitage T.G.
Armitstead P.R.
Armour R.H.
Armstrong C.P.
Ashby E.C.
Aston N.
Atkins P.
Auchincloss J.M.
Aukland P.
Ausobsky J.R.
Avill R.

Awad S.A.
Backhouse C.M.
Bagga T.K.
Bailey J.S.
Bailey M.E.
Baker A.R.
Baker P.
Baker R.
Baker R.H.
Bakran A.
Balfour T.W.
Ball C.
Bamford D.
Bancewicz J.
Banks A.J.
Bannister J.J.
Bardsley D.
Barker J.R.
Barlow A.P.
Barr H.
Barr R.J.
Barrett D.
Barrett G.S.
Barrie W.W.
Bartlett J.R.
Barwell N.J.
Basu H.K.
Bates T.
Bateson P.G.
Battersby R.D.E.
Baxter-Smith D.C.
Beauchamp C.G.
Beck J.M.
Belcher P.R.
Bell P.R.F.
Bellini M.J.
Belstead J.S.
Benfield J.
Bennett J.G.
Bentley P.G.
Bentley R.J.
Bernard Williams
Berry A.R.

Berstock D.A.
Best B.G.
Bett N.J.
Betts J.A.
Beverland D.E.
Bhamra M.S.
Bickerstaff K.I.
Bintcliffe I.W.L.
Bird R.
Bishop M.C.
Black J.
Black J.E.
Black R.J.
Blackburn C.W.
Blackett R.L.
Blacklay P.F.
Blacklock A.R.E.
Blake G.
Blakeway C.
Blamey R.W.
Blayney J.D.M.
Bodey W.N.
Boggon R.P.
Bolton J.P.
Bolton-Maggs B.G.
Bonnici A.V.
Bonser R.
Boobis L.H.
Booth C.M.
Boulos P.B.
Bowsher W.G.
Boyd P.J.
Bracey D.J.
Bradford R.
Bradley J.G.
Bransom C.J.
Brash J.H.
Brawn W.J.
Brearley S.
Brigg J.K.
Briggs T.W.R.
Brignall C.
Bristol J.B.

Britton B.J.
Britton D.C.
Brocklehurst G.
Bromige M.R.
Brooker D.S.
Brooman P.J.
Brotherton B.J.
Broughton A.C.
Brown C.
Brown G.J.A.
Brown J.G.
Brown M.G.
Brown M.W.
Brown R.
Brown R.
Brown R.F.
Browne M.J.
Browning A.J.F.
Brunskill P.J.
Bryan R.M.
Buchanan J.M.
Buckels J.A.C.
Bucknall T.E.
Budd D.W.G.
Budd J.
Bullen B.R.
Bulstrode C.J.K.
Bundred N.
Bunker T.D.
Burge D.
Burgess P.
Burke M.
Burman J.H.
Burnand K.G.
Burton V.W.
Butt M.A.
Cade D.
Callam M.J.
Callum K.G.
Calthorpe D.
Calvert C.H.
Cameron C.R.
Cameron M.M.

Campalani G.
Campbell A.J.
Campbell C.S.
Campbell D.J.
Campbell J.
Campbell R.
Carden D.G.
Cargill A.O'R
Carleton P.J.
Carr R.T.W.
Carty N.J.
Cassell P.G.
Cast I.P.
Cawthorn S.J.
Cetti N.E.
Chadwick C.J.
Chadwick S.
Challis J.H.
Chamberlain J.
Chan R.N.W.
Chana G.S.
Chant A.D.B.
Chappatte O.A.
Chapple C.R.
Charlesworth D.
Chauhan M.L.
Cheslyn-Curtis S.
Chilvers A.S.
Clark A.W.
Clark J.
Clarke D.J.
Clarke H.J.
Clarke J.
Clarke J.M.F.
Clarke N.M.P.
Clarke R.J.
Clay N.R.
Clayson A.
Cleak D.K.
Clegg J.F.
Clement A.
Clement D.A.
Clifton M.A.
Clothier P.
Coakham H.
Cobb A.G.
Cobb R.A.
Cohen G.L.
Colin J.F.
Colmer M.R.
Colton C.L.
Cook A.
Cooke D.A.P.
Cooke T.J.C.
Coombes G.B.

Cooper J.
Cooper M.J.
Copeland G.P.
Copeland S.A.
Copland R.F.P.
Corbett C.R.R.
Corder A.
Corfield A.P.
Corkery J.J.
Cornah M.S.
Corrigan A.M.
Cowen M.E.
Cowley D.J.
Crabtree S.D.
Craig B.F.
Crane P.
Crawford D.J.
Crawshaw C.C.
Craxford A.D.
Creagh T.A.
Creedon R.
Crisp J.C.
Crockard H.A.
Croft R.J.
Crosby D.L.
Cross A.T.
Cross F.W.
Crowson M.C.
Crumplin M.K.H.
Cumming J.A.
Cummins B.H.
Cunliffe W.J.
Curry R.C.
Curt J.R.N.
Curwen C.
Cuschieri R.J.
D'Arcy J.C.
D'Costa E.F.
Da Costa O.ST.J.
de Leval M.
d'E Meredith A.P.
Darke S.G.
Davidson B.R.
Davies C.J.
Davies H.L.
Davies J.N.
Davies J.O.
Davies S.J.M.
Davis C.H.G.
De K.R.
De Boer P.G.
De Bolla A.R.
De La Hunt M.N.
Deacon P.B.
Deakin M.

Deane G.
Deans G.
Dendy R.A.
Derodra J.
Derry C.D.
Desai J.B.
Deutsch J.
Deverall P.B.
Dhebar M.I.
Diamond T.
Dias J.J.
Dick J.A.
Dickson W.A.
Dilraj Gopal T.R.
Dinley R.R.J.
Dixon J.H.
Doig R.L.
Donaldson D.R.
Donaldson L.A.
Donovan I.A.
Dooley J.F.
Doran J.
Dorgan J.C.
Dormandy J.A.
Downing R.
Dudley N.E.
Duffield R.G.M.
Duffy T.J.
Dunster G.D.
Durrans D.
Duthie J.S.
Earnshaw J.J.
Eaton A.C.
Ebbs S.R.
Ebizie A.O.
Edge A.J.
Edmondson S.
Edwards A.N.
Edwards D.H.
Edwards J.L.
Edwards J.M.
Edwards P.W.
El-Aziz S.A.
El-Shunnar K.S.
Elder J.B.
Eldridge P.R.
Ellenbogen S.
Elliott B.
Elliott J.R.M.
Elliott M.J.
Ellis B.W.
Ellis D.J.
Elsworth C.F.
Emery S.J.
England P.C.

English A.H.
Evans A.G.
Evans C.M.
Evans G.A.
Evans G.H.E.
Evans H.J.R.
Evans J.
Evans P.E.L.
Evans R.A.
Everson N.W.
Eyre-Brook I.A.
Faber R.G.
Fagan A.M.
Fagg P.S.
Farrar D.J.
Fawcett A.N.
Fay T.N.
Feggetter J.G.W.
Ferguson G.
Ferguson J.
Ferrie B.G.
Ferro M.
Fiddian N.J.
Field E.S.
Field R.E.
Fiennes A.
Fillobos S.A.
Finan P.J.
Finch D.R.A.
Findlay G.F.G.
Finlay R.D.
Firmin R.K.
Fish A.N.J.
Flanagan J.P.
Flannigan G.M.
Fletcher M.S.
Flew T.J.
Flood B.M.
Flook D.
Flowerdew A.F.
Fogg A.J.B.
Fontaine C.J.
Fordyce M.J.F.
Forester A.
Forrest J.F.
Forrest L.
Forster I.W.
Forsyth A.T.
Forsythe J.L.R.
Fortes Mayer K.D.
Forty J.
Fossard D.P.
Foster R.P.
Fountain S.W.
Fowler C.G.

Appendix G - Participants (surgeons and gynaecologists)

Fox J.N.	Grabham	Harrison I.D.	Hook W.E.
Foy M.A.	Grace A.R.H.	Harrison J.D.	Hooper A.A.
Fraser I.	Grace P.	Harrison R.A.	Hooper T.
Fraser I.A.	Grange W.J.	Harrison S.C.W.	Hope P.G.
Frecker P.	Grant C.	Harrison T.A.	Hopkinson B.R.
Freedlander E.	Gray W.J.	Hart A.J.L.	Hopkinson D.A.W.
Fyfe I.S.	Green J.P.	Harvey C.F.	Hopkinson G.B.
Gale D.	Greenall M.	Harvey J.S.	Hopton D.S.
Galea M.	Greenhalf J.O.	Hasan S.S.	Horgan K.
Gallagher P.	Greenway B.	Hassan S.	Horner J.
Gallagher P.	Greiss M.E.	Hastie K.J.	Hosie K.B.
Galland R.B.	Griffith G.H.	Hatfield R.	Hosking S.W.
Galloway J.M.D.	Griffith M.J.	Hawe M.J.G.	Houghton P.W.J.
Gana H.B.	Griffiths A.B.	Hawthorn I.E.	Houlton M.C.C.
Gannon M.X.	Griffiths E.	Hay D.J.	Howell C.J.
Gardham J.R.C.	Griffiths M.	Hayes A.G.	Howell F.R.
Gardner N.H.N.	Griffiths N.J.	Hayes B.R.	Hudd C.
Gartell P.C.	Grotte G.J.	Haynes I.G.	Hughes R.G.
Gatehouse D.	Guillou P.J.	Haynes P.J.	Hughes-Nurse J.
Gear M.W.L.	Guly H.R.	Haynes S.	Humphrey C.S.
Getty C.J.M.	Gumpert J.R.W.	Heath A.D.	Hunt D.M.
Giddings A.E.B.	Gupta M.	Heath D.V.	Hurst P.A.
Gie G.A.	Guvendik L.	Heather B.P.	Hussain M.
Gilbert J.M.	Guy A.J.	Hedges A.R.	Hutchinson I.F.
Gill S.S.	Gwynn B.R.	Helm R.H.	Hyde I.D.
Gillatt D.	Haggie S.J.	Henry A.P.J.	Ibrahim Z.
Gillham N.R.	Halawa M.	Hershman M.	Iftikhar S.Y.
Gillison E.W.	Hale J.E.	Heslip M.R.	Imray C.H.E.
Gilroy D.	Hall C.N.	Hetherington J.W.	Inglis J.A.
Gingell J.C.	Hall G.	Heyse-Moore G.H.	Ingoldby C.J.H.
Gladstone D.J.	Hall R.	Hickey M.S.J.	Ingram G.
Glasgow M.M.S.	Halliday A.G.	Higgins J.R.A.	Ingram N.P.
Glass R.E.	Hamer D.B.	Higginson D.W.	Insall R.
Glazer G.	Hamilton A.	Higgs B.	Ions G.K.
Gleeson M.	Hamilton G.	Hill J.G.	Ireland D.
Glick S.	Hamilton J.R.L.	Hilton C.J.	Irvin T.T.
Goddard N.J.	Hamlyn P.L.	Hinchliffe A.	Irvine B.
Goiti J.J.	Hammond R.H.	Hinton C.P.	Irwin S.T.
Golby M.G.S.	Hancock B.D.	Hirschowitz D.	Iyer S.V.
Goldman M.D.	Handley R.	Hoare E.M.	Jackowski A.
Goldstraw P.	Hands L.	Hobbiss J.H.	Jackson R.
Gollapudi S.M.	Hanley D.J.	Hodgson S.P.	Jackson R.K.
Goodall R.J.R.	Hannah G.	Hoile R.W.	Jacob G.
Goode A.W.	Hannon M.A.	Holbrook M.C.	Jacobs L.G.H.
Gooding M.R.	Hannon R.J.	Holden M.P.	Jaganathan R.
Goodman A.J.	Harding-Jones D.	Holdsworth B.J.	Jaiyesimi R.A.R.
Goodwin M.I.	Hardwidge C.	Holdsworth J.D.	James M.I.
Gopalji B.T.	Hargreaves A.W.	Holdsworth P.J.	James S.E.
Gordon E.M.	Harley J.M.	Holl-Allen R.T.J.	Jamison M.H.
Gore R.	Harper P.H.	Holliday H.W.	Jefferiss C.D.
Gornall P.	Harper W.M.	Holme T.C.	Jeffery P.J.
Gough A.L.	Harris D.L.	Holmes F.J.	Jeffreys R.V.
Goulbourne I.A.	Harris P.L.	Holmes J.T.	Jenkins A.J.
Gourevitch D.	Harris V.G.	Holt S.	Jenkins D.H.R.
Gowland-Hopkins N.F.	Harrison B.J.	Hood J.M.	Jenkins J.D.

Appendix G - Participants (surgeons and gynaecologists)

Jessop J.	Kettlewell M.	Leese T.	McIntosh J.W.
Jeyapaul K.	Keys G.W.	Leicester R.J.	McIrvine A.J.
Jeyasingham K.	Khalil-Marzouk J.F.	Lemon G.J.	Mackenney R.P.
Johnson A.G.	Khan M.A.R.	Lennard T.W.J.	McKibbin A.
Johnson A.O.B.	Khan O.	Lennox J.M.	Mackinnon J.G.
Johnson B.F.	Khawaja H.T.	Lennox M.S.	McLaren M.I.
Johnson C.D.	Khoury G.	Leopold P.W.	Maclean A.D.W.
Johnson J.R.	Kidd M.N.	Lester R.L.	McLeod F.N.
Johnson M.G.	Kinder R.B.	Levack B.	McMahon M.J.
Johnson R.H.	King J.B.	Leveson S.H.	McPartlin J.F.
Johnson R.W.G.	King T.	Lewis A.A.M.	MacPherson D.S.
Johnson S.R.	Kingsnorth A.N.	Lewis C.T.	McWhinnie D.L.
Johnston D.F.	Kingston R.D.	Lewis J.	Mace P.M.
Johnston G.W.	Kipping R.A.	Lewis J.D.	Mackie C.R.
Johnstone J.M.S.	Kirby R.M.	Lewis J.L.	Mackie I.G.
Jones A.S.	Kirk S.	Lewis P.	Mackle E.J.
Jones B.M.	Kirwan P.	Lien W.	Magee P.G.
Jones C.B.	Kiwanuka A.I.	Lincoln C.	Maheson M.V.S.
Jones D.R.	Klimach O.	Linsell J.	Maheswaran S.
Jones D.J.	Klugman D.J.	Little D.J.	Mahir M.S.
Jones D.R.	Knight S.	Livingstone B.N.	Main B.J.
Jones D.R.B.	Knox A.J.S.	Lloyd D.M.	Mair W.S.J.
Jones M.	Knox R.	Lloyd-Davies E.R.V.	Majowski R.S.
Jones M.W.	Knudsen C.J.M.	Lock M.	Makin C.A.
Jones N.A.G.	Kolar K.M.	Locke T.J.	Makin G.S.
Jones P.	Kulkani R.P.	Lodge J.P.A.	Mal R.K.
Jones P.A.	Lake D.N.W.	Logan A.M.	Mallya U.N.
Jones R.A.C.	Lake S.P.	London N.	Maltby B.
Jones R.N.	Lallemand R.C.	Lord M.G.	Manners R.
Jones S.M.	Lambert D.	Lotz J.C.	Manning M.
Jones W.A.	Lambert M.E.	Loynes R.D.	Mansel R.E.
Jurewicz W.A.	Lambert W.G.	Lunn P.G.	Mansfield A.O.
Kar A.K.	Lamerton A.J.	Lye R.	Marcus R.T.
Karpinski M.R.K.	Lane G.	Lyttle J.A.	Marcuson R.W.
Karran S.J.	Lane I.F.	McAdam W.A.F.	Markham N.I.
Kavanagh T.G.	Lane R.H.S.	Macafee A.L.	Marks C.G.
Kaye J.C.	Lang D.	McArthur P.	Marsh C.H.
Keates J.R.W.	Langkamer G.	McBride D.J.	Marsh D.R.
Keenan D.J.M.	Lansdown M.	McCarthy D.	Martin D.H.
Kelly J.D.C.	Large S.R.	McCollum C.N.	Martin M.M.R.
Kelly J.F.	Larvin M.	McCreadie D.W.J.	Martin R.H.
Kelly J.M.	Lavelle M.A.	McCulloch P.G.	Mason J.R.
Kelly M.J.	Law N.	MacDermott S.	Mason R.C.
Kemeny A.A.	Lawrence D.	Macdonald A.P.	Massey C.I.
Kennedy C.L.	Lawson R.A.M.	Macdonald D.A.	Mathalone M.B.R.
Kennedy R.H.	Lawson W.R.	McDonald J.	Matheson D.M.
Kenny N.W.	Lawton J.O.	McDonald P.	Matthews H.R.
Kenyon G.S.	Layer G.T.	MacDonald R.C.	Matthews J.G.
Keown D.	Lea R.E.	MacEachern A.G.	Matthews M.G.
Kerr G.	Leach R.D.	McFarland R.J.	Mattock E.J.
Kerr R.S.C.	Leaper D.J.	McFarlane T.	Maurice-Williams R.S.
Kerr-Wilson R.	Lear P.A.	MacFie J.	Mavor A.I.D.
Kershaw C.J.	Lee M.J.R.	McGee H.	Maxted M.J.
Kershaw W.W.	Lee P.W.R.	McIntosh G.S.	Maxwell R.J.
Kester R.C.	Lees P.D.	McIntosh I.H.	Maxwell W.A.

Appendix G - Participants (surgeons and gynaecologists)

May A.R.L.	Mulligan T.O.	Pancharatnam M.	Psaila J.V.
May P.C.	Mundy A.R.	Panesar K.J.S.	Pugh D.H.O.
Maybury N.K.	Munsch C.M.	Pantelides M.	Puntis M.C.A.
Meadows T.H.	Murday A.	Parker C.J.	Pye G.
Mearns A.J.	Murdoch R.W.G.	Parr N.J.	Pye J.K.
Meehan S.E.	Murphy A.G.	Parrott N.R.	Pyper P.C.
Mehdian S.M.	Murphy K.	Parvin S.	Quayle A.R.
Meikle D.D.	Murphy P.D.	Parys B.T.	Quayle J.B.
Menzies D.	Murray A.	Pastorino U.	Quick C.R.
Menzies-Gow N.	Muscroft T.J.	Patel A.B.	Radcliffe A.G.
Meredith A.D.	Naftalin N.J.	Patel A.D.	Rahman A.N.
Metcalfe J.W.	Nair K.K.	Patel P.	Raimes S.A.
Metcalfe-Gibson C.	Nair U.	Patel R.L.	Raine G.E.T.
Meyrick Thomas J.	Nash A.G.	Paterson I.S.	Rainey A.E.S.
Michaels J.A.	Nasmyth D.G.	Paterson M.	Rainsbury R.M.
Miller A.J.	Neal N.C.	Pattison C.W.	Ramus N.I.
Miller D.H.T.	Neil W.F.	Pattisson P.H.	Rand C.
Miller G.A.B.	Neill R.W.K.	Payne S.R.	Rao G.N.
Miller I.A.	Nelson R.J.	Peace P.K.	Rao G.S.
Miller J.M.	Nevelos A.B.	Pearson H.J.	Rao N.S.
Milligan G.F.	Newman R.J.	Pearson J.B.	Ratliff D.A.
Mills R.G.S.	Nicholls J.C.	Pearson R.C.	Rawsthorne G.B.
Misra P.	Nicholson R.A.	Peet T.N.D.	Ray D.K.
Mitchell D.C.	Nicholson S.	Pena M.A.	Read L.
Mitchell I.C.	Norris M.G.	Pennie B.	Reddy P.
Mitchell R.D.	Norris S.H.	Pepper J.R.	Reddy T.N.
Mitchenere P.	North A.N.	Pereira J.H.	Reece-Smith H.
Moat N.	Nouri E.	Perry P.M.	Rees A.
Mobb G.E.	Novell J.R.	Peyton J.W.R.	Rees A.J.S.
Modgill V.K.	O'Boyle P.	Pierro A.	Rees B.I.
Mohan J.	O'Brien T.E.B.	Pietroni M.C.	Rees D.
Moisey C.U.	O'Dwyer S.T.	Pigott H.W.S.	Rees R.W.M.
Mollan R.A.B.	O'Neill J.J.	Pigott T.	Regan M.W.
Monaghan J.M.	O'Reilly M.J.G.	Pillai R.	Reid D.J.
Monro J.L.	O'Riordan B.	Pinto D.J.	Reilly D.T.
Monson J.R.T.	O'Riordan S.M.	Pittam M.R.	Rennie C.D.
Montgomery A.C.V.	Obeid M.L.	Pollard J.P.	Renton C.J.
Montgomery B.S.I.	Odom N.J.	Pollard R.	Rew D.A.
Moore A.	Older M.W.J.	Pollard S.G.	Reynolds J.R.
Moore V.C.	Ormiston M.	Porter M.L.	Rhodes A.
Morgan M.W.E.	Orr M.M.	Poskitt K.R.	Rhys-Evans P.
Morgan S.J.	Ostick D.G.	Powell M.P.	Ribbans W.J.
Morgan W.E.	Owen A.W.M.	Powis S.J.A.	Ribeiro B.F.
Morgan W.P.	Owen W.J.	Powley P.H.	Rich A.J.
Morrell M.T.	Owen-Smith M.S.	Pownall P.J.	Richards D.J.
Morris B.D.A.	Packer N.P.	Pratt D.	Richardson P.L.
Morris I.R.	Paes T.	Price J.J.	Rickett J.W.
Morris P.J.	Page R.D.	Price-Thomas J.M.	Rigby C.C.
Morritt G.N.	Pailthorpe C.A.	Primrose J.N.	Rigg K.M.
Mosley J.G.	Pain J.A.	Pring D.	Riley D.
Moynagh P.D.	Paley W.G.	Pritchard G.A.	Rintoul R.F.
Mughal M.M.	Palmer B.V.	Pritchett C.J.	Roake J.A.
Mulholland R.C.	Palmer J.G.	Proud G.	Roberts A.H.N.
Mullan F.	Palmer J.H.	Prout W.G.	Roberts J.G.
Muller P.W.S.	Panahy C.	Pryor G.A.	Roberts P.H.

Appendix G - Participants (surgeons and gynaecologists)

Roberts P.N.	Sewell P.F.T.	Smith M.	Tam P.K.H.
Robertson I.J.	Shafighian B.	Smith P.L.C.	Tasker T.P.B.
Robertson J.F.	Shafiq M.	Smith R.	Taube M.
Robson M.J.	Shah J.	Somerville J.J.F.	Taylor A.R.
Rodin R.A.	Shaikh N.A.	Soorae A.S.	Taylor B.A.
Roe A.M.	Shanahan D.J.	Souter R.G.	Taylor G.J.
Rogers H.S.	Shanahan M.D.G.	South L.M.	Taylor I.
Rogers K.	Shand J.E.G.	Southgate G.W.	Taylor J.L.
Rosen P.H.	Shand W.S.	Sparrow O.C.	Taylor M.C.
Rosenberg I.L.	Shandall A.	Spearing G.J.	Taylor P.
Ross A.H.M.	Shanker J.Y.	Spence R.A.	Taylor R.M.R.
Ross B.A.	Shanmugaraju P.G.	Spencer J.	Taylor S.A.
Ross E.R.S.	Sharif A.H.M.	Spigelman A.D.	Teasdale C.
Ross K.R.	Sharif D.	Spivey C.J.	Teddy P.J.
Rosson J.W.	Sharma V.	Spooner S.F.	Telfer M.R.
Rothnie N.	Shaw J.	Spychal R.T.	Terry T.R.
Rouholamin E.	Shaw M.D.M.	Spyt T.	Thacker C.R.
Rowe P.H.	Shaw S.J.	Squire B.R.	Thawait B.P.
Rowe-Jones C.	Shearman C.P.	Stacey-Clear A.	Thomas D.G.T.
Rowlands B.J.	Shedden R.G.	Stafford F.W.	Thomas D.R.
Rowntree M.	Sheikh K.M.	Stamatakis J.D.	Thomas E.J.
Roy S.K.	Sher J.L.	Stanley D.	Thomas J.M.
Rundle J.S.H.	Sheridan R.J.	Stark J.	Thomas M.H.
Russell C.F.J.	Sheridan W.G.	Steele S.C.	Thomas T.L.
Russell R.	Sherlock D.J.	Stephen I.B.M.	Thomas W.E.G.
Rutter K.R.P.	Shieff C.L.	Stewart D.J.	Thomas W.G.
Sabanathan S.	Shields M.D.	Stewart J.	Thompson C.E.R.
Sabin H.I.	Shore D.F.	Stewart M.	Thompson H.H.
Sagar S.	Shorey B.A.	Stewart R.D.	Thompson J.
Sagor G.R.	Shorthouse A.J.	Stewart R.J.	Thompson J.F.
Sainsbury J.R.C.	Shukla H.	Stirling W.J.I.	Thompson M.H.
Salam A.	Shute K.	Stirrat A.N.	Thompson M.R.
Sales J.E.L.	Sibly T.F.	Stockley I.	Thompson R.L.E.
Samuel P.R.	Silverman S.H.	Stoddard C.J.	Thomson A.A.G.
Sanderson C.J.	Simison A.J.M.	Stoker T.A.M.	Thomson H.J.
Sansom J.R.	Simms J.M.	Stone C.D.P.	Thomson W.H.F.
Sarkar P.K.	Simonds G.W.	Stone M.	Thurston A.V.
Saunders N.R.	Simonis R.B.	Stothard J.	Tilakawardane A.L.N.
Sauven P.	Simpson B.A.	Stotter A.T.	Todd B.D.
Savage P.E.	Simpson E.	Strachan C.J.L.	Towler J.M.
Scholefield J.H.	Simson J.N.	Strahan J.	Townsend E.R.
Schraibman I.G.	Singh S.M.	Strang F.A.	Travlos J.
Scott A.D.N.	Skene A.	Studley J.	Treasure T.
Scott D.J.A.	Skidmore F.D.	Sturzaker H.G.	Treble N.J.
Scott J.E.	Skinner P.W.	Sudlow R.A.	Tresadern J.C.
Scott N.	Slater E.G.W.	Sugar A.W.	Tricker J.
Scott R.A.P.	Slater R.N.S.	Sullivan M.F.	Triffitt P.D.
Scott W.A.	Smallpeice C.J.	Suman R.K.	Trotter G.
Scott Ferguson J.	Smallwood J.	Suraliwala K.H.	Tsang V.
Scurr J.H.	Smallwood C.J.	Surtees P.	Tudor Davies W.
Sells R.A.	Smedley F.	Sutton G.	Tuite J.D.
Senapati A.	Smith A.	Sutton R.	Turner A.
Sengupta R.P.	Smith E.E.J.	Sykes P.A.	Turner D.T.L.
Sergeant R.J.	Smith G.M.R.	Tait W.	Ubhi C.
Sethia B.	Smith J.A.R.	Talbot R.W.	Umpleby H.C.

Appendix G - Participants (surgeons and gynaecologists)

Ursell W.
Vafidis J.
Vale J.
Valerio D.
Varma J.S.
Varma T.R.
Vass A.C.R.
Vaughan R.
Vaughan-Lane T.
Vellacott K.D.
Venables C.W.
Venn G.E.
Vesey S.G.
Vickers R.H.
Vohra R.K.
Vowden P.
Waddington R.T.
Wade P.J.F.
Wake P.N.
Walker A.J.
Walker A.P.
Walker C.J.
Walker D.R.
Walker E.M.
Walker R.T.
Walker S.M.
Wallace D.M.A.
Wallace W.A.
Walmsley B.H.
Walsh M.E.
Walter P.
Ward A.S.
Ward D.C.
Ward H.C.
Ward M.W.N.
Ward P.J.
Ward R.G.
Waters J.S.
Waterworth M.W.
Watkin D.F.L.
Watkin G.T.
Watkins R.M.
Watkinson J.
Watt-Smith S.R.
Way B.G.
Weatherley C.R.
Weaver P.C.
Webb J.K.
Webb P.J.
Webster D.J.T.
Wedgwood K.R.
Weeden D.
Wells A.D.
Wells F.C.
Wenham P.W.

Westwood C.A.
Wetherill M.H.
Whelan P.
Whitaker I.A.
White B.D.
White C.M.
Whitehead S.M.
Whitfield H.N.
Whittaker M.
Wickstead M.
Wilkins J.L.
Wilkinson A.R.
Wilkinson M.J.S.
Willett K.
Williams B.
Williams C.R.
Williams D.H.
Williams G.
Williams J.P.R.
Williams K.G.D.
Williams M.
Williams M.A.
Williams R.J.
Williams R.J.
Williams T.G.
Wilson N.M.
Wilson-McDonald J.
Windsor C.W.O.
Wise D.I.
Wise M.
Wishart M.S.
Wisheart J.D.
Witherow R.O.N.
Wolfe J.H.N.
Wolverson R.L.
Wood R.F.M.
Wood S.K.
Woodward D.A.K.
Worlock P.H.
Wray C.C.
Wren M.
Wright J.E.C.
Wright J.T.
Wright P.D.
Wright V.
Wynne K.S.
Yeates H.A.
Yeo R.
Yeung C.K.
Yogasundram Y.N.
Youhana A.Y.
Young C.P.
Young H.L.
Young J.R.
Zeiderman M.R.

Appendix G - Participants (surgeons and gynaecologists)

Appendix H - Local Reporters

This list shows the local reporters as of 10 July 1997.

We recognise that there are many clinical audit and information departments involved in providing data, although we have in many cases named only the consultant clinician nominated as local reporter.

Anglia & Oxford

Addenbrooke's	Dr D. Wight
Bedford Hospital	None
Heatherwood & Wexham Park Hospitals	Dr M.H. Ali
Hinchingbrooke Health Care	Dr M.D. Harris
Horton General Hospital	Dr N.J. Mahy
Ipswich Hospital	Mr I.E. Cowles
James Paget Hospital	Mrs C.L. Eagle
Kettering General Hospital	Dr B.E. Gostelow
King's Lynn & Wisbech Hospitals	Miss J.M. Rippon
Luton & Dunstable Hospital	Dr D.A.S. Lawrence
Milton Keynes General	Dr S.S. Jalloh
Norfolk & Norwich Health Care	Dr B.G. McCann
Northampton General Hospital	Dr A.J. Molyneux
Nuffield Orthopaedic Centre	Dr K. Fleming (until July 1997)
Oxford Radcliffe Hospital	Dr K. Fleming (until July 1997)
Papworth Hospital	Dr N. Cary
Peterborough Hospitals	Dr P.M. Dennis
Radcliffe Infirmary	Dr K. Fleming (until July 1997)
Royal Berkshire & Battle Hospitals	Dr R. Menai-Williams
South Buckinghamshire	Dr M.J. Turner
Stoke Mandeville Hospital	Dr A.F. Padel
West Suffolk Hospitals	Mrs V. Hamilton

North Thames

Basildon & Thurrock General Hospitals	Dr S.G. Subbuswamy
Central Middlesex Hospital	Dr C.A. Amerasinghe
Chase Farm Hospitals	Dr W.H.S. Mohamid
Chelsea & Westminster Healthcare	Ms G. Nuttal
Ealing Hospital	Dr C. Schmulian
East Hertfordshire	Dr A. Fattah
Essex Rivers Healthcare	Mrs A. Bridge
Forest Healthcare	Dr K.M. Thomas
Hammersmith Hospitals	Dr I. Lindsay (Charing Cross Hospital) Dr G. Stamp (Hammersmith Hospital)
Harefield Hospital	Mr K.B. Robinson
Havering Hospitals	Ms C. Colley
Hillingdon Hospital	Dr F.G. Barker
Homerton Hospital	Ms S. Kimenye
Great Ormond Street Hospital for Children	Professor R.A. Risdon
Mid-Essex Hospital Services	Mr A.H.M. Ross
Moorfields Eye Hospital	Professor P. Luthert
Mount Vernon & Watford Hospitals	Mrs M. Hill (Mount Vernon Hospital) Dr W.K. Blenkinsopp (Watford General Hospital)
Newham Healthcare	Dr G. Russell
North Hertfordshire	Dr D.J. Madders
North Middlesex Hospital	Dr K.J. Jarvis
Northwick Park & St Mark's	Dr S. Boyle
The Princess Alexandra Hospital	Dr R.G.M. Letcher
Redbridge Health Care	Dr P. Tanner
Royal Brompton	Professor D. Denison
Royal Free Hampstead	Dr J.E. McLaughlin
The Royal Hospitals	Dr P.J. Flynn
Royal Marsden	Mr R.J. Shearer
Royal National Orthopaedic Hospital	None

St Albans and Hemel Hempstead	Dr A.P. O'Reilly
St Mary's	Ms R.A. Hittinger
Southend Health Care	Ms L. Bell
UCL Hospitals	Ms A.E. Glover Mrs J.A. Sullivan (The National Hospital)
Wellhouse	Dr J. El-Jabbour
West Middlesex University Hospital	Dr R.G. Hughes
Whittington Hospital	Dr D.C. Brown

North West

Aintree Hospitals	Dr W. Taylor
Blackburn, Hyndburn & Ribble Valley Healthcare	Mr R.W. Nicholson
Blackpool Victoria Hospital	Dr K.S. Vasudev
Bolton Hospitals	Dr S. Wells
Burnley Health Care	Mr D.G.D. Sandilands
Bury Health Care	Dr E. Herd
The Cardiothoracic Centre Liverpool	Mr M. Jackson
Central Manchester Healthcare	Dr E.W. Benbow
Chorley & South Ribble	Dr C. Loyden
Christie Hospital	None
Countess of Chester Hospital	Dr P.R.M. Steele
East Cheshire	Dr A.R. Williams
Furness Hospitals	Dr V.M. Joglekar
Halton General Hospital	Dr M.S. Al-Jafari
Lancaster Acute Hospitals	Dr R.W. Blewitt
Liverpool Women's Hospital	Ms C. Fox
Manchester Children's Hospitals	Dr M. Newbould
Mid Cheshire Hospitals	Miss H. Moulton
North Manchester Health Care	None
Oldham	Dr I. Seddon
Preston Acute Hospitals	Dr C.M. Nicholson

North West continued

Rochdale Healthcare	Mr S. Murray
The Royal Liverpool Children's	Mrs P.A. McCormack
Royal Liverpool & Broadgreen University Hospitals	Miss K. Scott
St Helens & Knowsley Hospitals	Miss C. Gittens
Salford Royal Hospitals	Mr M. McKenna
South Manchester University Hospitals	Dr P.S. Hasleton (Wythenshawe Hospital) Dr J. Coyne (Withington Hospital)
Southport & Formby	Dr S.A.C. Dundas
Stockport Acute Services	Dr P. Meadows
Tameside Acute Care	Dr A.S. Day
Trafford Healthcare	Dr B.N.A. Hamid
Walton Centre for Neurology & Neurosurgery	Dr J. Broome
Warrington Hospital	Dr M.S. Al-Jafari
West Lancashire	Mr A.D. Johnson
Westmorland Hospitals	Dr R.W. Blewitt
Wigan & Leigh Health Services	Ms S. Tarbuck
Wirral Hospital	Dr M.B. Gillett
Wrightington Hospital	Mr A.D. Johnson

Northern & Yorkshire

Airedale	Dr J.J. O'Dowd
Bishop Auckland Hospitals	Dr D.C.A. Senadhira
Bradford Hospitals	Dr B. Naylor
Calderdale Healthcare	Mr R.J.R. Goodall
Carlisle Hospitals	Dr E.D. Long
Cheviot & Wansbeck	Dr J.A. Henry
City Hospitals Sunderland	Miss K. Ramsey
Darlington Memorial Hospital	Ms C. Evans
Dewsbury Health Care	Dr P. Gudgeon
East Yorkshire Hospitals	Mr G. Britchford
Freeman Group of Hospitals	Dr M.K. Bennett
Gateshead Hospitals	Dr I.M.J. Mathias

Harrogate Healthcare	Miss A.H. Lawson
Hartlepool & East Durham	Mrs A. Lister
Huddersfield	Dr H.H. Ali
North Durham Acute Hospitals	Dr D. Wood (Dryburn Hospital) Dr S. Dowson (Shotley Bridge Hospital)
North East Lincolnshire	Dr W.M. Peters
North Tees Health	Dr J. Hoffman
North Tyneside Health Care	Dr F. Johri
Northallerton Health Services	Dr D.C. Henderson
Pinderfields & Pontefract Hospitals	Dr S. Gill (Pinderfields Hospital) Dr I.W.C. MacDonald (Pontefract General Infirmary)
Royal Hull Hospitals	Dr M.R.F. Reynolds
Royal Victoria & Associated Hospitals	Miss D. Robson (Royal Victoria Infirmary) Dr J.D. Hemming (Hexham Hospital)
St James's & Seacroft University Hospitals	Mr N.S. Ambrose
Scarborough & N E Yorkshire Health Care	Dr A.M. Jackson
Scunthorpe & Goole Hospitals	Dr C.M. Hunt
South Tees Acute Hospitals	Mrs L. Black
South Tyneside Healthcare	Dr K.P. Pollard
United Leeds Teaching Hospitals	Dr C. Abbott
West Cumbria Health Care	Dr D. Smith
York Health Services	Dr J.M. Hopkinson

South & West

Royal Bournemouth and Christchurch Hospitals	Ms K. Hatchard
Dorset Health Care	None
East Gloucestershire	Dr W.J. Brampton
East Somerset	Dr G. Purcell
Frenchay Healthcare	Dr N.B.N. Ibrahim
Gloucestershire Royal	Dr B.W. Codling
Isle of Wight Healthcare	Mr P. Donaldson
North Hampshire Hospitals	Dr J.M. Finch
Northern Devon Healthcare	Dr J. Davies

South & West continued

Plymouth Hospitals	Dr C.B.A. Lyons
Poole Hospital	Dr D.S. Nicholas
Portsmouth Hospitals	Dr N.J.E. Marley
Royal Cornwall Hospitals	Dr R. Pitcher
Royal Devon & Exeter Healthcare	Dr R.H.W. Simpson
Royal United Hospital Bath	Dr P.J. Tidbury
Salisbury Health Care	Dr C.E. Fuller
Severn	None
South Devon Healthcare	Dr D.W. Day
Southampton University Hospitals	Dr I.E. Moore
Southmead Health Services	Ms G. Davies
Swindon & Marlborough Hospital	Mr M.H. Galea
Taunton & Somerset	Mr I. Eyre-Brook
United Bristol Healthcare	Dr E.A. Sheffield
West Dorset General Hospitals	Dr A. Anscombe
Weston Area Health	Dr M.F. Lott
Winchester & Eastleigh Healthcare	Dr R.K. Al-Talib

South Thames

Ashford Hospital	Dr J.C. Dawson
Brighton Health Care	Mr M. Renshaw
Bromley Hospitals	Dr M.H. Elmahallawy
Crawley Horsham	Dr C. Moon
Dartford & Gravesham	Dr A.T.M. Rashid
East Surrey Healthcare	Mr M. Warman
Eastbourne Hospitals	Mr M.D. Bastable
Epsom Health Care	Dr T.J. Matthews
Frimley Park Hospitals	Dr G.F. Goddard
Greenwich Healthcare	Mr O. Smith
Guy's & St Thomas' Hospital	Dr. B. Hartley (Guy's Hospital) Professor S.B. Lucas (St Thomas' Hospital)

Hastings & Rother	Mr S. Ball
Kent & Canterbury Hospitals	Mr M. Guarino
Kent & Sussex Weald	Dr G.A. Russell
King's Healthcare	Dr S. Humphreys
Kingston Hospital	Mr R.D. Leach
The Lewisham Hospital	Dr C. Keen
Mayday Healthcare	Mr C. Fernandez
Medway	Mrs J.L. Smith
Mid-Kent Healthcare	Mr J. Vickers
Mid-Sussex	Mr P.H. Walter (Hurstwood Park Hospital) Dr P.A. Berresford (The Princess Royal Hospital)
Queen Mary's Sidcup	Dr E.J.A. Aps
The Queen Victoria Hospital	Mrs D.M. Helme
Richmond, Twickenham & Roehampton Healthcare	Mr M. McSweeney
Royal Surrey County Hospital	Dr B.T.B. Manners
The Royal West Sussex	Mr J.N.L. Simson
St George's Healthcare	Dr S. Dilly
The St Helier	Dr E.H. Rang
St Peter's Hospital	Mr R.H. Moore
South Kent Hospitals	Dr C.W. Lawson
Thanet Healthcare	Mrs B.M. Smith
Worthing & Southlands Hospitals	Mrs J. North

Trent

Barnsley District General Hospital	Dr M.A. Longan
Bassetlaw Hospital & Community Services	Dr P.A. Parsons
Central Nottinghamshire Health Care	None
Central Sheffield University Hospitals	Dr C.A. Angel
Chesterfield & North Derbyshire Royal Hospital	Dr P.B. Gray
Derby City General Hospital	Ms K. Hillier-Smith
Derbyshire Royal Infirmary	Mr J.R. Nash
Doncaster Royal Infirmary & Montagu Hospital	Dr J.A.H. Finbow
Glenfield Hospital	Mrs S. Clarke

Trent continued

Grantham and District Hospital	Dr D. Clark
The King's Mill Centre for Health Care Services	Ms J. Jenkins
Leicester General Hospital	Dr E.H. Mackay
Leicester Royal Infirmary	Ms D. Burt
Lincoln & Louth	Dr J.A. Harvey (Lincoln County Hospital) Mr E.O. Amaku (Louth County Hospital)
Northern General Hospital	Dr C.A. Angel
Nottingham City Hospital	Professor D.R. Turner
Pilgrim Health	Ms S. Cosgriff
Queen's Medical Centre University Hospital	Professor D.R. Turner
Rotherham General Hospitals	Mr R.B. Jones
Sheffield Children's Hospital	Dr C.A. Angel
West Lindsey	Dr J.A. Harvey

West Midlands

Alexandra Healthcare	Dr J.C. Macartney
Birmingham Children's Hospital	Dr F. Raafat
Birmingham Heartlands Hospitals	Dr M. Taylor
Birmingham Women's Healthcare	Dr T. Rollason
Burton Hospitals	Dr N. Kasthuri
The City Hospital	Dr. S.M. Abraham
The Dudley Group of Hospitals	Dr S. Ghosh Dr O. Stores
George Eliot Hospital	Dr J. Mercer
Good Hope Hospital	Dr J. Hull
Hereford Hospitals	Dr F. McGinty
Kidderminster Health Care	Dr G.H. Eeles
Mid Staffordshire General Hospitals	Dr V. Suarez
North Staffordshire Hospital	Dr T.A. French
The Princess Royal Hospital	Dr R.A. Fraser
Robert Jones & Agnes Hunt	Dr P.M. Pfeifer
The Royal Orthopaedic Hospital Trust	Dr A. Thomas

Royal Shrewsbury Hospitals	Dr R.A. Fraser
The Royal Wolverhampton Hospitals	Dr J. Tomlinson
Rugby	None
Sandwell Healthcare	Dr J. Simon
South Warwickshire General Hospitals	Mr M. Gilbert
University Hospital Birmingham	Professor E.L. Jones (Queen Elizabeth Hospital) None (Selly Oak Hospital)
Walsall Hospitals	Dr Y.L. Hock
Walsgrave Hospitals	Dr T. Guha
Worcester Royal Infirmary	Mr A. Singfield

Northern Ireland

Altnagelvin Hospitals	Dr J.N. Hamilton
Armagh & Dungannon	Mr B. Cranley
Belfast City Hospital	Mr S.T. Irwin
Causeway	Dr C. Watters
Craigavon Area Hospital Group	Mr B. Cranley
Down Lisburn	Mrs M. Gilgunn (Downe Hospital) Dr B. Huss (Lagan Valley Hospital)
Green Park Healthcare	Dr J.D. Connolly
Mater Hospital	Dr H. Mathews
Newry & Mourne	Mr B. Cranley
Royal Group of Hospitals	Ms M. Toner
Sperrin Lakeland	Dr W. Holmes (Erne Hospital) Dr F. Robinson (Tyrone County Hospital)
The Ulster, North Down & Ards Hospital	Dr T. Boyd
United Hospitals	Mr I. Garstin Mr P.C. Pyper (Mid-Ulster Hospital) Mr D. Gilroy (Whiteabbey Hospital)

Wales

Bridgend & District	Dr A.M. Rees
Carmarthen & District	Dr R.B. Denholm
Ceredigion & Mid-Wales	Mrs C. Smith

Wales continued

East Glamorgan	Dr D. Stock
Glan Clwyd District General Hospital	Dr B. Rogers
Glan Hafren	Dr M.S. Matharu
Glan-y-Mor	Dr A. Dawson
Gwynedd Hospitals	Dr M. Hughes
Llandough Hospital & Community	Dr J. Gough
Llanelli/Dinefwr	Dr L.A. Murray
Morriston Hospital/Ysbyty Treforys	Dr A. Dawson
North Glamorgan	Dr R.C. Ryder
Nevill Hall & District	Dr R.J. Kellett
Pembrokeshire & Derwen	Dr G.R. Melville Jones
Rhondda Health Care	None
Swansea	Dr S. Williams
University Dental Hospital	Dr A.G. Douglas-Jones
University Hospital of Wales Healthcare	Dr A.G. Douglas-Jones (University Hospital of Wales) Mrs P. Perrott (Cardiff Royal Infirmary)
Wrexham Maelor Hospital	Dr R.B. Williams

Guernsey / Isle of Man / Jersey

Guernsey	Dr B.P. Gunton-Bunn
Isle of Man	None
Jersey	Dr H. Goulding

Defence Medical Services

All perioperative deaths in Defence Medical Services hospitals are reported to NCEPOD by the Commanding Officer or by a person nominated by the Commanding Officer.

BMI/Columbia Healthcare

The Alexandra Hospital	Ms J.M. Whitby
The Blackheath Hospital	Mrs G. Mann
The Chaucer Hospital	Mr R. Muddiman
Chelsfield Park Hospital	Ms C. Poll

The Chiltern Hospital	Ms S. Hill
The Clementine Churchill Hospital	Dr I. Chanarin
Fawkham Manor Hospital	Mrs C. Pagram
Harley Street Clinic	Ms S. Thomas
Highfield Hospital	Mr C.J. Durkin
The Park Hospital	Ms S. Quickmire
The Portland Hospital	Miss A. Sayburn
Princess Grace Hospital	Ms D. Cunliffe
The Princess Margaret Hospital	Mrs J. Bevington
Priory Hospital	Dr A.G. Jacobs
Runnymede Hospital	Mrs P. Hill
The Sloane Hospital	Miss J.E. Wilson
The Somerfield Hospital	Ms N. Poulson
Thornbury Hospital	Mrs J. Cooper
The Wellington Hospital	Mr R.J. Hoff

BUPA

BUPA Alexandra Hospital	Mr N.R. Permain
BUPA Belvedere Hospital	Mr S.J. Greatorex
BUPA Cambridge Lea Hospital	Ms M. Vognsen
BUPA Chalybeate Hospital	Ms M. Falconer
BUPA Dunedin Hospital	Mrs C. Bude
BUPA Flyde Coast Hospital	Ms D. Revell
BUPA Gatwick Park Hospital	Mrs D. Wright
BUPA Hartswood Hospital	Ms N. Howes
BUPA Hospital Harpenden	Ms H. Banks
BUPA Hospital Bristol	Ms M. O'Toole
BUPA Hospital Bushey	Mr R. Lye
BUPA Hospital Cardiff	Dr A. Gibbs
BUPA Hospital Clare Park	Ms M. Wood
BUPA Hospital Elland	Ms M.E. Schofield
BUPA Hospital Hull & East Riding	Ms A. Meyer

BUPA continued

BUPA Hospital Leeds	Mrs D. Farrell
BUPA Hospital Leicester	Mrs C.A. Jones
BUPA Hospital Little Aston	Mr K. Smith
BUPA Hospital Manchester	Ms A. McArdle
BUPA Hospital Norwich	Mrs C. Wilkie
BUPA Hospital Portsmouth	Ms G. Gibson
BUPA Murrayfield Hospital	Mrs J. Poll
BUPA North Cheshire Hospital	Miss A.L. Alexander
BUPA Parkway Hospital	Mrs M. Hall
BUPA Roding Hospital	Ms A. Stevens
BUPA South Bank Hospital	Miss A. Tchaikovsky
BUPA St Saviour's Hospital	Mrs E. Biddle
BUPA Wellesley Hospital	Mrs L. Horner

Nuffield Hospitals

Birmingham Nuffield Hospital	Mrs P. Shields
Bournemouth Nuffield Hospital	Mrs S. Jackson
Chesterfield Nuffield Hospital	Miss P.J. Bunker
Cleveland Nuffield Hospital	Mrs S. Jelley
Cotswold Nuffield Hospital	Mrs J.T. Penn
Duchy Nuffield Hospital	Miss S.J. Gardner
East Midlands Nuffield Hospital	Mrs C. Williams
Essex Nuffield Hospital	Mrs B.M. Parker
Exeter Nuffield Hospital	Mrs A. Turnbull
HRH Princess Christian's Hospital	None
Huddersfield Nuffield Hospital	Miss S. Panther
Hull Nuffield Hospital	Miss V. Ward
Lancaster & Lakeland Nuffield Hospital	Miss A. Durbin
Mid Yorkshire Nuffield Hospital	Mrs M. Dunderdale
Newcastle Nuffield Hospital	Miss K.C. Macfarlane
North London Nuffield Hospital	Miss J. Ward

North Staffordshire Nuffield Hospital	Mrs A. Woolrich
Nuffield Acland Hospital	Miss C. Gilbert
Nuffield Hospital Leicester	Mrs S. Harriman
Nuffield Hospital Plymouth	Mrs T. Starling
Purey Cust Nuffield Hospital	Mr J. Gdaniec
Shropshire Nuffield Hospital	Mrs S. Crossland
Somerset Nuffield Hospital	Mrs J. Dyer
Sussex Nuffield Hospital	Miss J. Collister
Thames Valley Nuffield Hospital	Mrs S.E. Clifford
The Grosvenor Nuffield Hospital	Mrs J.L. Whitmore
Tunbridge Wells Nuffield Hospital	Mrs L.R. Lockwood
Warwickshire Nuffield Hospital	None
Wessex Nuffield Hospital	Mrs V. Heckford
Woking Nuffield Hospital	Miss B.E. Harrison
Wolverhampton Nuffield Hospital	Mrs I. Jones
Wye Valley Nuffield Hospital	Mrs W.P. Mawdesley

St Martin's Hospitals

The Devonshire Hospital	Miss C. Lewington
The Lister Hospital	Mrs J. Johnson
The London Bridge Hospital	Ms Y. Terry

Other independent hospitals

Benenden Hospital	Mr D. Hibler